THE DOWNTRODDEN
(CASTE TRIBE WOMEN)

THE DOWNTRODDEN
(CASTE TRIBE WOMEN)

Dr. Vijay Prakash Sharma

KALPAZ

ISBN : 978-93-5324-054-7

First Published, 2019

Published by

Kalpaz Publications
C-30, Satyawati Nagar,
Delhi – 110052
Ph.: 011-47034999, 9811692060
www.kalpazpublications.com
E-mail: kalpaz@hotmail.com

Printed at: G. Print Process, Delhi

Contents

Acknowledgements 7
List of Contributers 9
Preface 11

1. Untouchables and Scheduled Caste in Jharkhand 15
2. The Scheduled Tribes of Jharkhand 27
3. Unravelling the Nation: A Sociological Narrative of Tribal Deprivation 39
4. Can Tea Migrant Tribes of Dooars Be Develop? 53
5. Political Deprivation of Tribal People in Contemporary India 65
6. Socio-Economic Condition of Tribal in Mining Area of Saranda, Jharkhand 79
7. Tribal Deprivation in Contemporary India: a Case study from Jharkhand 89
8. Tribal Development Initiatives and Achievements in Jharkhand 99
9. World of Tribal Women, Work and Leisure with Special Reference to Jharkhand 115
10. Economically Challenged People of Palamu, Jharkhand 135
11. The Level of Population Growth of Pahari Korwa of Chhattisgarh 153
12. Economic Deprivation among the Lodha Tribe of West Bengal 181
13. Government Interventions for the Downtrodden in Jharkhand 195
14. Anthropology and Rural Development 217

15. Tribal Deprivation and Identities in Assam: A Sociological Study based on Deuri Tribe of Lakhimpur District in Assam 239

16. The Impact of Economic Deprivation of Santhal Tribe on Ajodhya Hill Area, Purulia 245

Bibliography 257

Index 259

Acknowledgements

My sincere thanks are due to the article contributors in this volume and my associates at Institute for Human Development, Eastern regional centre, Ranchi where I worked as Director, during compilation of this treatise 'The Downtrodden". I wish to put on record the assistance provided by Ashwani Kumar, Amit Kumar, Nutan Shashi Tigga and Ivshita Dutta.

I express my gratitude to Prof. Ramesh Sharan, Vice-Chancellor, Prof. Ganganath Jha and Prof. P.C. Deogharia of Vinoba Bhave University, Hazaribagh for their encouragements.

I am obliged to my Wife Manju and both sons Mrigank Prakash and Shashank Prakash for their constant care.

I am thankful to Sri Amit jee, Director, Gyan Books publishing Pvt. Ltd., New Delhi for publication of this book.

Vijay Prakash Sharma

List of Contributers

1. Abhishek Kumar, Assistant professor Department of Anthropology, Birsa College Khunti (Ranchi University).
2. Biswajit Ghosh, Faculty Member, Department of Sociology, Srikrishna College, Bagula and M.Phil. Research Scholar, Deptt. of Sociology, Jadavpur University, Kolkata.
3. Dilip Kumar Bhuyan, Kherajkhat College, Deotola, Lakhimpur, Assam.
4. Himeswar Borah, Kherajkhat College, Deotola, Lakhimpur, Assam.
5. Ivshita Dutta, Institute for Human Development, Eastern Regional Centre, Ranchi;.
6. Jagdeep Oraon, Assistant Professor, Department of Anthropology and Tribal Studies, Sidho kanho Birsha University, Purulia, West Bengal.
7. Kailash Chandra Department of Anthropology and Tribal Studies, Sidho kanho Birsha University, Purulia, West Bengal.
8. Kaushik Chattopadhyay, Assistant Professor, Department of Sociology, Prof. Syed Nurul Hasan College. Farakka.
9. Mithilesh Kumar Mishra, Tribal and Rural Development Institute, Jashpurnagar, Chhatishgarh.
10. Nisha Kumari, UGC-NET, Department of Tribal Studies, Central University of Jharkhand, Ranchi.
11. Nutan Shashi Tigga, Research Consultant, Centre for Health Policy, Asian Develiopment Research Institute (ADRI) Patna, Bihar.
12. Tarak Mohan Hazari, Department of Anthropology and Tribal studies,Sidho Kanho Birsha University, Purulia.
13. Vijay Prakash Sharma,Director, VAIDYAS-India, Jharkhand; Vice president- Institute of Applied Anthropology and Social Research, Bidisa, W.B, India; Vice President- Ranchi University Anthropological

Alumni Association; He is in editorial board of Journals, and member of governing bodies of several societies. Former Director, Institute for Human Development, Eastern Regional Centre, Ranchi; Adjunct Faculty, NIRD&PR, Ministry of Rural Development, Government of India, Hyderabad.

14. Rilamala Saren and Ishita Mukherjee, Department of Anthropology and Tribal Studies, Sidho kanho Birsha University, Purulia, West Bengal.

Preface

India is hugely diverse country with unity of thought and convictions. At one of hand it practices lofty ideals of "VASUDHAIYVA KUTUMBKAM" and at the other there are diverse customs and a feast of social practices. This book rumbles through timely discontent that reminds us the problem of "the downtrodden" which is the central argument of this tapestry.

Some of the articles on Tribal deprivation are those presented articles in the National seminar on "Tribal deprivation in contemporary India" organised by Institute of social research and applied anthropology, Bidisa, in Paschim Medinipur, West Bengal on 8-9 December 2018, contains empirical data and arguments are included as penned down by the authors.

A characteristic feature of the scheduled caste groups is their social exclusion in the past. The scheduled castes/scheduled tribes and women have been identified as downtrodden groups of Indian society needing special attention.

The word downtrodden denotes oppressed, suppressed and subdued group of society. To my mind the scheduled caste, the scheduled tribe and the women in India are the best example facing social seclusion. An attempt has been made in this volume to understand their status and challenges faced by them in modern India.

Inherited inequality is found in every stratified society. "The black in America and in South Africa, the Burakumin of Japan, the Harijan of India, and the barber and washer men of Swat, the Hutu or Twa of Ruanda have all faced similar conditions as individuals and they have responded to them in similar ways (Berremen 1972, 405).

The Scheduled Castes of present India or Bharat have been referred by the various connotations in the early history or traditional literature. In some scriptures they have been called 'Antyaj', 'Dalit' 'Chandalas',

'Patittas', 'Shudras', Pancham and Harijan in India, they have been referred to as 'Unclean castes', 'Depressed classes', 'Exterior castes' and the like. The stigma of pollution and poverty attached to them mainly because of their old defiling profession although most of them are not in such profession now but the stigma continues.

Since the enactment of the Government of India Act of 1935, they have been constantly referred to as Scheduled Castes and this continued in the Constitution of India 1950. Thus, many untouchable castes in India listed in the Act. Widespread practice of social discrimination, domestic violence, atrocities against scheduled caste is an index at tailor of promise made to these oppressed people of this country.

The constitutional and statutory agencies entrusted with the task of safe guarding the entitlements have measurably failed. The scheduled castes also now politically leveled as 'Dalits' continue to face wide range of economic, social disadvantages and day to day humiliations and degradation, denial of justice and violent atrocities. By and large their condition is marked by high incidence of poverty, low education, limited employment opportunities and marginalization in all spheres of life. The bulk of them are landless and destitute so they are subjected to social, economic, political and sexual exploitation.

The Scheduled Tribe - Famous anthropologist S.C. Dubey is of opinion that "In the Indian context the term tribe has never been defined precisely and satisfactorily. The undermining of the cultural potential of the tribal population in India leveling them 'uncultured' 'forest dwellers' make us to believe that their mobility in the direction of the mainstreams of Indian culture is incompatible. This again is a myth, because on the contrary there are evidences to suggest that the concept of tribe does not refer to a set of static economic, social and ideological parameter. Communities with their differential lifestyle have their equally rich cultures which have undergone the process of change, adaptation and acculturation like others while still maintaining their tribal identity. In India, the indigenous people are referred to as 'Adivasi', (original inhabitants) 'Vanavasi', (Forest dwellers) 'Girijana'(Inhabitants of Mountains) and sometimes 'Mulavasi' (Original inhabitants). These terms are significant, for this attempt to identify the tribal people as the original inhabitants of the land having connection with nature.

Women though are the prime movers of earning livelihood for their family but are subdued in Indian society. They are always on move from here to their performing the household and field services usually with very little leisure time at their disposal. Women in Jharkhand continue to live in extreme deprivation and discrimination. Evident from the recent estimates reported by the NFHS 4, a significant proportion of women continue to suffer from anaemia compared to men. Moreover, the nutritional status indicated by Body Mass Index, reveals a similar plight of women, i.e., more women are undernourished compared to men in Jharkhand.

The rights available to woman in India can be classified into two categories, namely as constitutional rights and legal rights. The constitutional rights are those which are provided in the various provisions of the constitution. The legal rights, on the other hand, are those which are provided in the various laws (acts) of the Parliament and the State Legislatures. In spite of this, Women in Jharkhand continue to live in extreme deprivation and discrimination. Evident from the recent estimates reported by the NFHS 4, a significant proportion of women continue to suffer from anaemia compared to men. They are worst sufferers of patriarchal chauvinism. This volume on the down trodden elaborately discusses the status and challenges before them. I am sure readers will be fascinated by the field data and interpretation reported in this volume.

Hope, The sociological interpretations and facts will be welcomed by administrators, socialanthropologists, sociologists, social managers and those interested in social solidarity of the country.

Makar Sankranti 2019, Ranchi **Vijay Prakash Sharma**

Chapter - 1

Untouchables and Scheduled Caste in Jharkhand

— Vijay Prakash Sharma

A characteristic feature of the scheduled caste groups is their social exclusion in the past. The scheduled castes have been identified as downtrodden groups of Indian society needing special attention.

Inherited inequality is found in every stratified society. "The black in America and in South Africa, the Burakumin of Japan, the Harijan of India, and the barber and washer men of Swat, the Hutu or Twa of Ruanda have all faced similar conditions as individuals and they have responded to them in similar ways (Berremen 1972, 405).

The Scheduled Castes of present India or Bharat have been referred by the various connotations in the early history or traditional literature. In some scriptures they have been called 'Patittas', 'Chandalas' and 'Shudras', in census, they have been referred to as 'Unclean castes', 'Depressed classes', 'Exterior castes' and the like. Since the enactment of the Government of India Act of 1935, they have been constantly referred to as Scheduled Castes and this continued in the Constitution of India 1950. Thus, many untouchable castes in India listed in the act.

Widespread practice of social discrimination, domestic violence, atrocities against scheduled caste is an index at tailor of promise made to these oppressed people of this country.

The constitutional and statutory agencies entrusted with the task of safe guarding the entitlements have measurably failed.

The scheduled castes also now leveled as 'Dalits' continue to face wide range of economic, social disadvantages and day to day humiliations and degradation, denial of justice and violent atrocities.

By and large their condition is marked by high incidence of poverty, low education, limited employment opportunities and marginalization in all spheres of life.

Thus, it is important to research in the areas of the problems faced by the Scheduled castes in Jharkhand as no such study or publication has been attempted so far.

Jharkhand came into existence on 15th November 2000 by bifurcating erstwhile Bihar state, as 28 th state of the Indian Union. As a new state, Government of Jharkhand implemented several projects to uplift the conditions of scheduled castes and scheduled tribes in the state. But no impact study has been taken up so far to report the current status of the scheduled castes in the state.

There are however, large state wise variations in the proportion of the scheduled castes population. The scheduled castes are concentrated in as per the Constitution (Scheduled Castes) Order, 1950 (PART III—Rules and Orders under the Constitution) 1[PART VIA— there are 22 SC groups in Jharkhand-Table-1

Sl. No.	*Groups*	*Sl. No.*	*Groups*
1.	Bantar	12.	Halalkhor
2.	Bauri	13.	Hair, Mehtar, Bhangi
3.	Bhogta	14.	Kanjar
4.	Bhuiya	15.	Kuraiar
5.	Chamar, Mochi	16.	Lalbegi
6.	Choupal	17.	Musahar
7.	Dabajar	18.	Nat
8.	Dhobi	19.	Pan, Sawasi
9.	Dom, Dhangad	20.	Pasi
10.	Dusadh, Dhari, Dharhi	21.	Rajwar
11.	Ghasi	22.	Turi

Socio-Economic Conditions among the Scheduled Castes:

Francis Buchanan conducted studies of Bengal during the year 1807-14 and wrote about the land and people of Bihar in general and the districts of Patna, Bhagalpur, Purnea and Shahabad in particular had some anthropological insight in the treatment of problems of the Scheduled Casters. His four volumes are pioneering in many ways. It goes without saying that they contain the firsthand account of the Scheduled castes in as early as 1807. Thus these information's about their marriage customs social positions etc. function as bench-line data for any scientific research on them.

Dalton's "Descriptive Ethnology on Bengal" published in 1872 may be regarded yet another source of information of the Scheduled castes and the Scheduled tribes in general. As is vivid from the very title of the book it is a descriptive account of some of them. There are some very brief ethnographic notes about these very little known Scheduled tribes and castes. This 11 study, despite limitations, has been helping the researchers like the Polar start since more than a century

W.W. Hunter's "A Statistical Account of Bengal" published in 1877 may also be regarded as a mile-stone in this regard. Though we do not get a systematic account of any Scheduled caste in it, it does preserve glimpses of their life. It contains the ethnical division of the people, Emigration and Immigration lists of castes, religious division of the people, village institutions, material culture, agriculture and commerce and much other useful information important from anthropological point of view.

Risley's "Tribes and Castes of Bengal" published in two volumes in the year 1891 may be regarded as monumental work for these volumes were the first to have anthropological insight. The author tried his best to touch important aspects of all the major Scheduled castes and tribes.

After the works of Risley there is rather a big gap for about thirty years as there is no published work about them except the census reports.

In the year 1920, S.C. Roy published his monograph on the Bhuiyas which may be regarded as the master-piece in the germane field. It comprises of social organisations, kinship system, marriage, inheritance, birth, childhood, puberty customs, death and death rites, and the like. S.C. Roy, as the father of Indian Anthropology, may be regarded as the first Indian to have taken the cause of the Scheduled castes and have written a volume on them.

G.W. Briggs published his monumental book "The Chamar" in 1920. Though this was mainly based on the fieldwork carried on among the Chamars of U.P., there are several references of the Chamars of Bihar also in this book. This is a rare work and the first full length monograph ever written on Scheduled caste.

Grierson's "Bihar Peasant Life" published in 1926 is yet another book where we find some information about the condition of some of the Scheduled castes in Bihar.

"The Myth of Caste System" by N. Prasad published in 1957 may be regarded as a wonderful work on the Scheduled castes of Bihar. Mr. Prasad has extensively worked on the Scheduled castes and has enriched the poor store of the study among the Scheduled castes.

R.R. Diwakar's "Bihar Through the Ages" published in 1959 may be taken as eventful for he has tried to analyse the social system of the various tribes and castes of Bihar right from the 12 early Vedic period till the book was published. Diwakar deserves congratulations for he could accommodate even the untouchables.

"Inside Bihar" by P.C. Roy Choudhary published in 1962 is very informative for the author has very carefully described the affairs of the Scheduled castes along with the Upper castes.

This work is especially useful for the researchers of Bihar, particularly those interested in the study of caste system and the like.

S.D. Prasad, the then Superintendent of the Census operations of Bihar took some special interest in the census of 1960 by providing a section of the ethnographic notes and also few village studies in the forms of monographs. These ethnographic notes and monographs also depicted the cultural life of Scheduled caste people and are useful for the obvious reasons.

The first anthropological treatise on Scheduled Castes of Bihar was published by L.P.Vidyarthi and Narayan Mishra in 1977 under the title "Harijan Today"." Economic Problems of Scheduled Caste of Bihar'(1975) is another important study by the above duo and is a comparative study of the scheduled castes of the tribal and Magahi linguistic zones of Bihar.

V.P.Sharma (the applicant author) lead a team of anthropological researchers to Nathdwara in Rajasthan in the year 1989 and conducted studies on Scheduled Castes problem of untouchability and published a paper "Gandhian Approach to untouchability: It's applicability at Nathdwara"(1992) highlighting the importance of human values in Indian society. This paper examines the contemporary situation of Harijans in Rajasthan. The author examined the relevancy of Gandhi in eradication of untouchability.

Unfortunately, no such sociological or anthropological researches were conducted in Jharkhand. The proposed study will fill up the gap in our knowledge of problems faced by 22 schedule caste communities inhabiting Jharkhand today.

M.K.Gandhi (1950) described the difficulties faced by the Harijans. In modern society untouchability is a serious social problem. The untouchables are subjected to hardships.

1. They are forbidden from using the public utilities of roads, tanks and wells.
2. They are denied entry into temples, burial grounds and similar institutions. Gopinath Dhawan (1951)2 has pointed out the

importance of the vow taken by Gandhi for removal of untouchability. It follows from the principle of the spiritual unity of all life. We are all sparks 13 of the same fire, the children of the same God. Therefore, he asks of every one to break down the barriers between man and man and between the various orders of being and to serve all life as one's own self. To him the removal of untouchability is "an issue of transcendental value, far surpassing Swaraj in terms of political constitutions."

Gandhi's views about social relations is based on the Law of Varna which he calls true socialism and which was intimately connected with nonviolence.

The Scheduled caste communities deserve more attention than those of scheduled tribes. Social scientists especially sociologist and social anthropologists have paid little or no attention towards these people inhabiting Jharkhand plateau .The scheduled castes are to some extent homogenous though they are heterogeneous groups so the problems will have similarities. By and large their condition is marked by high incidence of poverty, low education, limited employment opportunities and marginalization in all affairs of life. So far no work has been done in the direction of finding out problems of the Scheduled Castes in the state of Jharkhand. This is first anthropological and sociological attempt to study the wide ranging economic, social disadvantages and day to day humiliations and degradation problems and how far government programmes helped them to solve their problems. The constitutional and statutory agencies entrusted with the task of safeguarding the entitlements have measurably failed. Industrial progress of the state of Jharkhand is responsible to bring change in their life style but only little efforts have been made.

Social Ecology and demography of scheduled castes of Jharkhand

According to 2001 census, the Scheduled Caste (SC) population of Jharkhand is 3,189,320, constituting 11.8 per cent of the total population (26,945,829). It holds 14th position among all the States / UTs in terms of the Scheduled Caste population. The decennial growth of SC population has been 23.2 per cent which is almost the same as the growth of the total population (23.3 per cent). The State has a total of twenty two (22) Scheduled Castes and all have been enumerated at 2001 census. 2.The SCs are predominantly rural as 81.1 per cent of them reside in villages. At the district level, the SCs have registered the highest proportion (31.9 per cent) in

Chatra district, followed by Palamu (25.7 per cent) and Garhwa (23.9 per cent). Pakaur and Lohardaga have the lowest proportion of SCs (3.3 – 3.5 per cent). 3.Out of twenty two (22) SCs, Chamar is the most populous caste, having a number of 837,333, constituting 26.3 per cent of the total SC population. Bhuiya and Dusadh are the second and third largest SCs having population of 680,030 and 349,284 respectively. The other SCs in 14 descending order are Dhobi, Bhogta, Baurri, Turi and Rajwar along with Chamar, Bhuiya and Dusadh, eight SCs constitute 85.5 per cent of the total SC population of the State. Four castes, Musahar, Pasi, Ghasi and Dom having population in the range of 42,647-137,465, account for 11.3 per cent; the remaining 10 castes along with the generic castes constitute the residual 3.2 per cent of the State's SC population. Bantar, Choupal, Halalkhor and Kanjar are other Scheduled Castes which are small in number each having less than1000 population. Chamars are in large number in the districts of Palamu, Giridih, Hazaribagh and Garhwa. They have the highest percentage of the total SC population in Giridih district (49.7 per cent). Bhuiya constitute more than half of the total SC population in Chatra (52 per cent) district. Dusadh are concentrated in Palamu district and in respect of other five large groups, namely, Dhobi, Bhogta, Baurri, Turi and Rajwas, their concentration in Dhanbad, Chatra, Dhanbad, Giridih and Bokaro districts respectively.

Sex Ratio -The overall sex ratio of the Scheduled Caste population in Jharkhand is 944 females per 1000 males which are higher than the national average of 936 in respect of all SCs. 6.Among the numerically larger groups, Turi, Bhogta, Bhuiya, Baurri and Chamar have recorded over all sex ratio higher than the national average. Other three SCs, Rajwas, Dhobi and Dusadh have over all sex ratio lower than the national average.

The sex ratio in the age group 0-6 years (984) is also higher than that of the SCs at the national level. All the major SCs have recorded child sex ratio higher than the national average with Bhuiya and Turi having preponderance of girl children.

Category of Workers

'Agricultural Laborers' constitute the highest proportion of 47.1 per cent among the total workers. This figure is slightly higher than the national average of 45.6 per cent recorded by all SCs in this category. 'Other Workers' constitute 27.9 per cent which is comparable with the national average of 30.5 per cent in respect of all SCs. 'Cultivators' account for 19.3 per cent and this figure are at par with the national average (20 per cent). Workers engaged in Household Industry (HHI) constitute 5.7 per cent which is 1.8 per cent higher than the national average (3.9 per cent). Among the major castes, Bhuiya have the highest percentage of 'Agricultural Laborers' followed by Rajwas and Chamar. Baurri have the highest proportion of 'Other Workers'. Bhogta have the highest share of 'Cultivators' whereas Turi have the maximum share of HHI workers.

The data show that slightly more than half of the Scheduled Caste population is 'never married' (52 per cent) whereas 'married' persons constitute 43.9 per cent. 'Widowed' persons form 4 per cent while a negligible per cent (0.2 per cent) is of 'divorced and separated' persons. 17.The proportions of married girls below 18 years as well as married boys below 21 years (4 per cent each) among the SCs are higher if compared to those at national level (2.8 per cent for female & 3.1 per cent for male). 18. The mean number of children ever born per ever married SC woman (45 – 49 years.) is 4 which are same as that of all SCs at national level (4). Religion 19.Hinduism is the predominant religion of the 99.9 per cent of Jharkhand. Only a negligible number of SC persons profess Sikhism (1848) and Buddhism (1186) together constituting 0.1 per cent.

According to 2011 census, the Scheduled Caste (SC) population of Jharkhand is 3,985,644, constituting 12.08 per cent of the total population (32,988,134). The decennial growth of SC population has been 24 per cent. The State has a total of twenty-two (22) Scheduled Castes and all have been enumerated in 2011 Census. The SCs are predominantly rural as 79.10 per cent of them reside in villages and 21.89 per cent in urban areas. At the district level, the SCs have registered the highest proportion (32.65 per cent) in Chatra district, followed by Palamu (27.65 per cent) and Garhwa (24.19 per cent). Pakaur and Gumla have the lowest proportion of SCs (3.16 per cent and 3.17 per cent). Out of twenty-two (22) SCs, Chamar is the most populous caste, having a number of 1,008,507, constituting 25.3 per cent of the total SC population. Bhuiya and Dusadh are the second and third largest SCs having population of 848,151and 424,330respectively. The three castes constitute 57.23 per cent of the total SCs in the State. The other SCs in descending order are Dhobi, Bhogta, Turi, Rajwar, Bauri, Dom, Dhangad, Ghasi, Pasi, Hari, Mehtar, Bhangi and Musahar account for 39.87 per cent. The remaining 9 castes along with the generic castes constitute the residual 2.89 per cent of theState's SC population. Chamars are in large number in the districts of Palamu, Giridih, Garhwa and Deoghar. In Giridih, Chamars are the highest percentage of the total SC population in the district i.e. 46.71 per cent. Bhuiya constitute more than half of the total SC population in Chatra (51 per cent) district, followed by Hazaribagh (79 per cent) and Latehar (37). Dusadh are concentrated in Garwha and Palamu.

Sex Ratio-The overall sex ratio of the Scheduled Caste population in Jharkhand is 950 females per 1000 males which are higher than the national average of 945 in respect of all SCs. The sex ratio in the age group 0-6 years (976) is also higher than that of the SCs at the national level (933).

Literacy & Educational Level : Like in the State of Bihar, the literacy scenario among the Scheduled Castes of Jharkhand is low. Though there is an improvement in the over-all literacy rate of SCs from 37.6 per cent at 2001 census to 55.89 per cent at 2011 census, it is still lower if compared with that of all SCs at the national level (66.07 per cent). Male and female literacy rates (66.94 per cent and 44.2 per cent respectively) continue to be lower than those at the national level (75.17 per cent and 56.46per cent). Among the literates, 34.61 per cent are either without any educational level or have attained education below primary level. The proportions of literates who have attained education up to primary and middle level constitute 30.15 per cent and 16.23 per cent respectively. As many as 15.48 per cent literates are educated up to matric / secondary / higher secondary level. Graduates and above are 3.26 per cent.It may be discerned from the educational levels attained by all SCs that the drop-out rate increases sharply from the higher secondary level onwards. Similar trend has been shown by the major SCs in attaining education. Major proportion (69.28 per cent) SC children in the age group 5-14 years, have not been attending school. Out of 10.89 lakh children in the corresponding age group, 7.55 lakh (69.28 per cent) have been going to school.

Work Participation Rate (WPR) The Work Participation Rate (WPR) of the SC population is 37.6 per cent which is marginally lower than that of all SCs at the national level (40.4 per cent). Female WPR has increased from 24.3 per cent to 27.7 per cent whereas male WPR has registered a marginal decline from 48.8 per cent to 47 per cent during 1991-2001. Among the total workers, 58.2 per cent are main workers and this proportion is lower than that of all SCs aggregated at the national level (73 per cent).than the national average for all SCs whereas Chamar, Baurri, Dhobi, Dusadh and Rajwas have WPR lower than the national average.

Caste and Casteism and Caste Politics in India

Caste was unique system of maintaining social solidarity in India since last 2000 years. This is the basic structure of Indian social organization called JAATI in vernacular. The term caste was used for the first time by Garcia de orta in 1563. Many studies by Indian and foreign scholars like Iravati Karve, G.S. Ghurye, N.Prasad, D.N. Mazumdar, Andre Beetle. Mckim Marriot, Adrian Mayer, David Mandelbaum etc. are available, but I prefer to give more credit to G.S.Ghurye and Iravati Karve who used

Indian approach to look into the system. According to her, "Caste can be defined as an extended kin group''. (Karve 1953, 5).

In Indian literature both old and new, the Indian words are JATI, JATA or KULAM. Many castes having similar status and performing similar functions have names, one part of which 17 may be common. Thus, the Castes, engaged in the work of Goldsmith (sonar) as the common part of their name. In Maharashtra, for example, there are distinct castes doing work in GoldDaivadanya Sonar, Lad Sonar, Ahir Sonar etc. Each caste group is endogamous either at caste level or at its sub caste group. The term sub-castes were formed out of the bigger groups called castes. But in central India, Rajasthan and Gujarat there are many sets of castes styling themselves SONAR. In west Bengal they are called Swarn Banik. In every linguistic regions of India, there are priestly castes calling themselves some type of Brahmin with several sub castes like Maga, Panch Gaud, Panch Dravid etc. Iravati Karve is of opinion that, 'Endogamy, distribution over s definite region and a hereditary occupation are the characteristic of a caste. (Karve 1953).

After 1953, i.e. after this study by Karve, Indian caste system witnessed tides of attacks blaming it as hindrance in developments. Many social scientists trained by British Anthropologist joined hands with attackers and wrote several thousand pages to prove its demerit but in vain. Caste is still a reality in India.

Casteism and Caste Politics have in recent years emerged as rallying points to gain electoral support.

- A new political trend of caste based consolidation of voters has emerged that can be termed as Revitalizations of caste in India. Government of India further introduced class like Forward class and Backward Class, scheduled Castes and scheduled tribes to suppress the old Occupation based system of caste. This has created several confusions and caste based reservations in job further fueling the fire. The officials, trained in British traditions turned no nerve unstrained to publicize the European supremacy of Class system over caste and promoted **Class –Caste Dichotomy**.
- Castes exercises its impact in politics by specific caste groups coming together to vote en block for a candidate of their own caste, without considering the merit of the candidate by appointing the members of influential caste or caste groups in the party as well as in the constituency and to offices of profit.

- Although no political party openly accepts the fact of being totally identified with any particular caste group (of course with few exceptions), there are cases galore of certain castes lending open and strong support and the political parties gladly accepting the same.
- Thus while political parties struggle among themselves to win different caste groups in their favor by making offers them, caste group too pressurize parties to choose its members for candidature in election.
- If the caste group is dominant and the political party is an important one, this interaction is all the more prominent.
- In many political parties, in place of ideological polarization there occurs the determination of policies and programmes as well as the nomination of electoral candidates and extension of support to them on caste consideration.
- A caste wishing to exercise political power must have a considerable number of its members elected. This involves putting pressure on some particular party and different castes struggling against each other in a bid to have a majority of their caste candidates elected.
- The electoral field witnesses both competition as well as alliances among various caste groups in order to get a substantial number of their caste men elected. Caste, therefore, dominates the political field, especially at the lower level.
- The emergence of regional parties and the withering away of the national outlook and spirit thus set up another crisis. Candidates come to be selected not in terms of accomplishments, ability and merit but on the basis of caste. Ultimately caste becomes the deciding factor on selection.
- One caste, in the attempt to obtain political power is committing aggression on the other thus promoting criminal nexus. The caste based politics and castes are eroding the unity principle in the name of regional autonomy. The influence of muscle power in Indian politics has long been a fact of political life since 1952. This is also promoted on caste lines.
- However, in the backdrop of the hegemony of Dominant Castes in our society and scour age of the caste system pushing away certain castes from mainstream to margins.
- Thus, Caste is a social and economic and political reality of Indian society and its assertion for a right and just political space has to be accepted.

- Caste that was a unique system of maintaining social solidarity in India since last 2000 years is now withering out and is being politically utilized to weaken the social fabric of our country.

Bibliography

Andre Beetle. Cast: Old and New- Asia Publishing House, New York, 1969.

Buchanan, Francis. An account of District of Purnea in 1809-10, Bihar and Orissa Research Society, Patna, 1928.

Census of India, the Scheduled Caste (SC) population of Jharkhand, Jharkhand data highlights. Government of India Publication, New Delhi, 2001.

Census of India, the Scheduled Caste (SC) population of Jharkhand, Jharkhand data highlights. Government of India Publication, New Delhi, 2011.

Dalton, E.T. Descriptive Ethnology of Bengal, Calcutta, 1872.

Diwaker R. R. Bihar through the ages, Oriental Longmans, Calcutta, 1959.

Iravati Karve- Hindu Social Organization.

Mishra, N. and L.P. Vidyarthi. Harijan Today, Classical Publications, Delhi, 1977.

Mishra, N. and L.P. Vidyarthi Economic problems of scheduled Castes of Bihar, in JSR, Vol. XVIII, no. 2, Ranchi, 1975.

Mukherjee, B.M. The position and future of the untouchables of Bihar, in Research Journal of Ranchi University, Vol. XII & XIII, 1976-77.

Roy S.C. 1920 The Bhuinyan.

Sharma, Vijay Prakash. Gandhi's approach to untouchability and its application at Nathdwara, in V.P. Sharma ed. Contemporary Indian Society, Vol. II, Anmol Publications, New Delhi, 1995.

Chapter - 2

The Scheduled Tribes of Jharkhand

— Vijay Prakash Sharma

Jharkhand is the second largest state inhabited by Tribal. They constitute nearly 26.7% of the population. Marginalization of tribal and commercial exploitation of their land and forest dates back to the British period. After independence, the nexus between development administration and businessmen on the one hand, and laws governing their commons on the other, further deprived them of not only their livelihood, but also resulted in a loss of their identity. The acts of aggression both internal and external are dangerous for their future survival. The major government projects like link-high way project, Netarhat firing range and Damodar Valley Corporations have displaced a large member of tribal.

The undermining of the cultural potential of the tribal population in India leveling them 'uncultured' 'forest dwellers' make us to believe that their mobility in the direction of the mainstream s of Indian culture is incompatible. This again is a myth, because on the contrary there are evidences to suggest that the concept of tribe does not refer to a set of static economic, social and ideological parameter. Communities with their differential lifestyle have their equally rich cultures which have undergone the process of change, adaptation and acculturation like others while still maintaining their tribal identity. In India, the indigenous people are referred to as **'Adivasi'**, (original inhabitants) **'Vanavasi'**, (Forest dwellers) **'Girijana'**(Inhabitants of Mountains) and sometimes **'Mulavasi'** (Original inhabitants). These terms are significant, for this attempt to identify the tribal people as the original inhabitants of the land having connection with nature.

Tribal legacy is as old as Indian pre-history and tribal are the cultural heritage of Indian sub continent. They have their own age old culture based on friendship with nature and their own language. One of characteristics which make human a human being is language; Language is nothing but verbal and non-verbal symbols or codes which have social-cultural meaninglanguage is acquired as a member of society. Mother tongue is cultural heritage. Mother tongue is also not statics rather it is dynamic. In this way language is a social heritage. Each community has a mother tongue. Each individual acquires it from old generation and handed it down to young generation. In this way language is transmitted from one generation to the next and continues as a tradition since the acquisition of the language starts from the lap of mother. An infant spends most of period of his/her life during childhood and adolescence period with mother; it is natural to call it as mother tongue. Another anthropologist, L.P. Vidyarthi feels that "In the ancient history of India their names, in the ancient language, the Sanskrit, would appear to have been, respectively (i) Nisad's, Sabaras, Bhils and Kollas, (ii) Kiratas, and (iii) Dasas, Dasyus, Sudras, and Dravidian. The ancient and epic literatures the Vedas, the Puranas, the Ramayana and the Mahabharata, present good accounts about the peopling of India. All these emphasize that India is inhabits by several types of tribes or people."(Vidyarthi1976, 26).

When the Aryan immigrants entered the country they found in the Land the nonAryan people and called them Dasyus. The word Dasyu was to denote the people other than themselves. I.e. the Aryans. The rig-Veda teems with different name of the people which denotes the mixed population of Indian. The Dasyus of Vedic antiquity, the non-Aryans are mainly of two stocks, like the Kolarians and the Dravidians (Regozin, 1961:287). The Mundas the Santhals, etc., of today are considered to be the descendants traits of character. Of the Dravidian tribes they are scattered through the Central Vindhya region and have covered the tableland of Deccan. The major representative Dravidian tribes are the Gonds, the Kondhs (the Kandhs) etc. Both Kolarians and the Dravidians came into the land at a prehistoric period far anterior to the Aryan from two opposite directions, the Kolarians from the east or northeast, the Dravidians from the north-west. It is thought that the Kolarians came first and after spreading over the present north-eastern Himalayan region and Bengal encountered the Dravidian current somewhere in the Vindhya region. The Kolarians being broken up by the tide dispersed in the valleys and forests of Vindhya high-land. The Dravidians marched ahead and inhabited the south (Hewitt, 1888-89). Presenting a consensual view Pathak (1972) also holds the Dravidians responsible for building of the Indus Valley culture. During the regime of great king Asoka issued order to the tribal's not to kill animals & birds as he was the patron king of Buddhism.

The ancient Sanskrit words suggest that the Mundas and other cognate tribes occupied northern India before the forefathers of Aryan Hindus entered the country. Manu Sanmhitas suggest that the tribes which by loss of sacred rites became outcastes from the pole of the recognized castes and sub-castes are the Dasyus. The Bhagawata Purana, give still another story about the origin of the Kols. The Harivansha Purana (XXX, 1616) and the Vayu Purana refer to the Kola whose descendants are the Kols. Leuva (1963), quoting the Rig-Veda, considers the Asuras and now Asurs.

The Ramayana also tells us about some tribal people. It endorses that there were only two groups of people – the Aryans and the non-Aryans. Among the non-Aryans the important tribes were the Rakshasas and the Vanaras both being the aboriginal tribes of the Deccan. The other tribes were the Nishadas, the Sabaras, the Yakshas and the Nags (Vyas, 1967:24). The Rakshasas are regarded as the earliest inhabitants of southern India and Sri Lanka. Racially they were perhaps identical with the Dasyus of the Rig-Veda. It is also believed that the Dravidian tribes of the Deccan descended from them. The Vanaras are also regarded as the non-Aryan hill tribes of southern India. Their chiefs were Bali and Sugriva. The name Vanara stands for the monkey, but it does not convey the some meaning. It is however believed that the Vanaras were only somewhat in appearance. The members of Ram's army were the people, the Vanaras that are generally seen in the forests of India (Ramdas, 1925). The Gridhas or the Supernal were some of the Indian nomadic tribes of the Ramayana age who were called after the names of birds on account of their migratory habit. The reference of Sabari in the Ramayana as a devotee of Ram is also attached to a group of people. Apparently she belonged to the tribe of Sabaras. The Kols of middle India regard Sabari as their mother.

The Mahabharata also mentions a few tribes. It is believed that Siva Mahadeva took the form of a Kirata and went to meet Arjun (Elwin, 1961: 2). From the Vedic period the world "Kirata" has been used for the non-Aryan tribes (Chatterji, 1968) living in the mountains, particularly in the Himalayan region. In the accounts of the Mahabharata, the Great War, we hear Sanjay describing the arrangements of the Korana Army mentions the Mundas as one of the constituents of the allied army. The comparison of the Mundas to Danavas in the Mahabharata (Drona Parva, 117, 23) would seem to indicate that the reference was to an aboriginal people of the name of Mundas.

We have seen the early people of India and the contribution of the tribal, through ancient literatures. In the early historical period of India which coincides with the Hindu period, the tribal either compromised with the Hindu neighbours or went farther in the deep forest. All through the long centuries of the Hindu rule and Hindu neighbours, the tribal's find themselves assimilated to an extent with the Hindu culture. Ghurye (1963:18) has discussed the matter in detail and opines that "almost all the so-called aboriginal tribes of the region have a Hindu section, small or large, that they have been in fairly intimate contact with the Hindus for a long time and that they have common interest with the Hindus in matter of religion and gainful occupation".

There has been enough evidence to establish that Ravana was representative king of the Dravidian tribe. The Ravana battle was virtually the battle of two Cultures, Dravidian (Adivasi) and non-Aryans. This way the history of Tribal in the country is as old as the country is.

Till recently it has been established that the number of Tribal communities are 510 & 463 are recognised as ST. They live in the basis of geo-climatic & demographic Characters in the following regions:

- North-Western tribal region
- Western tribal region
- Southern Tribal region
- Central tribal region
- North-Eastern tribal region
- Island region.

The Tribal people live in the North Western part of India in the high altitudes zone of Himalaya & they were referred to as Gandharvas & Kirata in ancient history & culture. A good member of Tribal communities still lives in the region. The Tribal's of western region were referred to as Aparanta which was the generic name of tribes in ancient Indian history.

In the southern tribal region which all use ancient in origin both primitive & back word & the term Daksinataya was a generic name of tribes (Nagar & Kadar).

In the Central region the Indo Genetic basin, which comprises of great part of tribal in- habitation & the number of tribes is huge. In the ancient history their generic names were Yaksa and Rakshas etc. The North Eastern region the tribal communities who historically played the role of buffer communities are Marang Naga & Khasi, who are of Mongolian origin. Besides these Lepchas, Bhutia also live in the region.

In the Island region, tribal communities (Onge, Jarwa, and Great Andmanese) live in Andaman Nicobar & Lakshadweep. The region has long history. This was pre-occupied by tribal communities but latter external invasion and interference resulted in the adverse situation.

It is rather a recent phenomenon that the great divide between the tribal and non-tribal has emerged. The census enumeration of 1901 under Risley, 1911 under Gait, 1921 under Lewis 24 and 1931 under Hutton do not have exact lexical references to tribes in the Pre-British India. The process of 'tribal' 'non-tribal' divide made the tribal population to shy away from the rapid modernization and as a result they were left behind in the society as 'uncared for'

Scheduled Tribes

Article 366 (25) of the Constitution of India refers to Scheduled Tribes as those communities, who are scheduled in accordance with Article 342 of the Constitution. This Article says that only those communities who have been declared as such by the President through an initial public notification or through a subsequent amending Actor Parliament will be considered to be Scheduled Tribes. Article 342 provides for specification of tribes or tribal communities or parts of or groups within tribes or tribal communities which are deemed to be for the purposes of the Constitution the Scheduled Tribes in relation to that State or Union Territory. In pursuance of these provisions, the list of Scheduled Tribes are notified for each State or Union Territory and are valid only within the jurisdiction of that State or Union Territory and not outside. The list of Scheduled Tribes is State/UT specific and a community declared as a Scheduled Tribe in a State need not be so in another State. The inclusion of a community as a Scheduled Tribe is an ongoing process. The essential characteristics, first laid down by the Lokur Committee, for a community to be identified as Scheduled Tribes are– (a) indications of primitive traits; (b) distinctive culture; (c) shyness of contact with the community at large; (d) geographical isolation; and (e) backwardness. Tribal communities live, in various ecological and geo-climatic conditions ranging from plains and forests to hills and inaccessible areas. Tribal groups are at different stages of social, economic and educational development. While some tribal communities have adopted a mainstream way of life, at the other end of the spectrum, there are certain Scheduled Tribes, 75 in number known as Particularly Vulnerable Tribal Groups (PVTGs), who are characterized by (a) pre-agriculture level of technology; (b) stagnant or declining population; (c) extremely low literacy; and (d) subsistence level of economy.

One cannot dispute this categorization for it is based on a political criterion. According to constitution of India, certain communities can be included in the schedule of tribes. This administrative action makes each such community a "scheduled tribe" and entitles it to special protection and privileges.

Broadly the STs inhabit two distinct geographical areas – the Central India and the NorthEastern Area. More than half of the Scheduled Tribe population is concentrated in Central India, i.e., Madhya Pradesh (14.69%), Chhattisgarh (7.5%), Jharkhand (8.29%), Andhra Pradesh (5.7%), Maharashtra (10.08%), Orissa (9.2%), Gujarat (8.55%) and Rajasthan (8.86%). The other distinct area is the North East (Assam, Nagaland, Mizoram, Manipur, Meghalaya, Tripura, Sikkim and Arunachal Pradesh). The Graph above shows the states' share of ST population out of India's ST population:

Late B.D. Sharma, the former Commissioner for SCs and STs, a Constitutional officer reporting directly to the President has noted the followings " (i) the virtual collapse of the Constitutional regime with regard to the tribal people who are now being attacked and suppressed in a war like situation; (ii) the Fifth Schedule of the Constitution, regarded as a Constitution within the Constitution' provides for the governors of states to write an annual report on the administration of the tribal areas and the giving of directions by the President but no such directions have been issued in the last 60 years; (iii) the Constitutional machinery of the Tribal Advisory Council has become extinct; (iv) state power extends to the tribal areas subject to the provisions of the Fifth Schedule; (v) Panchayat (Extension to Scheduled Areas) Act, 1996 has remained virtually unimplemented; and so is The Forest Rights Act, 2006; and (vi) the history of broken promises, predatory administration, co-optation through development programmes and unconcern at the top over massive displacement have led to the multiplication of revolts, which have been met with a brutal paramilitary response."

The tribal leadership is passing through a phase of vacuum and the spread of Naxal movement in the tribal areas is an expression of people's anger. They need special attention of the Government for their all-round development.

Tribal Development

There are over 700 Scheduled Tribes notified under Article 342 of the Constitution of India, spread over different states and Union Territories of the Country. As per 2001 census, tribal population of the country is 8.43 crores, constituting 8.2% of the total population. 91.7% of them live in rural areas and 8.3% in urban areas. About 15% of the country's area is inhabited by the tribal communities, who live in various ecological and geo-climatic conditions ranging from plains and forests to hills and inaccessible areas.

Broadly, they inhabit two distinct geographical areas. A large segment inhabits Central India, i.e., Madhya Pradesh(14.51%), Chhattisgarh (7.85%), Jharkhand (8.4%), Andhra Pradesh (5.98%), Maharashtra (10.17%), Orissa (9.66%), Gujarat (8.87%) and Rajasthan (8.42%). The other distinct area is the North East (Assam, Nagaland, Mizoram, Manipur, Meghalaya and Arunachal Pradesh).

Map Showing Curent Status of Tribals in Jharkhand

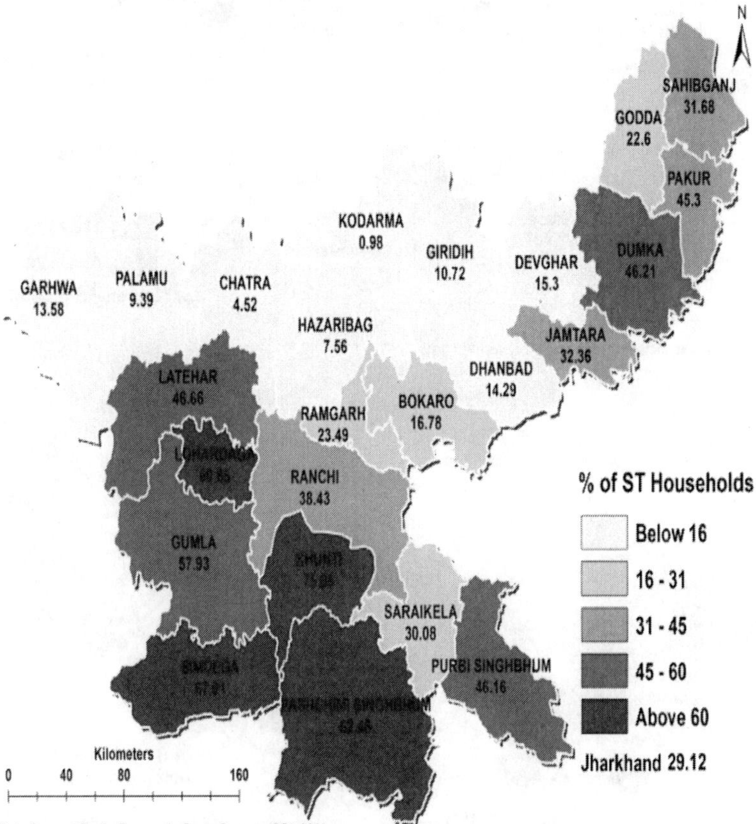

Data Source: Socio-Economic Caste Census, GOI, 2011

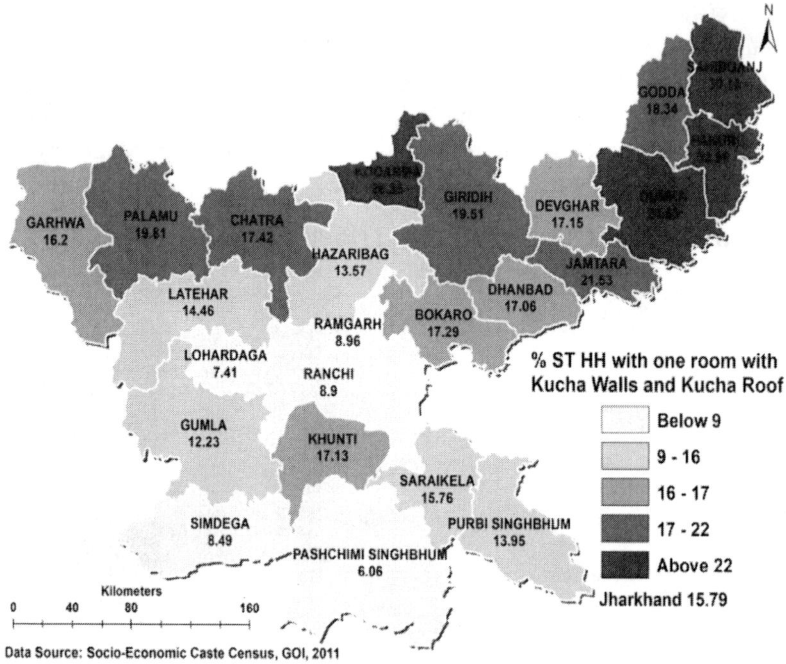
N
GODDA
18.34
GARHWA
16.2
PALAMU
19.81
CHATRA
17.42
GIRIDIH
19.51
DEVGHAR
17.15
HAZARIBAG
13.57
JAMTARA
21.53
LATEHAR
14.46
DHANBAD
17.06
RAMGARH
8.96
BOKARO
17.29
LOHARDAGA
7.41
RANCHI
8.9
GUMLA
12.23
KHUNTI
17.13
SARAIKELA
15.76
SIMDEGA
8.49
PURBI SINGHBHUM
13.95
PASHCHIMI SINGHBHUM
6.06
% ST HH with one room with Kucha Walls and Kucha Roof
Below 9
9 - 16
16 - 17
17 - 22
Above 22
Jharkhand 15.79
Kilometers
0 40 80 160
Data Source: Socio-Economic Caste Census, GOI, 2011

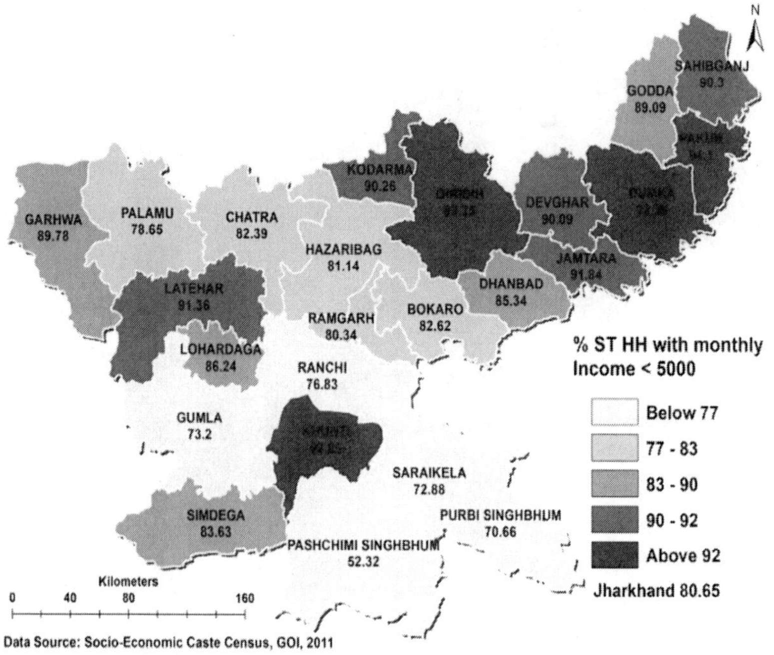
N
SAHIBGANJ
90.3
GODDA
89.09
KODARMA
90.26
GARHWA
89.78
PALAMU
78.65
CHATRA
82.39
DEVGHAR
90.09
HAZARIBAG
81.14
JAMTARA
91.84
LATEHAR
91.36
DHANBAD
85.34
RAMGARH
80.34
BOKARO
82.62
LOHARDAGA
86.24
RANCHI
76.83
% ST HH with monthly Income < 5000
GUMLA
73.2
Below 77
77 - 83
SARAIKELA
72.88
83 - 90
SIMDEGA
83.63
PURBI SINGHBHUM
70.66
90 - 92
PASHCHIMI SINGHBHUM
52.32
Above 92
Kilometers
0 40 80 160
Jharkhand 80.65
Data Source: Socio-Economic Caste Census, GOI, 2011

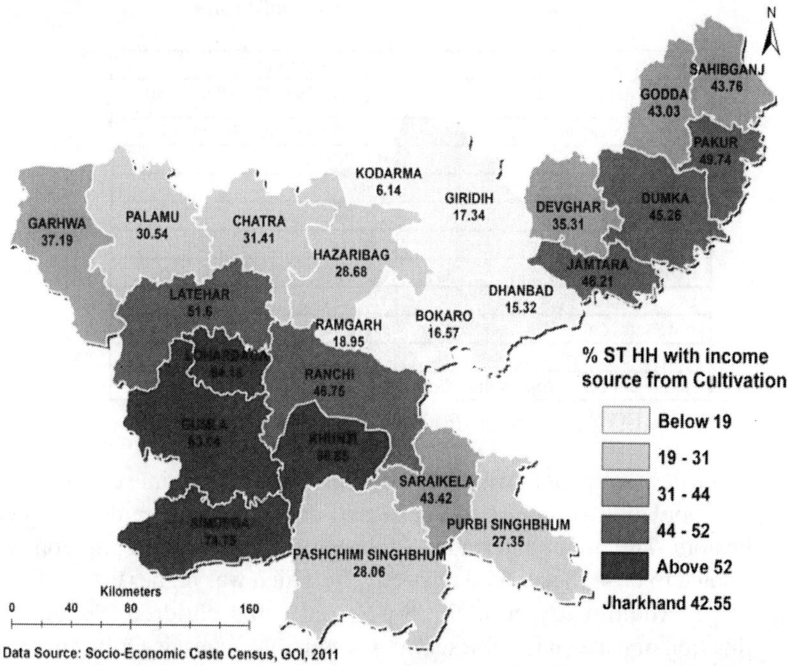

Data Source: Socio-Economic Caste Census, GOI, 2011

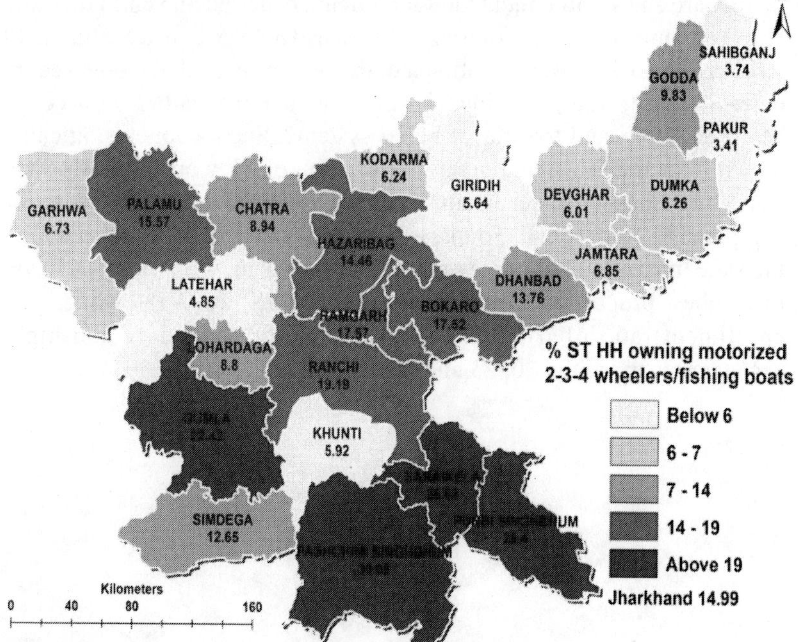

Data Source: Socio-Economic Caste Census, GOI, 2011

Table: Tribal Development Indicators

Indicators	Jharkhand
Infant Mortality Rate	46.8 (per 1000 live birth)
Under-5 Mortality Rate	64 (per 1000 live birth)
Anemia	78%
Gross Enrolment Ratio	
Primary	30
Secondary	23
Higher Secondary	22
Literacy Rate	57 (%)
Antenatal Care	7 (%)
Institutional Deliveries	49 (%)
Janani Suraksha Yojana Beneficiaries	50.8 (%)

Source: NFHS, 2015-16 and Jharkhand Economic Survey 2017-18.

The development of tribal in Jharkhand has been a prime concern. The tribal population continues to lag behind in various human development indicators. The infant and under-5 mortality of the tribal population was estimated to be 46.8 and 64.0 respectively, which was higher than the state average. Additionally, around 78 per cent tribal children are anemic. Utilization of maternal health services is equally appalling. Only 7 per cent of tribal women receive antenatal care in the state. Deliveries in health facility are an essential requisite for reducing maternal and child mortality. However, only 49 per cent of tribal women had deliveries in a health facility (NFHS 2015-16). Low institutional deliveries among tribal women cannot be attributed to the poor financial conditions alone, rather on access to health facilities and traditional belief systems. Such a conclusion can be drawn from the fact that a greater proportion of ST women are receiving financial assistance under Janani Suraksha Yojana to deliver in institutions compared to other social groups. Educational status of tribal population in the state, measured by literacy rate was 57 per cent, with Simdega having the highest proportion followed by Ranchi (JES, 2017-18) while; gross enrollment ratio of tribal children in primary, secondary and higher secondary was around 30, 23 and 22respectively.

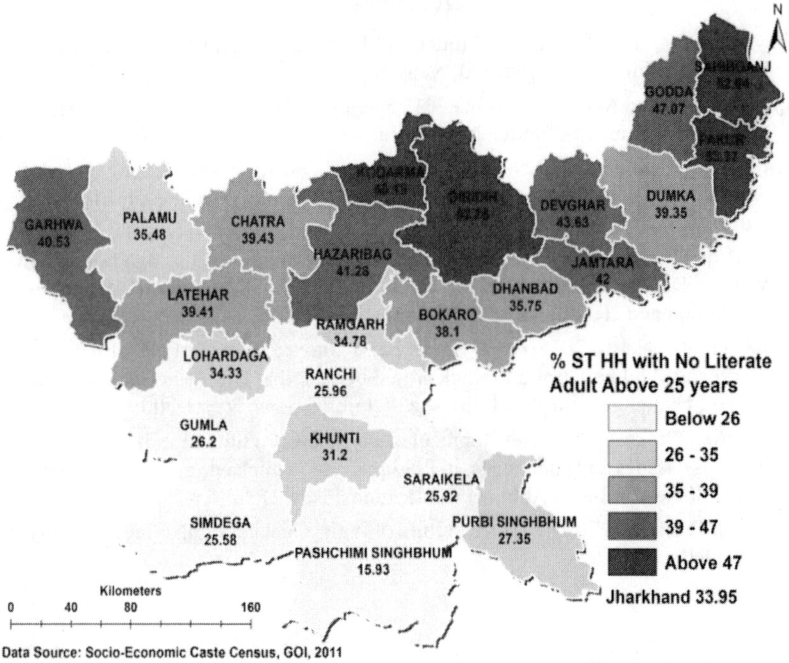

Data Source: Socio-Economic Caste Census, GOI, 2011

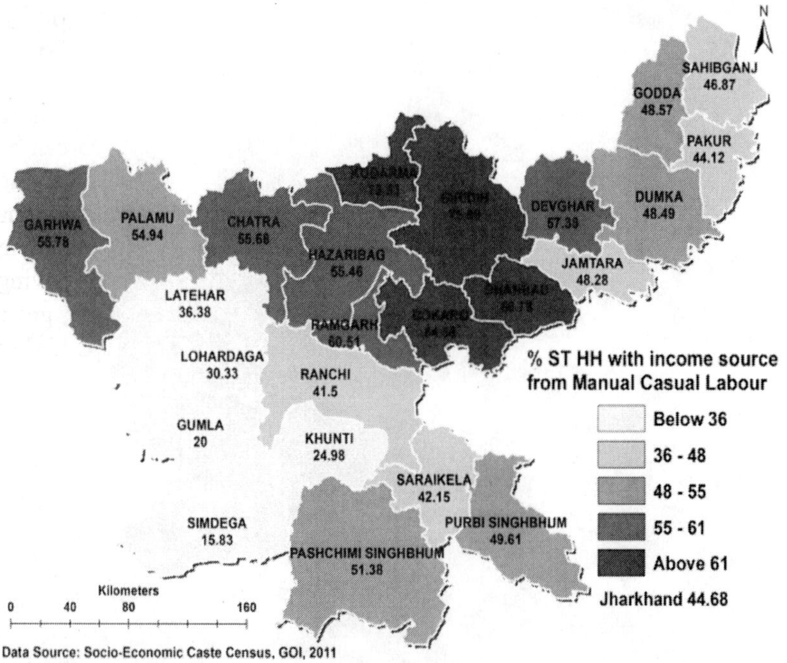

Data Source: Socio-Economic Caste Census, GOI, 2011

References

Dubey, S.C. 1977 Tribal Heritage of India, Vol I: Ethnicity, Identity and Interaction, Vikas Publishing House Pvt. Ltd, New Delhi.

Haque. Nurul S, and Ajay Narayan Jha 2012 Strategic Plan - 2012 – 2017 (Revised), MOTA, Government of India, New Delhi.

Sharma. Vijay Prakash, 2014 Need for Water and Land Resources among Tribe of Central India, published in B.M. Mukherjee edited book" Tribal People of Central India", K.K. Publications New Delhi.

Sharma. Vijay Prakash, 2014Thinking about Tribal Development through Integrated Village Development Model in Jharkhand, P. Dash Sharma edited book Livelihood and Health, Serial Publication, New Delhi.

Sharma. Vijay Prakash, 2015 Tribal Society and Unrest: A Case of Naxal Affected Jharkhand, Mukherjee and Mallick edited book Tribal Unrest in Central India-Causes, challenges and possibilities, K.K.Publications, New Delhi.

Sharma. Vijay Prakash, 2016 Development of Particularly Vulnerable Tribal Groups (PVTGs): issues and challenges, in Pradip K. Bhowmick edited book Changing Tribal Society in India, Abhijeet Publications, New Delhi.

Vidyarthi L.P. ET. al 1976 The Tribal Culture of India, Concept Publishing Company, New Delhi.

Chapter - 3

Unravelling the Nation: A Sociological Narrative of Tribal Deprivation

— Sri Biswajit Ghosh, Kaushik Chattopadhyay

Introduction

Presently we are passing through such a phase when the indigenous people of Indian society are being repudiated in the name of 'unity'. The woodlands are handed to the corporate houses on some developmental issues. These issues, as an obvious consequence, displace the jungle life style. The aboriginals' way of life is eventually becoming inconspicuous for the sake of 'Nation' construction.

These issues, though not new, but presently have gained a rapid momentum. Such description in anthropological tradition is eminently notable in the research works of Herbert Hope Risley, Franz Boas, Alfred Reginald Radcliffe-Brown, Bronislaw Kasper Malinowski, Nirmal Kumar Bose, Surajit Sinha, Probodh Kumar Bhowmick, Andre Beteille, and others. On a world scale anthropometric study depending on scientific research method, describes the indigenous people.

Without trailing the path of physical anthropology, we may observe the changes in the lives of 'adivasis' or 'vanvasi' or 'girijans' by explaining them through cultural and social anthropology (Majumdar, and Madan, 1956). From an ideal state with a self-contained unit, the study of tribal life has to be placed on historical perspective (Beteille, 1977). This interpretation may become sociological. A tribal group of people acclimatized in jungle life and habituated in forest-grown food, and another tribal group who are simultaneously living side by side in adjacent village society with modern life style, may be a matter of that discussion (Beteille, 1974; Sharma, 2001).

It is a matter of observation as how changes in group life and kinship bond, morality and language, rituals and ceremonies, and even change in marriage and dress code are emerging within their knowledge system (Bose, 2002). This primary subject in re-evaluating the conceptualization of tribal life is sailing through the anthropological tradition to sociological analysis for arriving at a consensus on few propositions.

The present endeavour tries to explore, especially in Indian society, how the tribes emerged; how their presence could be assessed; how different development programmes influence their dual livelihood; their stand after cultural assimilation, accommodation and diffusion is a point for analysis. And if it is an eventual result, then there rises a question: is detribalization inevitable? If we try to find out an answer to this fundamental question, it is necessary to make a sociological critical survey of the conceptualization of tribal development discourse.

Simultaneously, a query may arise – whose development? In what aspect there is development or in what expression underdevelopment is taken for granted? What are the parameters of tribal development? All these questions serially come to the fore. In the name of development, are we pushing the tribes to be rootless? This question becomes the central point of consideration.

Indian society and its first part of tribal identity formation

In the historical sociological aspect, this part is the first stage of globalization of aboriginal life in India. This is the first close connection with the external world by the Indian society. Vedic records, however, have failed to explain conclusively about this period. PreVedic literature lacks evidence. Yet on the basis of claims of Dr. Martin Haug, Dr. R. L. Mitter, Narayan Chandra Bandyopadhyay, and other social scientists, it may be held that the Iranians and Vedic Aryans were in special oneness about religious practices and holding of occasions. These two ethnic groups in the second and third B.C. constituted a racial mixture and claimed "themselves as Aryans". They were inhabitants of "hallowed land of the SaptaSindhavah" (Bandyopadhyay, 1938: 25). They could not vividly describe the then native people. No clear sociological explanation is available here about the tribe, clans and their ruling kinsmen. But what is available here, is the daily life-practices of the Aryans. The religious practices are praying for auspice and well being of their clans. They wanted expansion of their kingdom. They considered the enemies as polluting elements and by developing antagonistic relationship they fought against them. They marked it a weal to force them to surrender. These enemies were known to them as Jana (Chattopadhyay, 2017: 58-60).

These non-Aryans were enemies. They were not only separated in their physical characters, but also in their speech, manners, religion, and belief system – in all cases they differed (Dutt, 1925). In the process of Aryanization, Aryans named them as 'Jana' or tribe. The exclusive ethnic characteristics of this Jana are anâs (flat nosed) and mrdhra-vâc (hostile speech). Politically they were considered as Dâsyu (a race of hostile enemies). They had enough knowledge about the value of gold and silver and hold âyasi (forts), where Sambara (non-Aryan chief) lived. They are Dravidians.

Here a debate may arise as to how to justify the presence of the Dravidians in North India? Ethnological evidences and its philosophical explanations help to establish it scientifically. North Indian Gonds and Oraons are those Dravidians. Not only that, Brahuis of far-off Baluchistan are those Dravidians. They are racially and linguistically a branch of Dravidians. They are marked as Jana. In their Indo-Iranian contact and settlement Aryans forced 'Kol' people to serve them, were also a part of 'Jana'. North-West India was then divided into Aryans and non-Aryans. In subjugation and oppression, in forcible occupation –Aryans were victorious. Subjugated non-Aryans gradually shifted from their own cultural elements. This also is a kind of development. In one side, racial mixture, and on the other, it is the new saga of uprooted culture. According to Suniti Kumar Chatterji (1951: vii), "the civilization of India is the joint creation of her diverse peoples, Aryan, Dravidian, Austric (Kol) and Mongoloid."

If we look into the development of Indian tribal society through this phase of Jana identity formation, then it may be seen and explained as the first stage of globalization of tribal life. Here globalization does not integrate world market; rather it symbolizes local global nexus. Change occurred in the traditional quality of life of Jana. In one side there was emergence of varna and caste system, and on the other, the tribe's area-dependent environmental knowledge, medicinal practices, indigenous research procedure, started altering. The scenario of socio-economic background began change.

Jatinization, modernization and rethinking Indian society

Indian tribes live hilly or forested terrain. Barring North-East Himalayan areas of the tribes, the development on the lives of the tribes who live in Central and North-West region of India can be explained from three angles (Sinha, 1964). The first change can be termed as 'jatinization'. In Indian civilization, the development of agriculture, use of plough begot change in the caste hierarchy with the help of sanskritization process (Srinivas, 1952).

Similarly, such development paved the way of incorporation of the tribes within jati system (Elwin, 1955). The development of village based society and the rural life of tribal people ensured the success of jatinization. The tribal life based on venery (hunting) and collection of food and its preservation, changed by adopting the occupational skill of specific jati.

A specific caste based occupational skill can be adopted by a specific tribe (Mandelbaum, 1972). It is mentionable here that one jati organization was not only more flexible than that of tribal organization, but it also could easily include the others in the productive content. On the other hand for another two reasons jatinization could happen. Firstly, one tribe clearly maintained separation from its sub-tribes in the matter of customs, norms, and the estrangement of the kinsmen was considered as an ignominy and it influenced the rituals. As a result, violence occurred. To avoid such violence, tribe who lived within the peripheral position of the village society, wished to live inside the jati system. Secondly, in the interest of getting some benefits, the tribes were ready to drop their firm identity, close solidarity, religious satisfaction, and emotional security, and wanted to include themselves in Hindu jati-structure (Ghurye, 1932; 1955; and 1959). These may generally be material benefits or sharing of social resources. But they never wanted to shed off the status of a proud tribe and accept an inferior jati title. As an example, Kotas of Nilgiri Hills were proud to be aborigines; because they were the old inhabitants of that locality, and their artisan skills were of high quality. It is, however, true that it is difficult to differentiate between Hinduism and tribal religion. Daily communication, assimilation of cultural traits and religious practices of Hill or forest tribes very easily helped inclusion of tribal practices inside the Hindu community.

In the second aspect, multifaceted changes can be explained from two sides: firstly, Mughal invasion, and secondly, British colonization. Detailed discussion about influence of Mughal rulers on the Indian tribal socio-economic life is not noticeable. However, from scarce information available, it is found that the tribal communities in Mughal period remained isolated and intact (Habib, 2004). The changes that occurred in tribal life were specifically in Delhi and other such big townships (Padgi, 1952). In one word, North-Indian tribes embraced Muslim religion and got accustomed to Persi and Urdu. Even they separated themselves from the tribes of the Indo-Gangetic Plains (Gommans, 2002). Communication between Afghan and Iranian highlands' tribal people became clear at this point of time.

Surajit Sinha has done some excellent work in this field of study. He has mentioned about the influence of Vaisnava religion and specific norms of tribal food habit in his essay on "Vaisnava Influence on a Tribal Culture".

In this connection, Buddhism can also be mentioned here. The tribals had an affinity to Buddhism (Law, 1922; Coomaraswamy, 1943). Whatever may be the case, it can be indicated that in the era of Mughal Reign there existed no dichotomy between the tribal culture and the way of life of jati villagers. It is also to be noticed that the remote and isolated tribal groups were used to such cultural elements, there were some sort of similarity in everyday cultural and religious rites.

A huge change occurred in the Indian tribal community and in the tribal life at the advent of the British. Tribal life was enormously influenced by the British Raj on the ground that they used their administrative power in every nook and corner of India and, therefore, it grossly involved in creating societal process in a new order (Mahapatra, 1986). Example may be cited in respect of Irula, Badaga, Toda, Kola and Kurumba tribes of Nilgiri Hills of Tamil Nadu. In 1819, before British invasion in this area, and before construction of massive roads for easy transportability, every tribe had specific expertise and excellent economic and ritual activities which created in them a sense of self estimation and they maintained it for long time. But the British venture, crushed through its modernization project, changed that reciprocal relationship and amalgamates modern life with tribal life (Debo, 1940). This may be treated as a motivated outcome of development. This development was a short-to-medium term outcome of desirable targets. Indeed, it has been guided by motivation. Its focus point looks after only change and obliviates the most valuable part for ever.

The second perspective of development in India started becoming effective with the British rule. By using the centralized bureaucratic structure, development of all communities started framing in a common matrix (Desai, 1978; Chatterjee, 1996). Here one paternalistic assumption works and it is taken for granted that one set of universal values and characteristics will do well to all kinds of tribal way of life. Development here certainly indicates one kind of change and perhaps somewhere democratic, technocratic approaches are also taken. But there occurred obviously a form of exclusion, i.e. formation of compelling identity like "criminal tribe".

Incidentally, from Vedic age to pre-Mughal era, tribal development generally indicates that perspectives which may be called as long term process of structural and societal transformation. Mughal age did not influence tribal life much, but in this period unification may be described as a transitional phase. The kinds of development model used in British era were not short-to-medium term only; it ensured specific expected outcome with definite target fulfillment. The rites of taking food, dress code, occupational patterns etc. changed; as also extensive utilization of natural resource and forest wealth brought forth broad changes in their old-fashioned forest living. This is for the first time, development with displacement started to happen. Industrialization and new sort of division of labour brought wide-ranging changes in their traditional power structure in community life. Even some tribal communities, for example the Lodhas, Savaras, had been designated as criminal tribes (Bhowmick, 1963).

This may be described as a second wave of globalization in tribal life (Dutta and Chattopadhyay, 2016). In this phase, no clan group seemed eager to establish new redistributive relationship with their neighbouring clans. Old exchange related relationship started to efface. This second wave of globalization put a blow to the roots of tribal society. Old-fashion social conscience, community feelings, collective rituals, shared emotions, health consciousness started to transform. These changes started to govern their organizational role restructuring process. Urban tribes were fluent in using their own dialect, but subsequently they become expert in multilingual interactive space (Watters, 2003). It was certain for them to be attacked by new kinds of diseases.

Change in Tribal community life

In new zeal, independent India governs its administrative system for a fresh purpose. In the Preamble of the 1950-Constitution of India, these new aims have been targeted. Here arise the talks about social, economic, cultural, political, educational, health and hygiene related development programmes. It was intended to establish justice. Independent thinking, faith, religious practices, amenities and fraternity assure the dignity of the individual and the unity within diversity. To fulfill these aims, Babasaheb Ambedkar did a remarkable job of identifying 'depressed class' as Schedule Caste and Schedule Tribe. As this part of society (dalits and tribals) was the weakest section, it was decided to give them special protection. Special care was taken to protect their right in landed property (Bhowmick, 1963).

'Special advantages' speak about desirable outcome in all respects. That keeping the aims fixed, bringing change is an 'ahistorical' process, as Charles Gore (2000) demands. However, this perspective of development brought a radical change in the background of long-standing development process conjugated by sanskritization and jatinization. Infact, this change gave birth to "a confusion of choice of identity". As an example, we may talk about Bhumij tribe. These tribal people extensively live in Bihar and Ráàh areas of West Bengal. Numerically, they are about half a million. When natural and social level development process was mobile, then a big part of Bhumij were habituated to jati folk and achieved the status of

Kshatriya caste. As an example of upward social mobility, jatinization brought positive changes in the ensuring life of Bhumij tribe. Bhumij tribe is jatinized with BhumijKshatriya caste identity. But after independence, to avail of the advantages given to the Bhumij as Scheduled Tribe, a part of them stand for the collective identity of Adivasi (literally: first inhabitants). These Bhumij kinsmen demand that in comparison to their Kshatriya identity, they will reap more benefits with "identity of adivasi".

Surajit Sinha (1959) had conducted some relevant surveys on this subject. He observed that to be a partner of development the tribal society which had a "homogeneous character", the tribal society which was an example to the civilized society as an idea of community with "emotional security", was fragmented in two parts. Economically secured rich land-owners belonging to Bhumij wanted to remain akin to Kshatriya identity in the interest of having a high position in the society. They deserted Bhumij customs, norms, rituals, values and rites in an entirety. On the other hand, the marginal and poor Bhumij started living embracing their traditional norms, customs and values. As a religious custom, ploughing, marring a widow, and celebrating with rice beer in their ceremonies – these helped to bring their ancient identity as Bhumij.

Whatever may be the case, after independence, with a desire to realize the effective role of Indian Constitution, the government took initiatives in development programmes under Five Year Plans. Basically four contexts were emphasized. Firstly, development in communication facilities was initiated. Emphasis was given on road and railway development. Here North-East Hill Area could be mentioned as an example (Rao, 1975). Secondly, all attempts were made to develop educational and cultural facilities. For tribal children schools were founded during the fifties and sixties. Tribal teachers through the medium of their own language started receiving modern education. The third side is related to the facilities in the health, housing and water supply extending to the tribals. In the first two Five Year Plans decisions were taken to establish dispensaries in tribal areas and to arrange mobile health units. The fourth side is related to development vis-à-vis economic improvement. Here extensive changes were effected in old-fashioned mode of production. As a welfare measure, Government of India established Labour co-operatives in tribal area. And for the development of agriculture, seeds and irrigation facilities were arranged and for providing employment of tribal population on priority basis, the foundation of Cottage Industry was initiated. Technical supports were given to the tribal workers to enhance their efficiency and effectiveness. Through different work programmes economic developments of tribes were tried to be made more effective.

In the seventies some sort of changes were brought about in the short-term outcome centered planning in tribal development. Specifically, they were tried to be made effective in the fifth Five Year Plan. In 1974, Integrated Tribal Development Programme was formally launched. According to it, to realize the objectives of the programme, two perspectives have to be emphasized: (1) co-operation; (2) participation. The large sized Multi-purpose Cooperative Societies (LAMPS) were to play an important role in coordinating institutional finance, credit and marketing facilities for tribes. In every such developmental work, government expects that they will directly be involved. Integrated Tribal Development Project (ITDP) officials are directed to learn the language of the tribal clan with whom they are to work. This endeavour was undertaken to realize the target of participatory development. This is true that through this short-term goal-oriented programme when development takes place, simultaneous long-term social, economic, political, cultural and techno-structural transformation also comes out. Yet it is not in the old-fashioned constructed form. Impact of modernity and Indian variety of globalization had split that form.

The rhetorical discourses of tribal development in new millennium

In the eighties of the last century, Indian planning talked about self - sustained economy and that strengthen the technological development. Before the Annual Plans of 1990-92, Sixth and Seventh Five Year Plans influenced tribal development in two ways. Firstly, land-clan relationship was established solidly. Right to forest lands and connection with arable lands expressed tribal economy in a new dimension to modern market-based economy. Secondly, the extensive urbanization and progress of technology help in developing concepts like technocratic, bureaucratic tribesmen along with urban tribe, metropolitan tribe, etc.

In the nineties, liberalization, privatization and globalization organizationally dominated the economic-political scenario (Saren, 2013). Now we may observe this neoliberal globalization as the governing force of Indian economy for the first time and in the perspective of tribal development. We may call it the third wave. Here the dominance of America was much more than that of Europe. Conversion of religion of tribals is not related much to their welfare. Tribes give much stress on modern education, profession and expertise in their metropolitan living. This bestows their new identity. Their tribal identity here is somewhat grey. They keep relationship with those kinsmen who belong to such dignified position. They are the tribes of global village. They are part of network society.

Globalization here is interconnecting world metropolitan life with indigenous local identity (James, 2006; Chattopadhyay, 2017). This linking of tribal development makes delusions and disappointments face-to-face. We may call this contemporary nature as postdevelopmental stage, or post-colonial phase, or post-structural position. Whatever we say, the idea of development is strongly criticized. Criticism expanded gradually against the short term project in tribal development planning which was implemented by Government of India to achieve definite target. Development as an unintentional process progressively becomes an intentional activity. Questions arise as for whose interest is development? Is the rootless tribe as a 'lonely crowd' is the symbol of development? The 'independence of development research' is transformed from relative to absolute issue. It is evident that where the organizational research frame is financed by that monetary assistance, there the presence of secret cravings cannot be denied. Funding agencies give priority to their policy-oriented researches. Therefore, even if independent body does the research work, who are supplying funds and for which intention make the term development fishy?

Displacement for development is another side which torn the expectation of project based development (Mallavarapu, 2008). Displacement in tribal society happens for another reason. That is ethnic violence. Unequal development may cause violence among tribal clans. There are several other reasons. For political or electoral democratic means, or due to access to arms in place of old-fashioned power, or for cultural autonomy and array of new powerstructure, in any geographical area one tribe organizes violence on the others. Indeed, NorthEast India is the ideal place of ethnic cleansing. Specially, in Assam, Manipur, Nagaland, Arunachal Pradesh, Meghalaya, and partially in Tripura, such incidents of violence are happening. Through that question – Does development stabilize ethnic cleansing – both perspectives of development is being treated as inefficient.

For the reason of violence or to fulfill development project displacement brings change in everyday life. Especially this change is clearly revealed in language. This change happens inside the non-material cultural elements (Mahapatra, 1981). In respect of the tribal life, this is also a social fact. Specially in new habitat, social phenomena do happen and to express it in one sense or by giving a definition, if a tribe does not find the proper word from his own lexicon, then he borrows the words from dominant language (Misra, 2002). It is not their own, but they use it as new metanymy in their everyday speech. Their language loses its own flavour and flow. On the other hand in new areas, existing cultural elements of other people (those may not be tribes) entered inside their own ways abruptly. Such incidents are termed by Dipankar Gupta (1986) as the development for "divergence of tribal attitude."

Dipankar Gupta had observed the Santhals in the District of Birbhum, West Bengal. He found that extended Bengali society's nearness has brought change to the habitus of the Santhals. Eastern Blocks of Birbhum, where Bengalis are dominant in figure, the Santhal tribesmen, share-croppers or agriculture labourers or doing work somewhere else, are much more enduring in their behavioural nature by co-operation with other caste people. In their characteristics, even they are observant of religious practices, and in their behaviour with others the absence of gusto, the insouciance are notable. On the other hand, remote Western Blocks of Birbhum, where Santhals are dominant, they are aware of their racial history. They know who their legendary heroes are. In practical awareness they are strong in political matter. They can organize movements for the betterment of their community life.

Therefore, the conception of development in its long-term social and cultural transformation and short-term project based on desired goal assessment depicts the picture about detribalization process as demanded as development. Specially, keeping in mind Edward Said's (1978) proposition about "attitude of supremacy" and his knowledge about and knowledge of Orientals questioning who held native life as savage? Who told that they were underdeveloped? Through whose eyes estimation had been made about their everyday life processes? For this reason, contemporary development perspective views development as a dominant discourse of Western modernity. Not only identity, poverty and the rhetoric demand of high culture development frame are being constructed socially. By keeping and nurturing carefully this socio-cultural value and economic epistemes, the native life is stigmatized by bearing a compelling identity that unravels the nation.

Conclusion

In the long path of change, many Indian tribes had not deserted their religions, belief systems, values, habitations, food habits, ways of getting mates, traditions of treatment procedures, social solidarity and own history, they were also isolated from their traditional environment. They had forgotten their spiritual and cultural assets. On the other hand, they had not been able to keep pace with the modern life-style, high-mass-consumer behaviourism, and civilized manners. They were not habituated in the humanitarian agenda of liquid modernity.

Many tribal identities today are centred on the ideas of resistance and opposition. Some of them are taking part in money economy. Like other caste-women, somewhere tribalwomen have constituted self-help group of micro-finance, or participated in Mahatma Gandhi National Rural Employment Guarantee Act (MGNREGA) that offers a guarantee of hundred days of wage-employment in a year. Indeed, for the betterment of their family life, they include themselves in several Government welfare programmes, or in different private ventures. They even represent as elected members in several bodies of Government by winning seats which are reserved for the women candidates in democratic electoral system of India. In the meantime they alienate themselves from that knowledge tradition for which their woman ancestors, rather than their male counter-part, were more concerned. It was a familiarity with the medicinal plants of their local forests.

Postmodern perspective of development had forced the objective reality to be plundered. Everything is suspiciously observed. Following extreme in subjective dimension and various ethnographical studies of tribal social events, even if effective, but the capability in explaining alternatives to tribal development remains undefined (Maffesoli, 1988). What is important in postmodern post-development aspect? It is an interest in local culture and local knowledge. Postmodernists are well aware about oral traditions of native people. They know that migration, displacement and a new-settlement can easily disorder tribes' traditional habitus (Rao, 2005). It is not the farewell to reason; rather it is return to new reason. In such disordered form, postmodern approaches to the development theme can find an array which can alternatively be used as ways of capital hunting. Now knowledge is capital. Objectively it provides an alternative, which is important and this configures their 'compelling identity' and unravelling the nation.

Sociologists try to feel objectively the history of tribal communities, and their cultural traditions, elements of belief system, economic voices, and causes of socio-political movements. The tribes have to decide on their own development representation where Indian tribe will keep their own charisma and flourish as contemporary representative. It is probable that the researchers can find the solution of contemporary crisis of civilization from tribal ways of life. Consequently, retribalization will be considered as objective reality albeit of detribalization.

References

Bailey, F. G. (1960). (1960). Tribe, Caste, and Nation- A Study of Political Activity and Political Change in Highland Orissa. Manchester: Manchester University Press.

Bandyopadhyay, N. C. (1938). Development of Hindu Polity and Political Theories (Vol- 2). Calcutta: C.O. Book Agency.

Beteille, A. (1974). Six Essays in Comparatve Sociology. Delhi: Oxford University Press.

Beteille, A. (1977). "The Definition of Tribe", in Romesh Thapar (ed.), Tribe, Caste and Religion. Delhi: The Macmillan Company of India Ltd. Pp. 7-14.

Bhowmick, P. K. (1963). The Lodhas of West Bengal: A Socio-Economic Study. Calcutta: Punthi Pustak.

Bose, N. K. (2002). Tribal Life in India. New Delhi: National Book Trust, India.

Chatterjee, P. (1996). "Whose Imagined Community?", in Gopal Balakrishnan (ed.), Mapping the Nation. London: Verso. Pp. 214-225.

Chatterji, S. K. (1951). Kirâta-Jana-Krti. Calcutta: The Asiatic Society.

Chattopadhyay, K. (2017). "From Jana to Netibe: A Critique of Postmodern Conceptualization of Tribal Development", in D. Bhowmik & S. K. Das (eds.), Issues on Tribal Development. Kolkata: Rupali.

Coomaraswamy, A. K. (1943). The Hinduism and Buddhism. New York: Philosophical Library, Inc.

Debo, A. (1940). And Still the Waters Run: The Betrayal of the Five Civilized Tribes. Princeton, NJ: Princeton University Press.

Desai, A. R. (1978). "Tribes in Transition", in Akshay Ramanlal Desai (ed.), Rural Sociology in India. Bombay: Popular Prakasan Pvt. Ltd. Pp. 221-231.

Dutt, N. K. (1925). The Aryanisation of India. Calcutta: Self Published

Dutta, S. and Chattopadhyay, K. (2016). "Globalising Perspective of Tribal Life: A Sociological Understanding", in Vijay P. Sharma, Pradip K. Bhowmick and Palas C. Coomar (eds.), Globalization: The Missing Roads of Tribal's. Delhi: Kalpaz Publications. Pp. 43-48.

Elwin, V. (1955). The Religion of an Indian Tribe. London: Oxford University Press.

Ghurye, G. S. (1932). Caste and Race in India. London: Kegan Paul, Trench, Trubner and Co. Ltd.

Ghurye, G. S. (1955). Family and Kin in Indo-European Culture. Bombay: Popular Book Depot.

Ghurye, G. S. (1959). The Scheduled Tribes. Bombay: Popular Book Depot.

Gommans, J. (2002). Mughal Warfare: Indian Frontiers and High Roads to Empire, 1500-1700. London: Routledge.

Gore, C. (2000). 'The rise and fall of the Washington consensus as a paradigm for developing countries', World Development, 28 (5): 789–804.

Gupta, D. (1986). "Tribal Development in a West Bengal District : Programmes, Structure, and Process", in Economic and Political Weekly, XXI (1): 35-45.

Habib, I. (2004). Medieval India: The Study of a Civilization. New Delhi: National Book Trust, India.

James, P. W. (2006). Globalism, Nationalism, Tribalism: Bringing Theory Back In New Delhi: Sage Publications India Pvt. Ltd.

Law, B.C. (1922). Ksatriya Clans in Buddhist India. Calcutta: Thacker Spink & Co.

Maffesoli, M. (1988). The Times of the Tribes: The Decline of Individualism in Mass Society. Paris: Méridiens.

Mahapatra, S. (1981). Men, Patterns and Dust. Bhubaneswar: Bookland International.

Mahapatra, S. (1986). Modernization and Ritual: Identity and Change in Santal Society. New Delhi: Oxford University Press.

Majumdar, D. N. and Madan, T. N. (1956). An Introduction to Social Anthropology. New Delhi: Asia Publishing House.

Mallavarapu, R.B. (2008). "Development, Displacement and Rehabilitation: An Action Anthropological Study on Kovvada Reservoir in West Godavari Agency of Andhra Pradesh, India", in International Journal of Social, Behavioral, Educational, Economic, Business and Industrial Engineering, 2(5): 579-585.

Mandelbaum, D. G. (1972). Society in India. Mumbai: Popular Prakashan Pvt. Ltd.

Misra, R. N. (2002). Tribal Life and Habitat. Jaipur: Ritu Publications.

Padgi, S. R. (1952). Among the Gonds of Adilabad. Mumbai: Popular Book Depot.

Rao, N. (2005). "Displacement from Land: Case of Santhal Parganas", in Economic and Political Weekly, 40(41): 4439-4442.

Rao, V. V. (1975). A Century of Tribal Politics in North East India 1874-1974. New Delhi: S. Chand and Company Ltd.

Said, E. W. (1978). Orientalism. London: Routledge & Kegan Paul Ltd.

Saren, G. (2013). 'Impact of globalizations on the Santals: A study on migration in West Bengal, India,' in International Journal of Humanities and Social Science Invention, 2: 29-33.

Sharma, K. L. (2001). Reconceptualising Caste, Class and Tribe. New Delhi: Rawat Publications.

Shukla, H. L. (1988). Tribal History: A New Interpretation. Delhi: B. R. Publishing Corporation.

Sinha, S. (1959). "Bhumij-Kshatriya social movement in South Manbhum", in Bulletin of the Department of Anthropology, Government of India 8: 9-32.

Sinha, S. (1964). Tribal Polities and State Systems in Pre-colonial Eastern and North Eastern India. Calcutta: K.P. Bagchi and Company.

Srinivas, M. N. (1952). Religion and Society among the Croogs of South India. Bombay: Asia Publishing House.

Watters, E. (2003). Urban Tribes: A Generation Redefines Friendship, Family and Commitment. London: Bloomsbury.

Chapter - 4

Can Tea Migrant Tribes of Dooars Be Develop?

— Abhishek Kumar, Nisha Kumari

Introduction

Development doesn't mean only the self-development rather it refers the all-round development. The term Development refers to the practices, policies and innovation which helps to improve people's life in the society. According to Dudley Seers, the eminent British Economist "Development is the aim to make conditions that leads to realisation of the potentials of human personalities" and the realization comes with the fulfillment of physical necessities particularly food, job security, equal rights in the community, participation in government for helping themselves.

Development and Deprivation are always considered co-related to each other where Deprivation refers to the lack of material benefit which is considered as basic amenities for the people in the society. It has multifaceted dimension which includes Social deprivation, Economic, political and cultural deprivation. But as we know, plans provisions and development programme can only helpful for protection against deprivation. It is a strategy of planned social change which is considered desirable in the society. For fight out against the heavy odds, socio-economic advancement and political participation are necessary. That means if a community are far away from the development program and plans, they are of deprived class. This situation is more or less same in the region of *Dooars*.

Dooars is a geographical region which is also called as Terai. Border area of Bhutan and India are generally addressed by Dooars that etymologically means Door that displays the special significance for this region as its meaning here is Door to Bhutan. This is the lowest part of the

Himalaya range, located in North–East of India. It is also called the entrance of many languages and cultures. There are total 18 passes through which Bhutanese people contact Indians. This region is divided into two parts- East Dooars and West Dooars. Western Dooars and Eastern Dooars are also known as Bengal Dooars and Assam Dooars respectively. Presently, Dooars region spreads to the newly built Alipurduar of West Bengal, Coochbehar and Dubari, Kokrajhar, Barpeta, Goalpara and Bongaigaon in Assam Some parts of Assam and West Bengal comes under this area where major rivers like Sankosh, Teesta Torsa, Manas, Murti flow. The main source of economy of Dooars are 3T i.e. Tea, Timber and Tourism. Tea plantation plays important part for the econom y as weather condition of Dooars is favourable for tea plantation.

This is a multi-ethnic, multi-linguistic and multi-cultural zone where many community use to reside together. And it is also a tribal zone where the habitants of this area are mainly belongs to proto-australoid and mangoloid racial stock. Original habitant of Dooars belongs to mangoloid racial stock that means Dooars serves as cradle land for Mech, Rabha, Toto, Bhutia, Tamang, Lepcha and the tribe such as Oraon, Munda, Ho, Santhal and Mahali represents proto Australoid racial group. Some belong to Nepali groups. In short, this terrain is a mixture of linguistic, religious species and cultural sphere. In addition to tribal groups, large number of Bengali groups also reside, most of which are migrated groups after the partition of Bengal. This group is also merged with the local resident groups. This area is very important with the view of natural vegetation and also displays panoramic view of nature. This area, enriched with natural resources is excellent on account of Biodiversity. Under covered with wild life sanctuary & National parks, this area attracts tourists very much and it also provides a large amount of employment to the people.

As far as the tea migrant labourer are concerned, especially Oraon, Santhali, Munda, Kharia, Mahli, Lohra and Chik Baraik are residing here who were imported by the British from Chhotanagpur to Dooars region. Due to the increased demand of labour force, they were brought here with the family and settled in this region. Their livelihood totally depends on the Tea cultivation. These tribes of Chhotanagpur origin worked as a labourer in tea gardens since long back. They cleaned the forest and established tea garden. At present, major tribal population lives in Western Dooars. Here in this research paper an attempt will be made to explore the factors that affecting the labourer community of Dooars in all respect of life and the possibilities of development among them which will encourage the tea migrant worker to identify their status which helps them to fight out for their better livelihood, education, socioeconomic needs and also helps them to save from being deprived in these distressed and reduced circumstances.

Aims and ObjectiveS

For this research paper, I have included following aims and objectives:-

1. To understand the socio-economic and political deprivation among the tea migrant tribes of Dooars region.
2. To explore the factors related to deprivation that affects the living conditions of tea migrant labourers.
3. To know the possibilities of development that enhances social security and helps them to identify their status despite of deprivation.

Research Methodology Applied

The study of any research is incomplete without research methodology. Research methodologies provide direction to study and avoid disorientation. Present study is an empirical study based on field work for which sample has been taken mainly of tea laborers. Earlier studies among tea migrant settlers have also been collected. Officers of tea factories, workers of tea garden, N.G.O. workers, Govt. employees and Administrators of the area have also been selected under the coverage of the study. Both qualitative and quantitative data have been collected for this study. For compiling primary data, the technique such as observation, case studies, Life history, interview techniques have been applied. Both Diachronic & Synchronic approach have been used to collect the data. Diachronic approaches have been imposed to know the historical background of the tea migrant laborers whereas synchronic approaches have been used to know the current status of them. Informants have been interviewed on the basis of purposive sampling. Data are collected by the help of interview and focused group interview with the worker of tea garden, other officers who are working in tea estates and with the people who residing near the tea garden and who are related with the tea plantation whether directly or indirectly. Secondary sources have also been taken into consideration for fulfilling the research paper. Secondary data such as books, journals, internet and published and unpublished research articles have been taken to know the historical condition and also too know the reality of contemporary situation.

Area of the Study

For this study, we have chosen some tea gardens which are located in Hasimara under Dooars region. This research paper is primarily focused on the study of Satali Tea Garden, Bharnobari tea garden, Subhasini Tea

Garden and Madhu Tea Garden. All these tea gardens are in Kalchini block which falls under Alipurduar district. Alipurduar is a district of West Bengal which comes under the North- Eastern region of West Bengal. This entire area is called Dooars, which is the border area of Bhutan and India. This Terai area is considered best for the production of tea. Many tribal people such as Munda, Oraon, Kharia, Chikbaraik, Nepali Community, Rabha, Mech, Toto live together in this area which also shows diversities from ethnic perspectives. Due to the cultural, linguistic and social diversity of this area, it is also called Mini India. Due to the favourable environment for tea production, there are many industry flourished over here. These tea gardens were started in 1850 by the British in which some are converted into private and some are in public undertakings after independence. All tea plantations of the present study are private undertakings. Status of Satali tea garden and Bharnobari tea garden is better than Shubhasini tea garden and Madhu tea garden. The worst situation in all these gardens is of Madhu tea garden which is currently closed. The current study focuses on tea labourer entitled 'Can tea migrants of Dooars be develop?' On the basis of the study of these tea gardens, an overall figure will be drawn which describes the situation of tea migrant labourers in the whole region of Dooars.

Finding and Discussion

In this research paper presented, the following points have been taken to know the reality, development and denial of tea migrant settlers. This means that some sub titles have been created and explained to describe this research title which is as follows:-

Glimpses of Tea Migrant Labourers of Dooars

Dooars region are well known for the tea estate which constitutes the part surrounded by Bhutan, Assam, Coochbehar, Jalpaiguri in Northern part of West Bengal. Many local tribes are inhibiting here like Rabha, Mech, Toto, Rajbonshi but some other tribal group such as Oraon, Kharia, Ho, Karmali, Santhal, Munda are also used to reside here who are dominating this area but they are not the original or indigenous inhabitants of Dooars . They are migrated during the British colonial period. A large number of workers were needed after the settling down tea industry in Dooars. But it was not possible to fulfill the need by local people. Local people had agriculture based occupation, at that time they were not needy as compare to other tea migrant who was suffering with the state of turmoil before their migration. During 1850, these tribes are brought by the British for working as tea labourer in tea garden as tea cultivation is purely labour intensive industry. They are the main tea migrant settlers in the tea estate of Dooars. Though they are migrated and settled here from approximately 125 years but still they are deprived in all aspects of socio-economic and political perspective. Even after 70 years of independence, their status continued to fluctuate. They felt ignorance in every way of life despite some needful development. Yet their status seemed to be far away from the main stream.

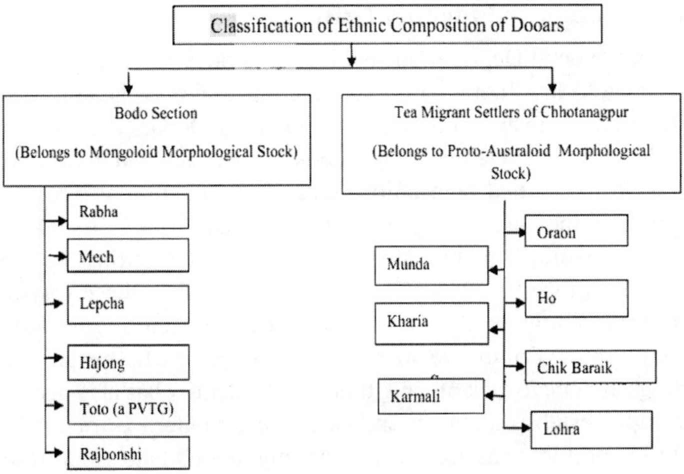

Source: Field Work, 2016-2017.

The above diagram depicts the overall ethnic figure of diversified culture of Dooars. The whole Dooars represent multi-cultural and multi-lingual diversities. Here emphasis has been made on many ethnic populations which belong to the two mongoloid and proto- Australoid morphological stock where tea migrant tribe belongs to proto-australoid racial stock. Bodo section such as Rabha, Mech,and Lepcha etc. are the original habitant here.

This research paper is confined to tea migrant settlers of Chhotanagpur. Maximum population of tea workers are residing in Satali tea estate, Bharnobari tea estate, Subhasini tea estate and Madhu tea estate in the district of Hashimara where Satali is one of largest tea estate and situated at a distance of 12.2 km from Kalchini Block. Satali tea garden village has population of 12,178 of which 6,170 are males while 6,008 are females where population of Schedule caste is 955 and Schedule tribe are 4,542 as per Census 2011. Total 4,854 labourers are working in the Satali tea garden village. In Satali tea garden village population of children with age 0-6 is 1,251 which make up 10.27% of total population of village. Average sex ratio of Satali tea garden village is 974 which is higher that West Bengal state average of 950. Child Sex ratio for the Satali tea garden as per Census is 931, lower than West Bengal average of 956. This village has lowest literacy rate compared to West Bengal. In 2011, literacy rate of Satali tea garden village was 71.46% compared to 76.26% of West Bengal. In Satali tea garden, Male literacy stands at 79.17% while female literacy rate was 63.57%. Even in rest of the tea estates, there are more or less similar figures can be seen.

Social Deprivation and Identity Crisis

The word 'Social Deprivation' is bit ambiguous and it has no proper definition. Due to low literacy rate, low income and poor health, tribal's are still far from mainstream of society. Tribals of Dooars are victims of the social destitution where mainly tea labourers are included in this. Since Tea migrant tribal settled here before three four generations ago as tea labourer but still they are not considered as the main tribe of the Dooars. During my fieldwork, I found that they are deprived of getting their own land and house. Since they haven't got the same status in these years and still considered as migrant, they loses their identity in their original habitat of Chhotanagpur. Tribal are always associated with the land and surroundings but due to lack of land, their social identity has also declined. With the rapid establishment of industries and modern infrastructure, Rehabilitation problem has come across among them due to victimization of land alienation. Even they get inadequate amount of compensation for their land if they have. They are recognised by their segmental solidarity, economical independence, common language, dialect, family and kinship. But now tea migrant workers are having problems even in establishing marriage relationship from their original habitant area of Chhotanagpur. Tribal on migration got socially isolated with the original habitant in this area and create socio cultural barriers between them which restrict their interaction. They are losing their cultural identity by intermixing themselves in other groups.

Culture has many diversifying aspects which allure people with their simplicity, behaviour and lifestyle. Illiteracy and lack of skills adds obstructions among the tea labourers on the way of developmental issues. They have lack of awareness among them for their own rights due to which they cannot keep their demands firmly in front of the government. But if we see the other aspect, it has only reached to the primary level of education even after attempting to make plans and affordable efforts by the government. Due to economic difficulties, the trend of people towards education decreases because ultimate fact is to obtain the basic amenities for them. Higher education is still a distant dream for them due to lack of infrastructure and awareness. Education and literacy creates awareness and helps in the emergence of public consciousness. Nowadays higher education is as much compulsory as primary education so that one can secure better opportunities for them otherwise they have confined to do work as labourer. On the other hand, children of the tea labourers who work in the tea garden for helping their parent can not able to save their time as the school time mismatch with their work. Since higher economic development carried by higher educational development and illiteracy is a huge obstacle in the road to development.

Apathetic attitude of tea labourer towards the education can be seen evidently because of language barriers. Language which binds the tribal society and acts as conductor of culture that moves from one generation to another generation. It means cultural elements such as customs, rituals, tradition, and taboos are transferred to the next generation. It is the special and unique feature of any community. But Tea migrant have begun to forget their language due to migration and intermixing with other culture. Therefore, collapsing and declining rate of language are also one of the causing factors for social deprivation.

Apart from this, lack of effective research and policies, lack of health, lack of medical facilities, nutrition and hygiene are also responsible for impoverishment. Earlier in my research area, there was health centre and hospitals in each of the tea estates but nowadays all are closed except there is only one health centre are still running in Bharnobari where only one nurse are working here and Doctors are nowhere available to attend the patient. Earlier they usually don't need to go anywhere for minor treatment and other medical facilities such as vaccination, free medicine but currently due to apathetic attitude of government and tea companies, they are depriving in health perspectives.

Economic Deprivation

It has been observed that Tea industry is an important industry in many ways as it is not only contributes for the national economy but also to earn the livelihood of people residing in Dooars region. Despite the increasing demand of cultivation and supply of tea, it is evident that most of the tea industry is gradually sinking. One of them is Madhu tea garden that is also a part of this study but currently this tea garden is closed due to the distressed and poor production. Today, after 70 years of independence, we can see much advancement among ourselves but despite these advancement tea estates are battling with the complicated situation. Also, Tea industries are facing problems such as poor financial support, and inadequate communication. Due to the poor production of tea, tea estates are started disintegrating and the problem of permanent employment arises among the tea migrant labourer. They are getting low wages for their work. Sometimes they do not find that much work so they used to indulge themselves for part-time work in tea garden on basis of daily wages and also they need to go outside for alternate source of work like pebble stone collection from the bank of the river, work in hotel, spa and garage, driver and even work as tourist guide as this area is considered tourist place because of so much biodiversity exist here. Even disparity in wages can be seen among male and female workers. Being a migrated labourer, they also find it difficult to get social and economic security by which they don't get job available for them in further generation. Few people are having job card by MGNREGA but despite having job card there are no work for them because where they are living, all are tea estates and these tea estate are private estate village. At presen t, Madhu tea garden has been closed so the habitant of this tea estate village are changing their mode of livelihood and going outside to earn for their basic needs.

As tea cultivation is labour intensive work, so they migrate here to work as tea labourer but currently demand for tea is increasing which has led to a problem of labour crisis in tea estates. Where the employment is present, the wages are so meager that running a household from that amount becomes difficult. Government and tea companies are not providing the proper solution for the permanent employment, low wages and also not providing the quarters and food grain to their employees that created factionalism and conflicts among them. It also misleads them and created tension between labourer and tea companies. Earlier, food grains were distributed in this area by the tea company for tea labourer, no such problems of food grain and nutrition had arises among them. But today, due to the disintegration and poor production, tea companies do not providing enough food so that they can able to consume food grain in whole month. All the grain and food related material last in just few days. Tea migrant labourers even get exploited by the money lenders.

Political Victimization of Tea Migrant Tribe

It is apparent that the tribal communities are highly dependent upon natural resources around them to sustain their life. Apart from this, political consciousness is also necessary to sustain the development in society. Many non-tribal planners failed to understand the relationship between tribal and their land, tea labourers also suffered from this. Sometimes the political motives and agenda are hidden behind this. For safeguarding their land and resources, conflicts arises between government and tea plantation workers.

As a result, they are divided into numbers of labour union and they started fighting for their rights separately. Under these circumstances, tea companies were compelled to negotiate with the tea labourers, local political leader and their own production. To protect the identity of the tribal's, many constitutional rights are given by the government but tea migrant settlers are still not got their complete identity of scheduled tribe by which they can avail the special privileges. Those rights which are given to the original habitant of Dooars are still not available for tea migrant settlers. So, for achieving their rights against tea companies and government, they formed trade union. Many trade unions are working for the rights of tea migrant labourers in this area. One of the oldest trade unions among the tea plantation labourers of Dooars was the communist controlled AITUC affiliated "Zilla Cha Bagan Workers Union", which starts from 1947. Apart from this, other trade union are also working in this area.

Since tea labourer recognize their power through numerical strength of tribe. Oraon population is abundant among tea migrant settlers in this area, so from political perspectives, status of Oraon tribes is far better than other tea migrant whose conditions are still remains the same. Tribal are also recognized by their own specific traditional political belief and system but due to the intervention of outsiders and modern political organization, a sense of awareness displays among them by which they now take more precautions for their rights. But still if the government tries to bring some developmental programs and policies to their area, they tend to be rejected and stalled due to lack of awareness. Even they are demanding persistently about 5th Schedule and PESA (Panchayat Extension of Scheduled Area) by which tea migrant and other tribe will get special recognition in this area and enhance their cultural identity. The main objectives of the Panchayat are to encourage tea migrant labourers to take up economic and political consciousness. Earlier tea planters has full control and grip over tea migrants but if PESA will implement in this area, they will lose their grip over tea labourer and then tea labourer will not be wholly depended on the tea planters. Even due to 5th schedule, interference of outsiders, tea planters, officials and government will decreases but still this act will not completely implemented and hence they are again deprived in political perspectives.

Development Programmes and its Reality

Many schemes are currently being run for the up-liftment of tribal development by the Central and State governments. Migrant tea worker based in Dooars is not fully entitled of the rights of tribal which receives by Rabha, Mech. The West Bengal government has kept them in the category of tribal but has limited the rights due to which, they cannot get full benefits of tribal related schemes and plans of the state government. On the other hand, tea workers do not have their own land, they remain in the accommodation given by the tea company. Due to lack of land, residential schemes such as Prime Minister Housing Scheme, Indira Housing Scheme, Aamar Baari Schemes cannot be availed of by them. The first condition of these schemes is their land which they don't have. They are not even eligible for this scheme, that's why they are facing housing problem. At the same time, food grains are also not available as food provided in advance as compensation but it is not enough for indigenization for the entire month. Due to being a tea worker, the government doesn't consider them unemployed and therefore they can not avail the benefits of employment schemes. In the absence of land they cannot able to constructor build toilets under the cleanliness drive. This means, whichever scheme is related to land, there is no place for tea migrant workers, which is affecting their development.

In view of the complex nature of the problems of the area, the various development strategies were introduced. Ultimately, improved situation of tea production will improve the condition and status of tea labourer. The government has framed various schemes to provide better wages and social security benefits for the plantation labourer. They introduced a scheme for reducing transport expenses by a considerable margin for tea workers. Concession and facilities, supplementary wages were available in many gardens. These includes land for cultivation, free housing, medical attendance, maternity benefit, fuel and grazing facilities and provision of food stuff and clothing at cheaper rates. Wages of daily rated plantation workers were revised time to time.

To resolve the problems of their constitutional rights, numbers of trade unions are formed for taking active participation in politics to strengthen their position as well as development of society. These trade unions help them to avail the facilities laid down by the government. The west Bengal labourer welfare board has been constituted by the government of west Bengal for rendering and promoting welfare activities amongst the workers. For restoration of health of the tea plantation, financial support and term loan are required from the government. But the plantation finance scheme remains non operative for the time being because of inadequate allotment of funds.

Despite of these development programmes, they are not availing the facilities which were given to them. They have lack of vocational training which they require to understand the tea industry. They must have the need to encourage themselves in every way about their own tradition, arts, cultural values to maintain their identity that can be done by recreational centers. Financial constraints for the development project can be frequently seen here which damages the condition of tea production. Due to financial crisis among tea migrant labourer, either we see enrolment of children is low or high number of drop outs. Government come up as failure to enlighten and awareness programme for this community by politicizing the issue of tea migrant labourer for creating vote bank only. Lack of coordination and integration at centre and state level is also a factor for social and economic deprivation.

Conclusion

On the basis of above discussion, we can state that tea migrant settlers who are surviving in the Dooars region are highly deprived in all respect of life. Since tea migrant settlers are solely depended on the tea industry as their main occupation here is work as tea labourer in the tea garden. But nowadays, the way tea industry is shutting down due to poor production of tea; it is not possible to live their lives. And above all, the tea labourer has to work on low wages due to which they are compelled to opt for the alternate option to earn their livelihood. Problem of land alienation is also faced by them due to being migrant settlers. They not only lost their lands and liberty but also lost their ethnicity and ethnic culture. Even in the field of education, tea migrant tribe are always victimized of their condition. They always want to educate their child but they are not able to provide proper education because children of the tea migrant settlers are also use to work with their parents so that they will able to help in obtaining the basic needs. In spite of living in this area from such a generation, tea migrant settlers have not attained the status of scheduled tribe till now. They are also demanding to implement the rule of 5 th schedule and PESA act so that it strengthen their morale and able to initiate some beneficial steps for improving their condition. By establishing the self-governance rule in this Dooars region, the scope of their rights or we can say constitutional rights will also become broad which can act as panacea to save their social- cultural and political identity and work for their all- round development.

Government always try to contribute their effort in making plans and provisions for the tribes but mostly it always left on the floor and not even able to implement that plans and provisions by which their struggle can be reduce a bit. Government programs for free and compulsory education are creating awareness among them for their personal and societal progress. Many housing plans and health awareness programmes have also been implemented in this area. Despite so many government efforts it is the issue of concern that they failed to provide the satisfactory result. Apart from this, the merciless control policies of tea planters are also responsible for the indeterminate, unbearable and hopeless life of the tea garden workers. But if this continued and the attitude of the government and the tea planters remained same for tea migrant tribes would they ever improve their position and situation?

There should not be such situation come in front of them that they need to migrate from here too. Since development doesn't mean the development in one area, true development is the all-round development of the community. So, ultimately tea migrant tribe need to make proper efforts mutually with the government to get rid of destitution and deprivation. But yet the question remains the same, *Can tea migrant tribe of Dooars will be developed*?

References

Bhowmick, Sharit K, Virginius Xaxa and Kalam.1996:Tea Plantation Labor in India. Fredrich Ebert Stifting, New Delhi. Bailey, F.G (1960): 'Tribe, Caste and Nation', Oxford University Press: Bombay.

Bhowmick, Sharit.1981: Class Formation in the Plantation System. People's Publishing House, New Delhi.

Bryceson, Deborah faby et.al., 2007: Identity and Networks : Gender and Ethnicity in a Cross-cultural Context. p.p. 54, Berghahn Books, New York.

Das, A.K. & R.N. Saha et.al (1991) ed.: 'West Bengal Tribes : Socio-economic and Cultural Life', Special Series No. 35, Bulletin of the Cultural Research Intitute, Schedule Castes and Tribes Welfare Department: Government of West Bengal.

Dasgupta, Pranab Kumar and Iar Ali Khan, 1983: Impact of Tea plantation industry on the life of Tribal Labours. Anthropological survey of India, Calcutta.

Hodgson, B.H., 1880: Reprint 1947 on the Aborigines of India. Essays on koch, bodo and dhimal tribe in miscellaneous essays relating to Indian subjects, vol.i& ii Turner and co., London .ISBN 0-415-24505-2.

Kar, R.K and Sharma, K.L, 1990: Ethnic Identity of Tea Labour: A Case study in Assam D. Pakem(ed) Nationality, Ethnicity and Cultural Identity in North East India ; Omsons.

Nolan, Riall. W, 2001: Development Anthropology:Encounters in the real world, West view Press: New York.

Ravisagar, 2002: Plantation Labourers: Know Your Rights, Guwahati: North Eastern Social Research Centre

Risley, H.H,1891: The Tribes and castes of Bengal, Calcutta, The Bengal secretariat press.

Sengupta, Sarthak, 2009: The tea Labourers of North East India: An Anthropo-historical perspective, Mittal Publication:New Delhi.

Chapter - 5

Political Deprivation of Tribal People in Contemporary India

— Jagdeep Oraon, Kailash Chandra

Introduction

"Deprivation" can be understood as the outright discrimination of tribal groups or, less extremely, as the non representation of tribal groups at the national or sub national level. The scheduled communities evolved out of the British colonial concern for the Depressed Classes who faced multiple deprivations on account of their low position in the hierarchy of the Hindu caste system. The degrading practice of untouchability figured as the central target for social reformers and their movements. The issue acquired strong political overtones when the British sought to combine the problems of the Depressed Classes with their communal politics. The Communal Award of August 4, 1932, after the conclusion of two successive Round Table Conferences in London, assigned separate electorates not only for the Muslims, Sikhs, Christians and several other categories, but also extended it to the Depressed Classes. This led to the historic fast unto death by Gandhi and the subsequent signing of the Poona Pact between B.R. Ambedkar and Madan Mohan Malviya on September 24th 1932. According to this agreement a new formula was evolved in which separate electorates were replaced by reserved constituencies for the Depressed Classes. The actual process of 'scheduling' of castes took place thereafter in preparation of the elections in 1937.

Before these the tribal's were fought against the British rulers for their rights time to time in the all over India. But Jharkhand is the prime place were several rebellions we can see in the past history which gives the political rights as well as identity for the tribal's. History has witnessed plenty of politically excluded tribal groups that have resorted to violence against the British Government and have succeeded in overcoming their deprivation. Before India free form the British crown the important rebellions were like Tilka Manjhi Revolt (1784), Great Kol Revolt (1832), Santhal Revolt (1855), Birsa Munda Revolt (1895), Tana Bhagat movement (1914) etc. established the political rights of the deprived people of this areas.

The Tribal communities are believed to be original/earliest inhabitants of the country, mainly occupying the forest region and far from the civilized people. The third largest tribes of India are the Santhal Tribe and also the largest indigenous tribe in Jharkhand in terms of population. According to census 2011 there were 8645042 tribal people in all over Jharkhand, where most of people belong from Santhal tribe. In Jharkhand total Santhal population 2754723, where male 1371168 and female 1383555. Dhanbad is a district of Jharkhand state where total tribal population 233119 including 182173 Santhal populations (male 91091 and female 91082). Santhals are found in few regions of India basically in West Bengal, Orissa and Jharkhand and also in Assam. In Dhanbad district, Saharaj is a Santhal village where total Santhal population is 515 including 267 male and 248 female.

Besides their many organisations political organisation played an important role of their life. They had a primitive political organisation which used to control their society. There are seven posts like Manjhi, Paranik, Jog-Manjhi, Jog-Paranik, Godit, Nayke and Kudum-Nayke and rest of the villagers, are the member of this political system. It concerned with the control and regulation of the use of physical force and regulation of relations between groups or members of different groups within the society at large.

But now in contemporary India this traditional political organization is going to extinct. It was deprived due to modern political system or Panchayati Raj Institution. Elections in all over India level, growth of factions and parties in the villagers, formation of regional political parties are also causes their traditional setup or now they deprived in various ways of life through the change in their life or adapting the modern politics. Modern politics hinders their political life or attract to spoil their traditional political life. The present government passed the ordinance against the CNT and SPT Acts and tries to snatch the land rights of the tribal's. State government suppressing their voice and rights through passing such rules and regulations by which the tribal identity is in danger.

This article contributes toward filling this gap and asks whether rebellions by deprived tribal groups help to overcome political deprivation. Violent rebellions and civil wars are bloody endeavours that disrupt and traumatize societies, sometimes even two or three generations. Considering the bloodshed and atrocities associated with civil wars, rebellions are hardly ever efficient. But are they effective – that is, do they put governments under enough pressure so that they at some point grant the rebel groups political rights?

Objectives of this Article

1. To know about Santhal tribal community and their traditional political system.
2. To highlight the major factors affecting their political system.
3. To know the present status of their political organisation.
4. To know how they are depriving politically.

Research Methodology

The data for the study have been collected from primary and secondary sources. The primary sources included Government Acts, Rules, Regulations, Documents, Assembly proceedings, handouts and interviews conducted with persons well versed on the subject. It was conducted orally to elicit informations and questionnaires/schedule was also used to elicit opinion. The secondary sources were drawn from published and unpublished books, seminar proceedings and other printed materials, journals, newspapers, etc.

Study Area

The area of the study was conducted at village Saharaj, block Gobindapur under Dhanbad district of Jharkhand State. It is a fully Santhal village. In the northern side of the village Barakar River (about 10 km from the village), in the southern side Gerua Hill, in the eastern side Maithan Dam and western side Harkara Hill was situated.

Findings

There are two type of political organisation found in village Saharaj, one is traditional and other is modern political system. This village is not belongs to PESA Act 1996, so they did not get that facilities which are given by PESA Act through our Constitution to the schedule area. That is why they belong from General Panchayat System.

A. Traditional Political System of Santhal in the Study Village

For better control their own society they built up a political system and it was running from the primitive time. In this village the traditional political system has a great value to control the village. There was a traditional panchayat system which built up by the villagers 64 of this village. All villagers are the member of this panchayat. They sit together and discuss the every matter of their village and come to a decision which supported by the villagers. Although the all villagers of this village are the member of this panchayat but also there are seven main post found on the basic of type of work which are **Majhi, Paranik, Jog-Majhi, Chakladar, Godit, Nayke** and **Kudum Nayke**. They have different type of work. This post was inherited from one generation to next generation and only for male candidate. If there was no male candidate on the next generation than the villagers sit together and discuss about it. And finally they select a candidate for each of the following positions from the villagers...

Majhi is the head or chief man of this village and also the traditional panchayat system. All responsibilities of this village are entrusted on him. From birth to death each and every rituals nothing can be done by his instruction. He tries to clear all type of problem from this village. When Majhi could not cleared the problem the then they called the five Majhi from five village and the five Majhi make a decision after discussion the matter or problem. **Satrughan Hembram** is the Majhi of this village.

Paranik is the assistant of Majhi. He does the all work of Majhi on absence of him. If anyone of the villager doing something wrong then Paranik fined him or her. It measured by the type of guilty. It may up to 250 Rs. The fine was collected, which was used for the development for the village. **Pargan Hansda** is the Paranik of this village. Basically he tries to solve the every type of problem of families of this village. He also leads the youth of the village. **Dulal Marandi** is the Jog-Majhi of this village. He makes the final decision of any type of issue. **Parameswar Murmu** is covering this great post of the traditional political panchayat.

Godit is the messenger of Majhi. If a meeting to be called, the godit informs the villagers on behalf of the Majhi. During festivals and rituals he plays a big role. Here Chhutu **Dom** was appointed on this post.

Nayke is the village priest. He performs all the rituals and worship. Here Majhi and Nayke is the same person. **Satrughan Hembram** is the Nayke of the village.

Kudum nayke is the assistant of the Nayke, and the worshipper of forest and nature. If necessary, he sacrifices his own blood, so that evil spirits cannot harm the villagers. **Dulal Marandi** is the Kudum Nayke of this village.

B. Modern Political System

In India, apart from the traditional political system of tribal's, the modern political system (Lok Sabha, Rajya Sabha, Vidhan Sabha, and

Panchayati Raj Institution etc.) has also found. The framers of the Indian constitution took note of the fact that certain communities in the country were suffering from extreme social, educational and economic backwardness. This disadvantaged position of deprivations to which they are exposed is rooted in the hierarchical structure of the Indian society and is maintained by legitimized traditions of discrimination and suppression of rights. The strength of traditions can be seen most clearly in the persistence of caste-designated occupations among disadvantaged groups. The framers of the Indian constitution were, thus, occupied with the thought of making the newborn India a better place to live, of securing economic and social justice for various people subject to centuries of exploitation. In other words, they tried to ensure that in independent India, no one is discriminated on grounds of colour, caste, religion and gender, i.e., no one would be excluded arbitrarily from public life and all would be equal before the law. They realized that this is impossible to translate into a reality without ensuring special treatment for the deprived.

Guided by this understanding, the Indian constitution provided preferences/reservations for the weaker sections (STs) of the society. Preferential treatment policies in India are a system of quotas for disadvantaged groups in education (Articles 15 (4) and 29), employment (Articles 16 (4), 324 (4) 333 and 335) and legislatures (Articles 330 and 332). 1 Like affirmative action policies in other countries, preferential treatment policies in India aim to increase opportunities for under-represented groups. In India, positive discrimination is increasingly being seen as an instrument of social transformation. The STs owe their existence in the legislative bodies to the political base provided by the provisions of protective discrimination. Thus, preferences provide for a substantial quantitative presence of this group that would otherwise be lacking.

Since there have been numerous studies on the effect of political deprivation on the Scheduled Castes (SCs) or the Other Backward Classes (OBCs), but there is hardly any major work that tries to study the working and impact of policies in the context of preferences for STs in Jharkhand. However, this paper is confined on electoral reservations as well as the political deprivation for STs. This paper is directed towards understanding the impact of 66 political deprivation for STs in Jharkhand. It also makes an attempt to explore the political problems faced by the tribal community in Jharkhand.

The general political characteristics of the modern societies of the first type are:

(i) The existence of a nation-state as the political community,

(ii) The existence of political parties, pressure groups and political movements,

(iii) The election of the political executive by universal adult suffrage, and

(iv) The administration of public affairs by a large bureaucracy.

Panchayats (Extension to Scheduled Areas) Act, 1996 (PESA)

Article 243M of the Constitution, while exempting the Fifth Schedule areas from Part IX of the Constitution, provides that Parliament may by law extend its provisions to the Scheduled and Tribal Areas subject to such exceptions and modifications as may be specified in such law and no such law shall be deemed to be an amendment to the Constitution. On the basis of the report of the Bhuria Committee submitted in 1995, the Parliament enacted the Panchayats (Extension to Scheduled Areas) Act, 1996 (PESA) to extend Part IX of the Constitution with certain modifications and exceptions to the Scheduled areas of 10 States (in 2018) viz. Andhra Pradesh, Telengana, Chhattisgarh, Gujarat, Himachal Pradesh, Jharkhand, Madhya Pradesh, Maharashtra, Odisha and Rajasthan. The Ministry of Panchayati Raj is the nodal Ministry for implementation of the provisions of PESA in the States.

Objectives of the Act

1. To extend the provision of Part IX of the Constitution relating to panchayats to the scheduled areas with certain modifications
2. To provide self-rule for the bulk of the tribal population
3. To have village governance with participatory democracy and make the Gram Sabha a nucleus of all activities
4. To evolve a suitable administrative framework consistent with traditional practices
5. To safeguard and to preserve the traditions and customs of tribal communities
6. To empower panchayats at the appropriate levels with specific power conducive to tribal requirements
7. To prevent panchayats at the higher level from assuming the power and authority of panchayats at the lower level of the Gram Sabha

Features of the Act

1. Panchayats in the Scheduled areas shall be in consonance with the customary law, social and religious practices and traditional management practices of community resources.

2. Village shall be ordinary consist of a habitation or a group of habitants comprising a community and managing its affairs in accordance with traditions and customs.
3. Every village shall have a Gram Shabha consisting the persons whose names are included in the electoral rolls for the panchayat at the village level.
4. Every Gram Sabha shall be competent to safeguard and preserve the
   (a) Traditions and customs of the people,
   (b) Their cultural identity,
   (c) Customary mode of dispute resolution.
5. Every Gram Sabha shall –
   (a) Approve of the plans, programmes and projects for social and economic development before they taken up for implementation by the panchayat at the village level.
   (b) Be responsible for the identification of beneficiaries under alleviation and other programmes.
6. Every panchayat at the village level shall be required to obtain from the Gram Sabha a certification of utilisation of funds for the above plans, programmes and projects.
7. Reservation of seats in the scheduled areas in every panchayat shall be in proportion to the population of the communities for whom reservation is sought to be given under part IX
8. Scheduled tribes shall not be less than one-half of the total number of seats.
9. Further, all seats of Chairpersons of panchayats at all level reserved for the scheduled tribe.
10. State government may nominate such scheduled tribes which have no representation in the panchayat-not exceed 1/10 of the total members to be selected in the panchayat.
11. Gram Sabha or the panchayata at the appropriate level shall be consulted before making the
    (a) Acquisition of land in the scheduled areas for development project and
    (b) Before resetting or rehabilitating persons affected by such projects in scheduled area.
12. Planning and management of minor water bodies

13. Gram Sabha or the panchayats shall be mandatory for grant of prospecting license or mining lease for minor minerals.
14. Panchayats at the appropriate level and the Gram Sabha are endowed specifically
    (a) The power to enforce prohibition or to regulate or restrict the sale and consumption of any intoxicant
    (b) The ownership of minor forest produce
    (c) The power to prevent alienation of land in the scheduled areas and to take appropriate action to restore any unlawfully alienated land of a scheduled tribe
    (d) To power to manage village markets
    (e) To power to exercise control over money lending to the scheduled tribe
    (f) To power to exercise control over institution and functionaries in all social sectors
    (g) To power to control local plans and resources for such plans including tribal sub plans
15. State legislature shall Endeavour to follow the pattern of the Sixth Schedule to the Constitution while designing the administrative arrangements in the panchayats at district level in the scheduled areas.

FIFTH SCHEDULE [Article 244(1)] Provisions as to the Administration and Control of Scheduled Areas and Scheduled Tribes:

Part A- General

1. **Interpretation.**— In this Schedule, unless the context otherwise requires, the expression "State" does not include the States of Assam, Meghalaya, Tripura and Mizoram.

2. **Executive power of a State in Scheduled Areas.**—Subject to the provisions of this Schedule, the executive power of a State extends to the Scheduled Areas therein.

3. **Report by the Governor to the President regarding the administration of Scheduled Areas.**— The Governor of each State having Scheduled Areas therein shall annually, or whenever so required by the President, make a report to the President regarding the administration of the Scheduled Areas in that State and the executive power of the Union shall extend to the giving of directions to the State as to the administration of the said areas.

Part B- Administration and Control of Scheduled Areas and Scheduled Tribes

4. Tribes Advisory Council.— (1) There shall be established in each State having Scheduled Areas therein and, if the President so directs, also in any State having Scheduled Tribes but not Scheduled Areas therein, a Tribes Advisory Council consisting of not more than twenty members of whom, as nearly as may be, three-fourths shall be the representatives of the Scheduled Tribes in the Legislative Assembly of the State: Provided that if the number of representatives of the Scheduled Tribes in the Legislative Assembly of the State is less than the number of seats in the Tribes Advisory Council to be filled by such representatives, the remaining seats sha ll be filled by other members of those tribes.

(2) It shall be the duty of the Tribes Advisory Council to advice on such matters pertaining to the welfare and advancement of the Scheduled Tribes in the State as may be referred to them by the Governor.

(3) The Governor may make rules prescribing or regulating, as the case may be,—

(a) The number of members of the Council, the mode of their appointment and the appointment of the Chairman of the Council and of the officers and servants thereof;

(b) The conduct of its meetings and its procedure in general; and

(c) All other incidental matters.

5. Law applicable to Scheduled Areas.— (1) Notwithstanding anything in this Constitution, the Governor may by public notification direct that any particular Act of Parliament or of the Legislature of the State shall not apply to a Scheduled Area or any part thereof in the State or shall apply to a Scheduled Area or any part thereof in the State subject to such exceptions and modifications as he may specify in the notification and any direction given under this sub-paragraph may be given so as to have retrospective effect.

(2) The Governor may make regulations for the peace and good government of any area in a State which is for the time being a Scheduled Area. In particular and without prejudice to the generality of the foregoing power, such regulations may—

(a) Prohibit or restrict the transfer of land by or among members of the Scheduled Tribes in such area;

(b) Regulate the allotment of land to members of the Scheduled Tribes in such area;

(c) Regulate the carrying on of business as money-lender by persons who lend money to members of the Scheduled Tribes in such area.

(3) In making any such regulation as is referred to in sub-paragraph (2) of this paragraph, the Governor may repeal or amend any Act of Parliament or of the Legislature of the State or any existing law which is for the time being applicable to the area in question.

(4) All regulations made under this paragraph shall be submitted forthwith to the President and, until assented to by him, shall have no effect.

(5) No regulation shall be made under this paragraph unless the Governor making the regulation has, in the case where there is a Tribes Advisory Council for the State, consulted such Council.

Part C- Scheduled Areas

6. Scheduled Areas.— (1) In this Constitution, the expression "Scheduled Areas" means such areas as the President may by order declare to be Scheduled Areas.

(2) The President may at any time by order—

(a) Direct that the whole or any specified part of a Scheduled Area shall cease to be a Scheduled Area or a part of such an area;

(a, a) increase the area of any Scheduled Area in a State after consultation with the Governor of that State;

(b) Alter, but only by way of rectification of boundaries, any Scheduled Area;

(c) on any alteration of the boundaries of a State or on the admission into the Union or the establishment of a new State, declare any territory not previously included in any State to be, or to form part of, a Scheduled Area;

(d) rescind, in relation to any State or States, any order or orders made under this paragraph, and in consultation with the Governor of the State concerned, make fresh orders redefining the areas which are to be Scheduled Areas; and any such order may contain such incidental and consequential provisions as appear to the President to be necessary and proper, but save as aforesaid, the order made under sub-paragraph (1) of this paragraph shall not be varied by any subsequent order.

Part D- Amendment of the Schedule

7. Amendment of the Schedule.— (1) Parliament may from time to time by law amend by way of addition, variation or repeal any of the provisions of this Schedule and, when the Schedule is so amended, any reference to this Schedule in this Constitution shall be construed as a reference to such Schedule as so amended.

(2) No such law as is mentioned in sub-paragraph (1) of this paragraph shall be deemed to be an amendment of this Constitution for the purposes of article 368.

C. Causes for Political Deprivation

Article 330 provides for reservation of seats for SCs and STs in the Lok Sabha. In pursuance of this Article, 106, out of 545 seats are reserved for members of SC/ST communities. In the 11th, 12th, 13th Lok Sabha, there were respectively 123 members of Parliament belonging to SC/ST communities, which indicates that besides the reserve Constituencies SC/ST candidates are elected against unreserved Lok Sabha seats also. Here we can see the interest of tribal people in modern political system.

With the enactment of the Panchayats (Extension to the Scheduled Areas) Act, 1996, (No 40 of 1996), the provisions of part IX of the Constitution relating to Panchayats have been extended to the Scheduled Areas subject to exceptions and modifications that a Legislature of a State Shall not make any law inconsistent with any of their own practices like Customary law, social and religious practices and traditional management practices of community services. But this village does not belong under this Panchayats (Extension to the Scheduled Areas) Act, 1996. That is why they are politically deprived.

D. Recent Situation

The study village Saharaj is not under the PESA Act. It is the main causes for their deprivation. It is under the general panchayat system. Where Mukhia and most of the members are belongs from other caste. Only two female people are the members of this panchayat system.

In this picture shows the members list of Gram Panchayat of Saharaj Village. Where only two members were (no.4 Bandani Hembram and no. 5 Pratima Tudu) belonged from scheduled tribe.

Now BJP is the ruling party in this state as well as in this village. JMM (Jharkhand Mukti Morcha), JVM (Jharkhand Vikash Morcha), BSP (Bahujan Samaj Party), AJSU (All Jharkhand Student Union) etc. political parties were also found. Mostly the younger are interested in this political system. Here every person wants a chance for be a part of this system.

Now a day the traditional and modern political systems are going parallel and that is why there traditional political system is going to deprive.

For example, in any kind of problems or situations the villagers believed on modern political system more than their traditional political system. Here we examine to understand the present politics how deprive the tribal people then find that the life is became the individualistic so the old people or the tradition political heads are not giving the appropriate decisions so the Santhals took the decision to approach the modern politics.

Here traditional political system played a vital role from ancient time. The members of this system could understand their problems very closely and also from humanistic way. Because they have we felling. So in this traditional political system the villagers are getting free from every type of problem through some fine and these fine also used for village development. The traditional political system was not complicated. All type of problems used to solve in their village level. But now day's the villagers are facing many difficulties due to more believe of modern political system. This time the villagers are go to the local police station for their every kind of problems which were used to solve through their traditional political system from many days. When police station unable to solve their problems they sent to the district court. That is why they were harassed through mentally and physically. Besides these they also are spending time and money and harass whole life.

Conclusion

According to the above discussion we get a clear knowledge about the traditional political system of Santhal tribe of Jharkhand district and how this system is played an important role in their life. But in modern India the modern political system is spreading in all over India. This modern political system is effecting to the tribal traditional political system as well as tribal life or tribal identity.

If this village will enlist to the schedule area and under the PESA Act, the villagers will get a chance to preserved their traditional political system and survive according to their own culture and tradition.

Bibliography

Bodding. P.O. 1960 Tradition and Custom of Santhal, Oriental Foundation Press, Manchester (U.K.).

Deoganakar S.G. 1988 Tribal Administrative and it's Development, Concept Publishing Company, New Delhi, 100014.

Dubey,S.C. 1977 "Tribal Heritage of India: Ethnicity, Identity and Interaction". Vol. I, Vikas Publication House, New Delhi.

Hasnain. N, 1991 Tribal India, Palaka Prakashan, Delhi, 110035.

Jagannath. Ambag, 2006 Standing At The Edge : Representation and Electoral Reservation for Scheduled tribe of Orissa, The Indian Journal of Political Science Vol. LXVII, No. 2, Apr. -June.

Jha. M. 1994, An Introduction to Social Anthropology, Vikash Publishing house Pvt. Ltd., Noida.

Pesadarpan.gov.in

Rajbhavan-maharastra.gov.in

Tribal.nic.in

Vidyarthi L.P. & B.K. Roy, 1976, Tribal Culture of India, Concept Publishing Company, New Delhi.

Chapter – 6

Socio-Economic Condition of Tribal in Mining Area of Saranda, Jharkhand

— *Vijay Prakash Sharma*

Introduction

Socio-economic survey in five villages of West- Singhbhum district was conducted in a scientific manner. The villages selected in West-Singhbhum are located in Iron Ore Rich Saranda forest division.

A structured questionnaire was formulated and pre-tested for user interface in Saranda Villages. Dynamic youths with positive mindset were identified as Field Investigators and trained extensively on survey methodology and questionnaire. The Field Investigators carried out the survey under close supervision and guidance of Project Coordinator. The data generated from the survey were analysed using specially designed software package.

Study Area:

The area is in West Singhbhum District of Jharkhand State bounded by 22° 11' - 22° 11' 38" North and longitude 85° 21' 54" East covered by Survey of India Topo sheet No. 73 F/8. The following five survey villages are under Nawamundi block of West Singhbum district:-

Villages	*No. of Households*
Bokna	106
Boraiburu	144
Kantoria	52
Diriburu	167
Tatiba	187s

The area has hilly terrain with maximum elevation 789 mtrs above MSL in the southern portion. The minimum RL is 460 mtrs above MSL in the eastern part. The prominent slope of the area is towards southeast and north east as it makes local water divide.

The rainfall varies from 1300 – 1600 mm and nearly 86% of it is received in Monsoon season. Maximum rainfall recorded in a day is 439.2 mm. The maximum Temperature recorded is 43.2° C and Minimum is 7.2° C. Relative humidity varies from average 78% to as low as 26%.

Study Objectives

- To understand the present Socio- economic situation of the people and the area.
- To identify development needs of the people.
- To identify potential persons with leadership quality.
- To identify available resources in and around the villages for proper channelisation.
- To design sustainable development strategy for the region.
- To understand existing government schemes.

Socio - Economic Profile of five Villages

Boraiburu

The village is at a distance of 10km from Badjamda. An all weather pitch road connecting Badjamda and Kiriburu connects it. This is the closest village to the Vijay II Iron Ore Mines located at a distance of some 2km from the mines. Pattern of settlement in the village is sporadic. The population in the village is Ho tribes who stay close to their agriculture land. Total household numbers 144. The dependency on mine for livelihood is to the tune of 81% as daily labourer. The village Munda plays a key role in all decision making pertaining to the village. All villagers have respect for the village Munda. The Munda also collects land revenue within the village and deposits the same with the Govt. The Munda gets a sum of Rs75/- per month for his service. The village Dakua who is responsible for disseminating administrative information in the village died his work is now under control of Munda. Sri Junu Purti is the village Munda of Boraiburu village. He is a positive minded person and is very much convinced that development in agriculture, education and other resources is essential for sustainable all round development of the community. The village is divided into following tolas: Boraiburu bustee, Indira Awas Colony, Teliahatting, Thaparhatting, Sasang hating.

Bokna

The village is at a distance of 3km from Baddajamda. An all weather pitch road connecting Badjamda and Kiriburu connects it. Usha Martin Industries is in the process of acquiring land in this village for setting up its crusher unit. Pattern of settlement in the village is sporadic. The population in the village comprises of Ho tribe who stay close to their agriculture land. Settlement in Bokna is spread across six hamlets namely Bokna Basti, Tondanghatu Toli, Gauhatu Toli, Pakota Sahi, Tirilpi Toli, Konarko Toli. There are 106 households in the village. The primary occupation of the villagers of Bokna is agriculture but 51% peoples are dependent on mines for livelihood as labourer & 24% are in service. Kolai Munda is the Govt. recognised Munda of Bokna village who is now too old to perform active duty so at present Ganguram Champia is treated as Munda of the village for all practical purposes. The village is politically sensitive. Ganguram Champia has affiliation with the Kolhan Sangh and works under the direction of Mr. K.C. Hembrom who stays at Jhinkpani. It is worthwhile to mention that Mr. Hembrom is the first leader to voice for separate KOLHAN as nation.

Tatiba

The village is at a distance of 12km from Badajamda. The village is connected by 10km of pitch road and 2km of metalled road with Badajamda. Pattern of settlement in the village is sporadic. The village is well surrounded by Reserve Forest.Agriculture is the primary occupation of the villagers of Tatiba but people also depend on mines for livelihood to great extent. Village Munda, Haja Hembrom plays a crucial role in all village decisions. All villagers have high respect for the village Munda. The village is distributed in the following tolas: Hembram Sahi, Bari Sahi, Burusahi, Ratanlal hating, Rotubatu, Saranda, Gandkutur.

Diriburu

The village is located at a distance of 5Kms from Badajamda. The village is connected by metalled road. To reach the village one has to take a left turn from the PHC Barajamda. Unlike other villages the settlement pattern in this village is not sporadic. People live in 164 households divided into three tolas - Khas Diriburu, Nuagaon and Kusumsai. The main occupation in this village is agriculture. Some also work as labour in mines. Shyam Singh Champia is Village Munda. Mr. Bangra Champia is another influential person in the village.

Kantoria

The village is located at a distance of 7Kms from Badajamda. The village is connected by metalled road. To reach the village one has to take a left turn from the PHC Barajamda.The settlement is sporadic. 92% villagers are engaged in paddy cultivation in patches. Some villagers also work in mines as labour. Bikram Sirke is the Munda of this village and takes keen interest in village development. The only educated person in Kantoria village is Miru Sirke.

Demographic Profile

- This survey covered 653 households with 2612 People residing in five villages of Iron ore mine project area at Nawamundi block of west singhbhum district.
- Out of the total population in five villages in the project area, 50.49% are males and 49.50% are females.

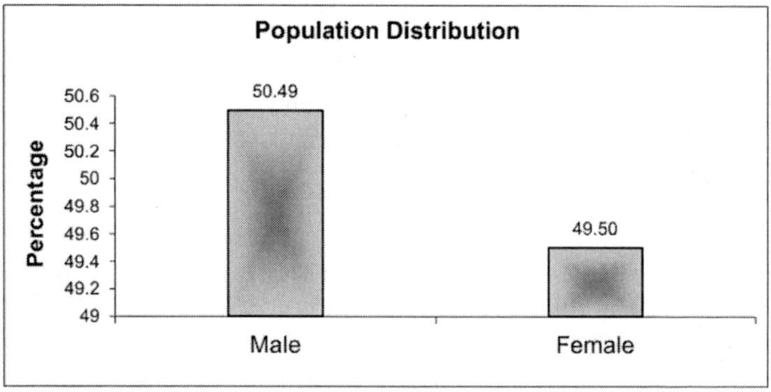

- Out of the total population in five villages in the project area 52.56% are married and 43.80% are unmarried. 1.79% of the people are widow.
- Average house hold size is 4.

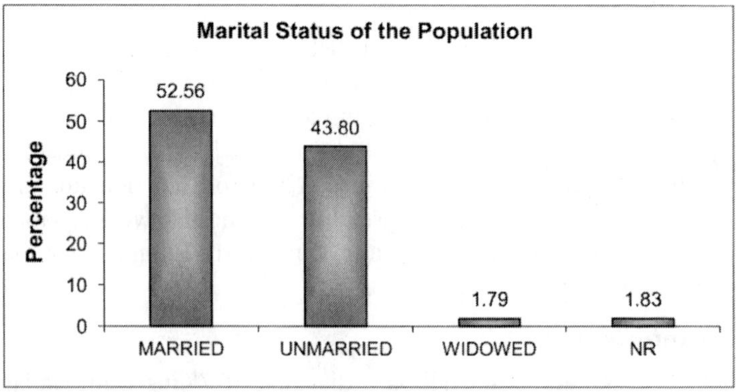

- There are 99% Kachcha houses and 3.67% pacca houses in the study area.
- The 'Ho' tribe people construct rectangular type Kachcha houses on the bank of river, high clefts & near water resources in rows.

Table: Village wise Housing characteristics

Villages	*% Pucca*	*% Kutcha*	*% with Toilet Facility*	*% with Separate Kitchen*
Bokna	-	99.05	-	-
Boraiburu	11.80	86.80	02.77	-
Kantoria	01.92	96.15	01.92	01.92
Diriburu	01.82	96.34	0.61	24.19
Tatiba	01.07	96.25	02.14	02.13

- There is no facility of electricity in 95.71% of the households in five villages only 1.53% population avail electricity facility.

Table: Village wise Households and Population figure

Villages	*Number of HH*	*% Population*			*Average HH Size*
		Total	*Male*	*Female*	
Bokna	106		51.66	48.33	4
Boraiburu	144		49.12	50.87	4
Kantoria	52		49.21	50.78	4
Diriburu	167		51.92	48.07	4
Tatiba	187		50.91	49.08	4

Cultural Profile

Including Sarana members of HO tribes, the majority of inhabitants i.e. 86% are Hindu. The 'Ho' practice spirit worship. 'Bongaism' is the main feature of 'Ho' religion. They believe that natural objects exercise a benevolent influence on their life and happiness; as such they offer periodic prayers and offerings as a part of thanks giving service. The sun, the moon, the rivers and the mountains are the principal 'Bongas' of the 'Ho'. Sun God is 'Sing bonga' – the chief of Bongas, Each village has a second grove where villageprotecting spirit 'Desauli' is believed to sta. They place of worship is called 'Sarana' like Munda of Jharkhand.

The 'Ho' are patrilineal and patrilocal tribe. They are devided into 'Killis'. Their 'Killi' are named after Plant, animal or some materials, which are totemic in nature. The members of a 'Killi' are considered as blood relations so they don't marry within Killis. The 'Ho' cannot marry outside their community otherwise they will be excommunicated. They practice Cross – cousin marriage. They collect Gonong ('Bride price) FOR marriage of girls. In the absence of any marriage proposal a girl may grow into a maiden and remain spinster all her life.

They perform sacrifices at different festivals. They observe following festivals – Maghe porab in February, Baha Porob in March – April, Hero Porob in July – August, Batauli Porob in July – August, Joma nema in August – September, Buru Bonga in August – September, Govar puja in September – October, in addition they also worship Kali- ma, Durga – ma and Hanumanjee. Deori- the village priest conducts worship at the secred grove called 'Jaher' on the occasion of all-important festivals.

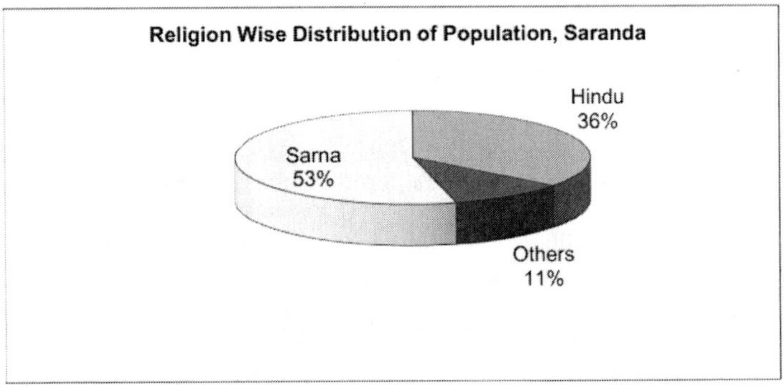

- The mother tongue of most of the people in the project area is tribal "HO" dialect. This belong to Austro – Asiatic linguistic group.

Economic Profile

- 69.83% of respondents are marginal farmers having below 5 acres land.

  Only 3.6% of the population in the project area has land holdings above 10 acres and 8.11% own land between 5 to 10 acres.

Table: Village wise landholding pattern

Village	*% Households Landless*	*Land Holders*		
		% Owning Below 5 Acres	*% Owning 5 – 10 Acres*	*% Owning Above 10 Acres*
Bokna	09.43	86.79	02.83	-
Boraiburu	72.22	22.91	-	-
Kantoria	03.84	94.23	-	-
Diriburu	08.53	73.17	15.24	09.75
Tatiba	47.05	75.40	09.62	03.20

The average household annual income of the people in five villages in the project area is Rs 15564 out of this they spent Rs. 13368.00 and save Rs. 2196.00 on average. Expenditure priority if food, cloth, festivals, health & drinks. Second expenditure priority they give to education, transport and smoking.

Table: Village wise Income & Expenditure percentage households in each category

Village	*Income*			*Expenditure*		
	Below 5000	*5000 – 10000*	*Above 10000*	*Below 5000*	*5000 – 10000*	*Above 10000*
Bokna	01.88	32.07	66.03	02.83	34.90	60.37
Boraiburu	13.19	61.80	25.00	25.47	54.16	17.36
Kantoria	100.00	-	-	94.23	01.92	-
Diriburu	06.70	25.00	67.68	05.48	25.61	68.90
Tatiba	-	31.01	66.31	01.07	63.63	31.55
Bokna	01.88	32.07	66.03	02.83	34.90	60.37

Table on Average Annual Expenditure by Items :-

(Given average for all the five villages) –

Items	*Average Annual Expenditure (Rs.)*
Food	7021
Festivals	1569
Health	478
Clothing	1321
Education	238
Transport	282
Drinks	789
Smoking	108
Electricity	18
Others	496

- The 'Ho' people do not depend only on agriculture they are also earring from mines and industry as industrial workers / labours. The village population is involved in following occupation:-
  1. Agriculture - 8.45%
  2. Labourers - 32.21%
  3. Service - 1.45%
- Source of Income as responded by people of five villages is as follows: -
  1. Agriculture - 29%
  2. Daily Labourers - 49%
  3. Service - 11%

- There are 244 ploughs in the five villages of project area. The number of other agriculture implements in these five villages is 710 includes Nail (Wooden plough), Kudal (Spade), Datrum (Sickle), Hake (Axe). Affluent group uses Bihar Hall i.e. the iron plough.
- The major crop in the villages is paddy (21.63%), wheat (9.72%) & maize (3.72%) followed by pulse crop like Rahar (7.38%), Khesari (11.80%), Moong (2.17%), Urad (1.86%) & Bajra (1.80%)

Health & Education

- 81.16% respondents said that malaria is the common disease in the area. 1.22% said that cough & cold is the common disease, 1% said fever is the common disease. 11.79% respondents identified diarrhea is the common disease in the area and 0.61% said T.B is the common disease. Special drive to control Malaria & Diarrhea should be taken up at the earliest.

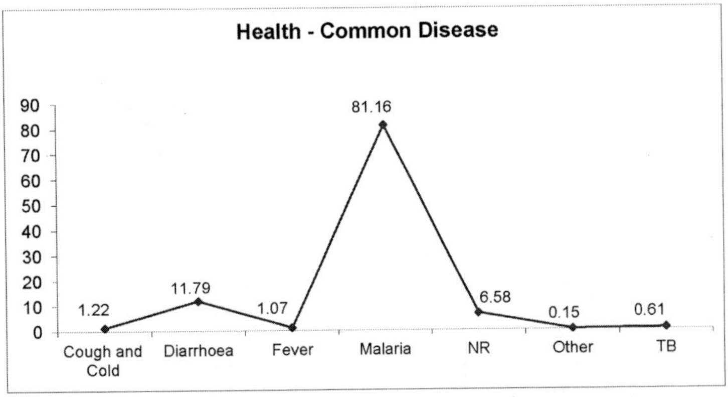

- Only 12% respondents had knowledge of Family Planning.
- 80.53% were aware about Primary Health Centre, 9.8% about Sub Health Centre, 49% had information about Health Centres in Bokna, Boraiburu and Badajamda (PHC).

The educated population in the village is 28.8%. AT present 392 children are studying in educational institutions. All five villages have primary schools. In Tatiba one school is privately run by Bharat Sevashram Sangh. Setu vidyalaya for drop out children are also operational in the villages. Jharkhand Shiksha Pariyojna is running a primary school at Bokna.

Table: Village wise common diseases in the locality

Villages	*Malaria*	*Cough & Cold*	*Fever*	*Diarrhea*	*T.B.*
Bokna	95.28	-	-	-	-
Boraiburu	90.97	01.38	03.47	0.69	0.69
Kantoria	94.23	-	-	-	-
Diriburu	96.95	0.61	-	-	-
Tatiba	03.62	02.68	01.07	40.64	01.60

Gender

The village women take part in family decisions. A girl cannot inherit father's landed property but her husband gets movable property.

- 89.73% of the respondents in the project area felt that the status of women in the villages is lower than male whereas only 9.95% felt that women's status is high.
- 49% respondents said that cowdung making and fetching water are the leisure timework of women.

  Many of them also take part in preparation and sale of HARIA (RICE BEAR) in weekly HAATS.
- The HO collects Gonong (Bride price) for marriage of girls. In the absence of any marriage proposal a girl may grow into a maiden and remain spinster all her life.

Political profile

- Among the political parties 16.53% favoured BJP and rest did not responded.
- 57.27% respondents did not responded to political questions. Out of those who responded, 27.56% named Haza Hembram as their leader, 16.53% knows Mangal Singh Gilua, 1.37% named Junu Purti as leader, 0.15% named Karmu Mahto as new emerging leader.
- The traditional political system divides area into 'Pirs'. Each Pir have five to ten villages. 'Manki' is the divisional Headman and 'Munda' is the headman of a village. Manki and Munda are assisted by 'Dakuas', who are the 'Chaukidars' appointed by Mundas to protect village during night. The system is popularly known as MANKI – MUNDA_- SYSTEM.

Chapter - 7

Tribal Deprivation in Contemporary India: a Case study from Jharkhand

— *Vijay Prakash Sharma*

Introduction

The Scheduled Tribes, in Constitutional term were isolated physically and socially, which is often considered as a reason of their relative or absolute deprivation. Merely 10% of the tribal population reside in the urban areas, while almost 90% continue to live in rural areas (Census, 2011). Following the Tendulkar Committee, the percentage of ST Population Below Poverty Line during in 2011-12 was 45.3 in the rural areas and 24.1 in the urban areas. The human development indicators of the STs in India lag far behind when compared to the nonST population. The literacy rate of the STs was 59%, while that of non STs was 73% in India in 2011. Infant mortality rate and under-five mortality rate of the STs was 44 per 1000 population and 57 per 1000 population respectively as estimated by NFHS 4 (2015-16). Moreover, the facility regarding delivery of children among the STs is low compared to other communities according to NFHS 4. Additionally, only 30.8% of the ST households covered by a health scheme or health insurance (NFHS-4, 2015-16). The estimates provided by Annual Employment-Unemployment Survey (2015-16), reveal that only 46% of the STs aged between 15 and above worked for 12 months. These figures are an indication that the STs continue to live in severe deprivation amidst various constitutional amendments and interventions.

Earlier studies confirm extreme deprivation among the STs compared to other population groups. A study by Dubey (2009), concludes the existence of disparities in mean consumption and poverty incidence between the STs and Other population groups. He also mentioned there was a rise in the disparities between the two groups based on the mean consumption and poverty incidence. A study by Sujatha (1999), concluded that the education outcomes among the STs were lower compared to SCs, with severe variation across the states. The author attributed the low educational achievement levels among tribals to schoolrelated variables along with social and locational factors.

A study by Sandip Sarkar et. al (2006), "Development and Deprivation of Scheduled Tribes" presents estimates of the human development index, human poverty index and gender development index for the scheduled tribes in India. The HDI and HPI for STs are found to be around 30 per cent lower than the corresponding all-India indices. In an international comparison, development and deprivation among the STs of India are similar to that in the poorer countries of sub-Saharan Africa to survive beyond age of 40 years. To illustrate just how serious the situation of deprivation is, we take a closer look of Orissa, which, as mentioned above, is already a state with a low human development. Within Orissa, the districts with the lowest HDI values (as calculated in the Orissa Human Development Report, 2004) fall in one contiguous belt in the south and south-west region of the state. There is a concentration of ST population in this belt. Not only were there very high levels of poverty, going up to 92 per cent for STs in southern Orissa, but this is a region where the incidence of poverty actually increased between 1993-94 and 1999-2000. This increase occurs in spite of the certainty that the 1999-2000 poverty figures are on the whole understated. When comparing the incidence of poverty of STs in Orissa with Africa, it is easily seen that almost no other country has a similar incidence of poverty. Of course, this is based on the assumption that we can compare these poverty rates. (Sandip Sarkar, Sunil Mishra, Harishwar Dayal, Dev Nathan, 2006)

According to a study on tribes of Kerala reported in Shodhganga chapter -vi human development and deprivation of Tribal in Kerala (Shodhganga 2014), Health is regarded as a vital component in the growth and development of a society or a nation. Ill health can lead to capability deprivation and hence poverty, causing a substantial loss of financial and human resources. Poverty caused by poor health further reinforces ill health; poverty leads to low food intake and nutritional deficiencies, deprived of basic amenities like sanitation and clean drinking water cause infections. The health and nutrition problems of the vast tribal population of India are as varied as the tribal groups themselves who present a bewildering diversity and variety in their socio-economic, socio-cultural and ecological settings. The malnutrition is high among the tribal population, especially the mothers and preschool children. Nutritional deficiency leads to diseases like endemic goiter, anemia, etc. The deficiency may result from improper diet. Nutritional anaemia is a major problem for women and children in India and more so in the rural and tribal belt. This is particularly serious in view of the fact that both rural and tribal women and children have a heavy workload and anemia has a profound effect on psychological and physical health. Anaemia lowers resistance to fatigue, affects working capacity under conditions of stress and increases susceptibility to other diseases. Maternal malnutrition is quite common among the tribal women, especially those who have many pregnancies too closely spaced. Tribal diets are generally grossly deficient in calcium, vitamin A, vitamin C, riboflavin and animal protein. Nutritional deprivation is overwhelmingly the largest factor in overall poverty. The type and use of sanitation facility is one of the important indicators of development of a region or a group. During the field survey, it was observed that the majority of the tribes do not give much care for neatness and cleanliness. They do not give any importance to their daily health.

Research Methodology

Socio- economic status is an important determinant of the human development status of a family or a society. Maintaining a decent standard of living is an essential ingredient of human development.

Income is the most commonly used indicators of standard of living. Nevertheless, the mere receipt of income does not imply improvement in human standard of living, although it provides the potential for that.

Therefore, assets and amenities also have to be assessed, in addition to income, to get a reasonable idea about the standard of living dimension of human development.

This paper presents tribal deprivation status in Jharkhand based on socio-economic analysis of secondary data collected from government and academic sources.

Discussion

The Tribal communities are believed to be original/earliest inhabitants of the country, mainly occupying the forest region. In India, the tribal concentration is dominant in the Central and North-Eastern region.As per the Census 2011, the tribal population of the country is 10.43 crore, constituting 8.6% of the total population.More than half of the Scheduled Tribe (ST) population is concentrated in states of Madhya Pradesh, Chhattisgarh, Jharkhand, Andhra Pradesh, Maharashtra, Orissa, Gujarat and Rajasthan and the North East. There are705 individual ethnic groups notified as Scheduled Tribes across 30 States/UT's. There are Tribes which are known as Particularly Vulnerable Tribal Groups (PVTGs), owing to their dependency on pre-agriculture level of technology; their stagnant or declining population; extremely low literacy; and subsistence level of economy.

1. Source of Monthly Household Income

As per Socio-Economic and Caste Census of India, 2011, the household income of majority(**44.68 %**) of tribals in Jharkhand depends on manual casual labour followed by cultivation(**42.55%**). **Table 1**.

Table 1: District wise STHouseholds by Source of Monthly Household Income in Jharkhand, 2011

Sl. No.	*District Name*	*Total ST House holds*	*% ST Households by Income Source*						
			Culti-vation	*Manual Casual Labour*	*Part time or Full Time Domestic Service*	*Foraging Rag Picking*	*Non agri-cultural Own Account Enterprise*	*Begging/ Charity/ Alms collection*	*Others*
	All India	19719299	37.94	51.34	1.99	0.22	0.63	0.23	7.60
1.	Garhwa	31164	37.19	55.78	3.28	0.20	0.47	0.22	2.85
2.	Chatra	7922	31.41	55.68	1.65	0.04	0.61	0.28	10.34
3.	Koderma	945	6.14	73.33	0.63	2.96	0.53	0.11	16.30
4.	Giridih	41141	17.34	75.99	1.43	0.08	0.10	0.15	4.91
5.	Deoghar	33142	35.31	57.38	1.89	0.07	0.15	0.08	5.11
6.	Godda	55081	43.03	48.57	2.04	0.09	0.16	0.09	6.02
7.	Sahibganj	65187	43.76	46.87	2.97	0.11	0. 63	0.08	5.58
8.	Pakur	78702	49.74	44.12	0.90	0.05	0.96	0.07	4.16
9.	Dhanbad	37285	15.32	68.78	2.79	0.13	0.27	0.37	12.33
10.	Bokaro	46458	16.57	64.58	2.59	0.12	2.37	0.19	13.58
11.	Lohardaga	48460	64.18	30.33	1.31	0.08	0.27	0.12	3.70
12.	Purbi Singh bhum	126107	27.35	49.61	10.18	0.44	0.76	0.15	11.51
13.	Palamu	30543	30.54	54.94	5.26	2.23	0.26	0.17	6.60
14.	Latehar	60141	51.60	36.38	2.79	0.09	0.58	0.11	8.45
15.	Hazaribagh	21033	28.68	55.46	2.49	0.13	0.36	0.11	12.76
16.	Ramgarh	36613	18.95	60.51	2.41	0.06	0.82	0.15	17.09
17.	Dumka	121357	45.26	48.49	1.23	0.07	0.17	0.12	4.66
18.	Jamtara	45259	46.21	48.28	1.64	0.05	0.10	0.14	3.57
19.	Ranchi	133072	46.75	41.50	2.73	0.33	0.52	0.18	7.00
20.	Khunti	71400	66.85	24.98	3.02	0.21	0.61	0.08	4.24
21.	Gumla	99915	63.04	20.00	6.05	1.24	1.12	0.32	8.23
22.	Simdega	72374	74.75	15.83	3.21	0.94	0.53	0.44	4.31
23.	Pashchimi Singhbhum	154862	28.06	51.38	9.66	2.17	0.78	0.23	7.72
24.	Saraikela Kharsawan	50474	43.42	42.15	5.50	0.57	1.59	0.11	6.67
Jharkhand		1468637	42.55	44.68	4.13	0.55	0.65	0.18	7.17

Source: Socio-Economic and Caste Census of India, 2011.

2. Deprivation Situation –

As per Socio-Economic and Caste Census of India, 2011, District wise Deprivation Situation among ST Households in Jharkhand,, 15.79 5 tribal's have only one room with kucha walls and kucha roof; 33.95% have no literate adult above 25 years; 13.23% are Landless households deriving major part of their income from manual casual labour.

Table 2: District wise Deprivation Situation among ST Households in Jharkhand, 2011

Sl. No.	*District Name*	*Total ST House-holds*	*% of Deprived ST Households with deprivation criteria*			
			Only one Room with kucha walls and kucha roof	*No adult member between age 16 to 59*	*No literate adult above 25 years*	*Landless households deriving major part of their income from manual casual labour*
	All India	19719299	22.12	3.74	39.29	29.82
1.	Garhwa	31164	16.20	4.88	40.53	10.37
2.	Chatra	7922	17.42	1.70	39.43	10.19
3.	Kodarma	945	26.35	2.12	50.16	40.32
4.	Giridih	41141	19.51	2.06	52.26	12.20
5.	Deoghar	33142	17.15	2.40	43.63	8.60
6.	Godda	55081	18.34	2.60	47.07	16.97
7.	Sahibganj	65187	30.16	2.30	52.64	18.77
8.	Pakur	78702	32.96	1.78	53.37	15.11
9.	Dhanbad	37285	17.06	1.70	35.75	15.42
10.	Bokaro	46458	17.29	2.01	38.10	12.09
11.	Lohardaga	48460	7.41	2.85	34.33	6.36
12.	PurbiSinghbhum	126107	13.95	2.15	27.35	20.12
13.	Palamu	30543	19.81	2.62	35.48	10.21
14.	Latehar	60141	14.46	2.89	39.41	6. 70
15.	Hazaribagh	21033	13.57	1.86	41.28	10.37
16.	Ramgarh	36613	8.96	2.11	34.78	14.37
17.	Dumka	121357	24.53	2.76	39.35	9.32
18.	Jamtara	45259	21.53	2.64	42.00	8. 29
19.	Ranchi	133072	8.90	2.49	25.96	12.12
20.	Khunti	71400	17.13	3.57	31.20	5.83
21.	Gumla	99915	12.23	2.72	26.20	4.66
22.	Simdega	72374	8.49	3.43	25.58	6.24
23.	PashchimiSinghbhum	154862	6.06	1.81	15.93	27.44
24.	Saraikela-Kharsawan	50474	15.76	2.38	25.92	13.94
Jharkhand		1468637	15.79	2.49	33.95	13.23

Source: Socio-Economic and Caste Census of India, 2011.

3. Asset and income Situation –

If we look at % ST Households with Asset and income Situation then you will be not surprised to learn that only14.99% Households owning motorized two/three/four wheelers/fishing boats 1.78% Households having kisan credit card with the credit limit of Rs. 50,000 and above; 3.49 % Households with any member as government employee; 5.14% Households with any member earning more than Rs. 10,000 p.m; Only 3.31% tribal Households paying income tax.

Table 3: District wise Asset and income Situation among STHouseholds in Jharkhand

Sl. No.	*District Name*	*Total ST*	*% STHouseholds with Asset and income Situation*				
		House-holds	*Households owning motorized two/three/four wheelers/ fishing boats*	*Households having kisan credit card with the credit limit of Rs. 50,000 and above*	*House-holds with any member as government employee*	*House-holds with any member earning more than Rs. 10,000 p.m*	*House-holds paying income tax*
	All India	19719299	9.89	1.65	4.37	4.48	3.35
1.	Garhwa	31164	6.73	1.61	2.08	1.79	0.96
2.	Chatra	7922	8.94	0.87	5.04	7.38	6.13
3.	Kodarma	945	6.24	3.07	6.77	6.77	4.87
4.	Giridih	41141	5.64	0.73	2.41	2.18	1.53
5.	Deoghar	33142	6.01	1.05	3.01	2.94	2.31
6.	Godda	55081	9.83	1.65	3.27	3.41	2.55
7.	Sahibganj	65187	3.74	2.03	2.36	2.93	1.73
8.	Pakur	78702	3.41	0.77	1.72	1.51	1.08
9.	Dhanbad	37285	13.76	1.08	7.78	8.58	8.02
10.	Bokaro	46458	17.52	0.81	7.02	9.19	7.20
11.	Lohardaga	48460	8.80	2.62	4.27	3.91	3.69
12.	PurbiSingh bhum	126107	28.40	1.74	2.83	6.53	3.35
13.	Palamu	30543	15.57	2.01	4.59	6.22	3.17
14.	Latehar	60141	4.85	1.11	3.53	3.53	2.33
15.	Hazaribagh	21033	14.46	0.71	6.11	9.91	8.51
16.	Ramgarh	36613	17.57	0.99	9.10	13.78	13.47
17.	Dumka	121357	6.26	0.64	3.69	2.94	2.11
18.	Jamtara	45259	6.85	0.92	2.98	2.21	2.38
19.	Ranchi	133072	19.19	2.05	4.21	5.34	4.23
20.	Khunti	71400	5.92	1.31	2.96	2.38	1.99
21.	Gumla	99915	22.42	2.03	4.75	8.06	3.27
22.	Simdega	72374	12.65	1.25	2.70	5.39	2.16
23.	Pashchimi Singh bhum	154862	30.05	4.42	1.23	6.96	2.87
24.	Saraikela Kharsawan	50474	26.68	2.67	2.60	5.13	3.04
Jharkhand		1468637	14.99	1.78	3.49	5.14	3.31

Source: Socio-Economic and Caste Census of India, 2011.

Conclusion

The Tribal communities are believed to be original/earliest inhabitants of the country, mainly occupying the forest region. In India, the tribal concentration is dominant in the Central and North-Eastern region.As per the Census 2011, the tribal population of the countryis 10.43 crore, constituting 8.6% of the total population.More than half of the Scheduled Tribe (ST) population is concentrated in states of Madhya Pradesh, Chhattisgarh, Jharkhand, Andhra Pradesh, Maharashtra, Orissa, Gujarat and Rajasthan andthe North East. There are705 individual ethnic groups notified as Scheduled Tribes across 30 States/UT's. There are Tribes which are known as Particularly Vulnerable Tribal Groups (PVTGs), owing to their dependency on pre-agriculture level of technology; their stagnant or declining population; extremely low literacy; and subsistence level of economy.

Source of Monthly Household Income

As per Socio-Economic and Caste Census of India, 2011, the household income of majority(44.68 %) of tribals in Jharkhand depends on manual casual labour followed by cultivation(42.55%). Table 1.

Deprivation Situation –

As per Socio-Economic and Caste Census of India, 2011, District wise Deprivation Situation among ST Households in Jharkhand,, 15.79 5 tribal's have only one room with kucha walls and kucha roof; 33.95% have no literate adult above 25 years; 13.23% are Landless households deriving major part of their income from manual casual labour

Asset and income Situation –

If we look at % ST Households with Asset and income Situation then you will be not surprised to learn that only14.99% Households owning motorized two/three/four wheelers/fishing boats 1.78% Households having kisan credit card with the credit limit of Rs. 50,000 and above ; 3.49 % Households with any member as government employee; 5.14% Households with any member earning more than Rs. 10,000 p.m ; Only 3.31% tribal Households paying income tax.

References and Bibliography

Badgaiyan (1986): "19 th century in Chotanagpur and Santhal Parganas – Political Economy of migration", in M.C.A. Rao (ed) Studies in Migration, Manohar Publication, New Delhi.

Bose, N.K. (1941): The Hindu Method of Tribal Absorption., Science and Society, (7): 188.94. (quoted in Xaxa, Virginius (2004): "Women and Gender in the Study of Tribes in India", Indian Journal of Gender Studies, 11:3, Sage Publications New Delhi/Thousand Oaks/London).

Burman B.K. Roy (1971): "Redistribution of Scheduled Tribe of India", Census Centenary Monograph, No. 7, Census of India, pp – 483 – 538.

Burman B.K. Roy (1978): "A Tribal India – Population and Society", Indian Anthropologist, vol.8, p. 75-76.

Burman B.K. Roy (1988): Challenges of Development and Tribal Women, in J.P. Singh et al. (eds.), Tribal Women, pp. 14. (quoted in Xaxa, Virginius (2004): "Women and Gender in the Study of Tribes in India", Indian Journal of Gender Studies, 11:3, Sage Publications New Delhi/Thousand Oaks/London).

Choudhury N.C. & Bhowmic S.K. (1986): "Migration of Chotanagpur Tribes to West Bengal", in M.C.A. Rao(ed) Studies in Migration, Manohar Publication, New Delhi.

Corbridge Stuart (1988): "The Ideology of Tribal Economy and Society: Politics in the Jharkhand, 1950-1980", Modern Asian Studies 22, 1 (1988), pp.22.

Das S. Childhood undernutrition: A comparative analysis of scheduled tribes and others in the mid-Indian tribal region. Social Change. 2008; 38:64.

Dhebar, U. N. (Chairman) (1962) Report of the Scheduled Castes and Scheduled Tribes Commission (New Delhi: Government of India Press).

Dubey, A. (2009). Poverty and Under-nutrition among Scheduled Tribes in India: A Disaggregated Analysis. IGIDR Proceedings/Project Reports Series PP-062-13.

Dube, S C, (1977) "Tribal Heritage of India, Ethnicity, Identity and Interaction", Volume 1, Vikas Pub.

Firdos, Sohel (2005): "Forest Degradation, changing workforce structure and population redistribution: the case of Birhors in Jharkhand", Economic and Political Weekly, Vol. 40, No. 8, Feb. 19-25.

Jharkhand Economic Survey 2017-18, CFS, Department of Planning and Finance, Government of Jharkhand.

Kosambi, D.D. 1975. The Culture and Civilization of Ancient India in Historical Outline, Delhi: Vikas Publishing House. (quoted in Xaxa, Virginius (2004): "Women and Gender in the Study of Tribes in India", Indian Journal of Gender Studies, 11:3, Sage Publications New Delhi/Thousand Oaks/London).

Maharatna, Arup and Chikte, Rasika (2004): "Demography of tribal population in Jharkhand 1951-1991", Economic and Political Weekly, Vol. 39, No. 46-47, Nov. 13-26, pp. 5053.

Moonis Raza and A. Ahmad (1990): An Atlas of Tribal India, New Delhi: Concept Publication.

Sachchidananda. (1988): Tribal Women in the Throes of Development, in J.P. Singh, et al. (eds.), Tribal Women, pp. 80. (quoted in Xaxa, Virginius (2004): "Women and Gender in the Study of Tribes in India", Indian Journal of Gender Studies, 11:3, Sage Publications New Delhi/Thousand Oaks/London).

Sarkar, Sandip, Sunil Mishra, Harishwar Dayal and Dev Nathan (2006): Scheduled Tribes of India: Development and Deprivation, Institute for Human Development, Delhi.

Shodhganga 2014 Human Development and Deprivation of Tribal In Kerala chapter –vi

Singh K S (1978) "Colonial Transformation of the Tribal Society in Middle India', Economic and Political Weekly, Vol. 13, No. 30 (Jul. 29, 1978), pp. 1221-1232.

Socio-Economic and Caste Census of India, 2011, Government of India.

Subba Rao (1958): Personality of India, Baroda: University of Baroda.

Sujatha, K. (1999). Education of India: Schedule Tribes. A study of community schools in the district of Vishakapatnam, Andhra Pradesh. UNESCO working Paper Series on Strategies of Education and Training for disadvantaged groups UNDP (2004): Human Development Report, Oxford University Press, New York.

Xaxa, Virginius (2004): "Women and Gender in the Study of Tribes in India", Indian Journal of Gender Studies, 11:3, Sage Publications New Delhi/Thousand Oaks/ London, pp. 351.

Xaxa V. Protective Discrimination: Why scheduled tribes lag behind scheduled castes. Economic and Political Weekly. 2001; 36(29):2765-72.

Chapter - 8

Tribal Development Initiatives and Achievements in Jharkhand

— *Vijay Prakash Sharma*

As per the Census of India, 2011, the population of Scheduled Tribes in Jharkhand is 8.65 million, which is 26.2 per cent of the total population of the State. Of the total Tribal population, 4.32 million are males and 4.33 are females. Table 15.1 gives the demographic statistics of the STs in Jharkhand for 2001 and 2011. The decadal growth of ST population in Jharkhand was 22 per cent.

Table A.: Demographic Statistics of STs in Jharkhand (2011)

State	*Year*	*Jharkhand*
Total Population	2001	26,945,829
	2011	32,988,134
Decadal Growth in Percent	2001	22.4
ST Population	2001	7,087,068
	2011	8,645,042
Total Male Population	2011	4,315,407
Total Female Population	2011	4,329,635
Decadal Growth in Percent	2011	22
Percent STs in State to total population of State		26.2
Percent STs in the State to total ST population in India		8.3

Source: Census of India, 2001 and 2011.

The majority of the tribal population in Jharkhand resides in the rural areas i.e. 91 percent. The proportion of tribal population across the districts is shown in Map15.1. The districts having a high concentration of tribal communities are Khunti, Simdega, Gumla and Paschimi Singhbum. Alternatively, Koderma has the lowest proportion of ST population in the State followed by Chatra.

Table B. provides a list of notified STs in the State. There are 32 tribes in the State of Jharkhand.

Map A Percentage of ST population in Jharkhand

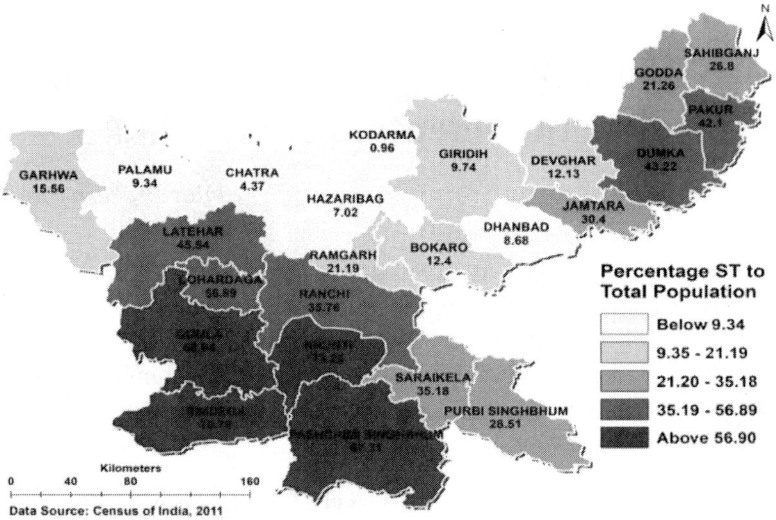

Source: Census of India, 2011.

Table: B. List of notified Scheduled Tribes in Jharkhand

1.	Asur (Agaria, Amendment No-10 of 2003- 7 Jan 2003)- Particularly Vulnerable Tribal Group (PVTG)
2.	Baiga
3.	Banjara
4.	Bathudi
5.	Bedia
6.	Binjhia
7.	Birhor- Particularly Vulnerable Tribal Group (PVTG)
8.	Birjia- Particularly Vulnerable Tribal Group (PVTG)
9.	Chero
10.	Chik Baraik
11.	Gond

(*Contd...*)

12.	Gorait
13.	Ho
14.	Karmali
15.	Kharia (Dhelki Kharia, DudhKharia, Hill Kharia-Amendment No-10 of 2003- 7 Jan 2003)
16.	Kharwar
17.	Khond
18.	Kisan (Nagesia Amendment No-10 of 2003- 7 Jan 2003)
19.	Kora (Mudi Kora- Amendment No-10 of 2003- 7 Jan 2003)
20.	Korwa- Particularly Vulnerable Tribal Group (PVTG)
21.	Lohara, Lohra
22.	Mahli
23.	Mal Paharia (Kumarbhag Paharia Amendment No-10 of 2003- 7 Jan 2003) (PVTG)
24.	Munda (Patar Amendment No-10of 2003- 7 Jan 2003)
25.	Oraon (Dhanga Oraon- Amendment No-10 of 2003- 7 Jan 2003)
26.	Parhaiya- Particularly Vulnerable Tribal Group (PVTG)
27.	Santal
28.	Sauria Paharia
29.	Savar- Particularly Vulnerable Tribal Group (PVTG)
30.	Bhumij (in North Chotanagpur and South Chotanagpur divisions and Santal Parganas)
31.	Kol (Amendment No-10 of 2003- 7 Jan 2003)
32.	Kawar (Amendment No-10 of 2003- 7 Jan 2003)

Note: Hill Kharia-PVTG has been shown in central list that makes Nine PVTGs in Jharkhand.

Socio-economic status of SCs/STs in rural Jharkhand

Economic Status of STs

The rural ST households, compared to the rural SC households in Jharkhand, although reveal a better picture evident from the State average, the disparity across the districts is disheartening. Districts like Pakur, Dumka, Giridih, Khunti have more than 92 per cent rural ST household with a monthly income below 5000, much higher than the State average (82 per cent).

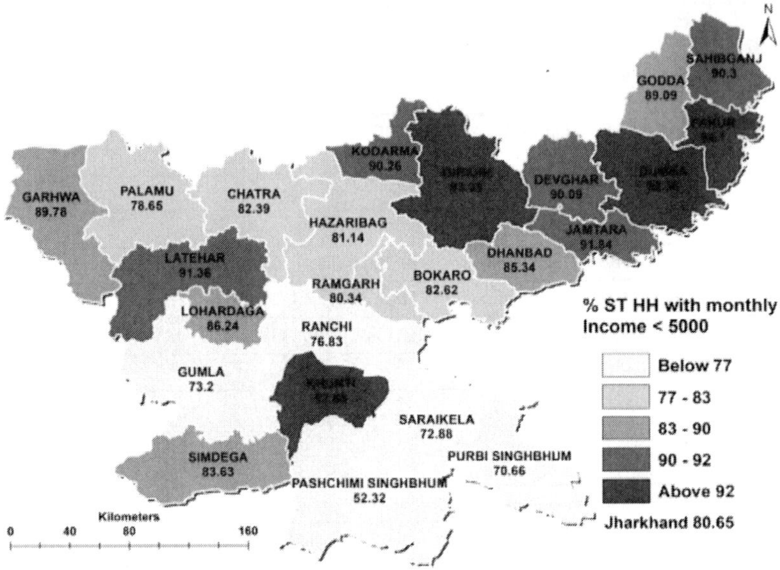

Source: Socio-Economic Caste Census, 2011.

Map 1: Percentage of ST households with monthly income <5000 (Rural) (2011) (%)

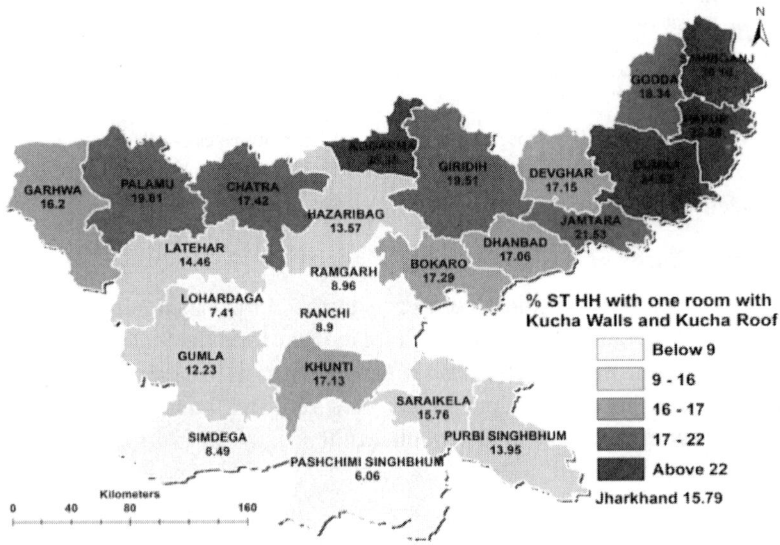

Source: Socio-Economic Caste Census, 2011.

Map 2: Percentage of ST households with one room with Kucha walls and Kucha Roof (Rural) (2011) (%)

Housing Conditions of STs

Even after 17 years of formation of the State, the tribal households in the rural Jharkhand (around 16 per cent), are living in one room with Kucha walls and Kucha roof. Across the districts, the proportion is further worse. The district with greater proportion of rural ST 104 households living in one room with Kucha walls and roof is Pakur (32 per cent), followed by Sahibganj (30 per cent).

Educational status of SCs/STs

In Jharkhand, The proportion of rural ST households with no literate adult s above 25 years was highest in the district of Pakur followed by Sahibganj. The proportion of ST households with no literate adults in these districts was much higher than the State average of 34 per cent.

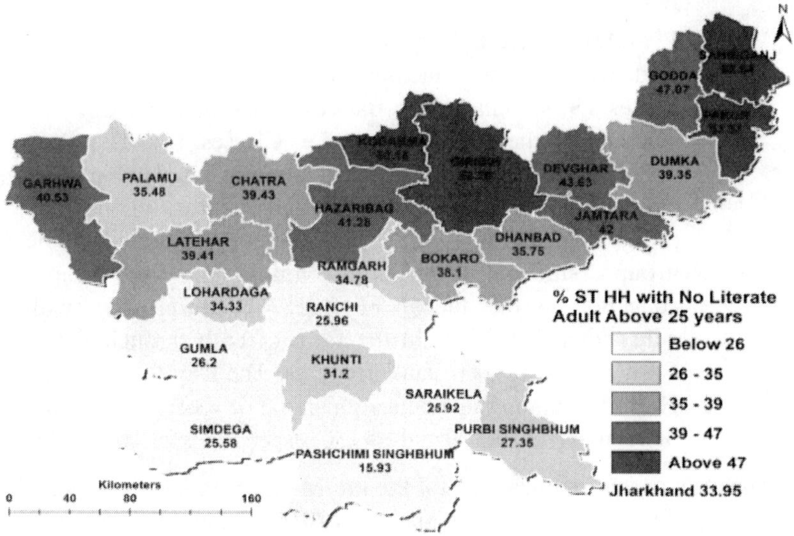

Source: Socio-Economic Caste Census, GOI, 2011.

Map 3: Percentage of ST households with No literate adults above 25 years (Rural) (2011).

Welfare Department, Government of Jharkhand

The Department of Welfare is mandated to look after the welfare of the most underprivileged sections of the society namely the Scheduled Tribes, Scheduled Castes, Backward Classes and Minorities and the task of bringing all-round development of these sections.

Welfare Schemes for the Tribal and other vulnerable groups in Jharkhand

The Scheduled Tribes (STs), Scheduled Castes (SCs), Other Backward Classes (OBCs), Religious Minorities, Senior citizens or Aged persons, Differently-abled etc. are considered as the vulnerable or disadvantaged groups of the society in terms of education, health, social security etc. This section seeks to portray a status report of the various schemes initiated by the Central/State Governments which were operational during the year 2017-18 and review their performance.

(i) Education-related Welfare Schemes for the Vulnerable Groups:

- **Scholarship:** The Scheduled Tribes (STs), Scheduled Castes (SCs) and Other Backward Classes (OBCs) have poor educational attainments as well as poor access to educational infrastructure at all educational levels. To encourage their enrolment, the government provides scholarships at Pre-and Post-Matric levels.
- **Pre-Matric Scholarship Scheme** provides cash to the poor students belonging to the Scheduled Tribes (STs), Scheduled Castes (SCs) and Other Backward Classes (OBCs) 106 studying at the Primary level i.e. Classes 1-4. The Day-Scholars and Hostellers receive a monthly Scholarship of Rs 50 and Rs 150 respectively for 10 months. In order to promote education at higher levels among these vulnerable groups, students undertaking Middle and High-school education i.e. the students of Class 5-10 are provided with educational incentives in the form of cash through Direct Cash Benefit in their bank accounts. The Day-Scholars and Hostellers among this educational cohort receive a monthly Scholarship of Rs 100 and Rs 150 respectively for 10 months.

The status of the applications for the Pre-Matric Scholarship targeted for the Minority community during the years 2016-17 and 2017-18 depict that 20625 scholarships were renewed in 2016-17. A total of 15449 scholarships were renewed in 2017-18.In 2016-17, 40411 applied for scholarship, while 68752 applied for the fresh scholarship in 2017-18.

(Source: Department of Social Welfare, Government of Jharkhand)

- **Post-Matric Scholarship Scheme** provides a yearly scholarship upto Rs 50,000 to ST/SC students whose family income is maximum Rs 2.5lakh a year, and OBC students whose family income is maximum Rs 1 lakh a year. Scholarship can be availed by the students enrolled in technical colleges both within and outside the state. Provision of pre-matric and post matric scholarship in the year 2016-17 amounted to Rs 52839.57 lakh. To provide scholarships in the year 2017-18, Rs 34090 lakh has been estimated for the pre-matric scholarship and Rs 41389 lakh for post matric scholarship, which has been proposed.

Sports Scholarship

The scholarship aims to encourage the students in sports at District, State and National level. It is awarded to the ST/SC/OBC students for their outstanding sports performance. Other provisions of the scholarship provide assistance in the organization of sports events and provide sports tools and equipments.

Exemption from examination fees

This is state initiated scheme aimed to increase education among the students of the deprived community of ST, SC and OBC. They are exempted from the examination fees in matriculate and Intermediate examinations conducted by the Jharkhand Academic Council. This encourages the students to continue their schooling, who would have otherwise dropped out 107 due to the inability to pay the examination fees. They are exempted from paying Rs 125 in matriculation and Rs 175 in intermediate.

Cycle Distribution

The distance from the school is one of the primary reasons for non-enrolment or low attendance. The problem is more serious among the students of ST/SC/OBC who already have fewer means to send their children to school. The scheme provides Rs 3000 through DTB to the students of ST/SC/OBC and other minority groups enrolled in class 8. About 11.43 lakh students have benefitted through the scheme as on 2016-17.

Pahariya Mid-Day Meal Scheme

The scheme aims to provide the especially backward tribal communities with good education and nutrition. The 32 Pahariya schools in the Santhal Pargana provide books, copies, stationary and other study material. It also provides nutritious mid-day meal to the students. The scheme covers the cost of Rs 10.90 per meal per child. This promotes education and health in the tribal areas of the Santhal Pargana.

- **Guaranteed Education Loan Scheme:** The scheme aims to ensure that the continuation of higher education among the poor students belonging to ST, SC and OBC. The government has launched this new scheme to guarantee the provision of education loan through the banks to such students.

(ii) Healthcare related Welfare Schemes for the Vulnerable Groups

Health Assistance

It provides free medical assistance to the poor families of ST/SC/OBC. The District Welfare Officer provides a maximum of Rs 3000 and District Commissioner provides Rs 10,000 through the district committee.

- **Pahariya Health Scheme:** The health condition among the tribals of Santhal Parganais poor. They often remain excluded and inaccessible to the medical facilities. This scheme makes medical facilities accessible as well as affordable to them. There are 18 Pahariya health-care centres opened in the Pargana area by the Welfare Department. The centres provide facilities of medical checkup, Auxiliary Nurse Midwifery (A.N.M.), Male Health Specialists and medicines. Each centre has received a remuneration of Rs 108103596 for A.N.M., Rs 103596 for Male Specialists, Rs 19200 for medical checkups, and Rs 1,40,000 for medicines. Thus, a total of Rs 366392 has been allotted to each medical centre in the Santhal Pargana.
- **Rural Hospital:** The ST, SC and other minority groups often livein geographically remote areas, making basic facility such as health, mostly inaccessible. Therefore, the scheme aims to provide health facilities in such rural areas by establishing hospitals with both OPD and IPD. Currently, 9 rural hospitals are to be established for the 50 rural identified areas.

(iii) Welfare Schemes of Housing for the Vulnerable Groups

- **Birsa Munda Awas Yojna:** The STs have been homeless or live with less stable residence. This makes them more susceptible to health, financial and social exploitation. This State initiated scheme provides ST families with free residence at the rate of Rs 1.35lakh per household.

(iv) Welfare Schemes for Social Security and Social Protection of the Vulnerable Groups

The ST and SC are considered minority not just in educational or economic terms, but because they face immense social discrimination and exploitation. The government implements the following Acts to protect them from any acts of atrocity.

- **ST Pension Scheme:** This scheme provides a monthly pension of Rs 600 to the 9 tribes: *Asur, Birhiya, Birhor, Birjiya, Korwa, Mal Pahadiya, Sariya Pahariya and Sabar.*
- **ST/SC Prevention of Atrocities Act:** This Act protects the members of ST and SC community from atrocities, which can be physical or verbal. The culprit can be charged any amount from Rs 10,000 to Rs 2lakh, depending on the nature and degree of the atrocious act. If such an act leads to the death or inability of the prime earner of the family, then Rs 2lakh is compensated to the family. Further, in case of physical and sexual violation of a female, a compensation of Rs 50,000 is provided.
- **Village Development of the Martyr Scheme:** This new scheme seeks to reward the martyrs of the ST/SC community and promote rural development. Under the scheme, the villages of such martyrs are developed through road construction, better connectivity, house construction, provision of drinking water, Anganwadi and health centres. The government provides free residence to the villagers at Rs 2.63lakh per household.
- **Implementation of Forest Rights Act, 2006:** The Act is for the welfare of the STs residing in the forests and other traditional forest-dwellers. Due to the fast rate of industrial development, the tribes who traditionally dwell and depend on the forest, often come in conflict with the outsiders over the use of land and forest. The Act issues legal land rights, patta, to traditional forest dwellers, residing there for more than75 years, and to Scheduled Tribes, who have been residing there for more than 5 years.
- **Citizen Protection Act, 1955:** The Act aims at better governance and prevention of discrimination against the members of ST and SC at public places. It criminalises discriminatory entry at restaurants, hotels, worship places etc. The District Magistrates are expected to spread awareness through hoardings and street-plays.
- **Article 275(1) of Constitution:** The Act is for the promotion of welfare for the STs of the tribal areas. It provides for the development of Eklavya schools, P.C.C. roads, health centres, rural hospitals, tribal art and culture centres, hostels, solar lights and drinking water.

(v) Welfare Schemes for Livelihood security among the Vulnerable Groups

Grants via Pre-Jha Foundation for Skill Development

This scheme aims to generate employment among the ST/SC/OBC

and other minority groups. Many skill development centres have been opened through the Welfare Department at the district level to provide necessary skills to the unemployed youth. The centres run through the grants provided by the Pre-Jha Foundation. This will increase self-employment and income among such minority groups.

- **Training centre for lac cultivation:** The people from ST still derive their income from the forest resources. To facilitate their livelihood, the government has launched **Lac Development Scheme**. One of the provisions of the scheme is to provide them with training related to lac cultivation. For the purpose, 98 training centres for lac cultivation have been established.
- **Livelihood Training:** The scheme aims to encourage self-employment among the ST, SC, OBC and other minority groups. For the purpose, many skill development training centres will be established. These centres will impart skills to the unemployed persons belonging to these disadvantaged groups to be self-employed.
- **Jharkhand Tribal Empowerment and Livelihood Project:** The project aims to increase self-employment, ensure food security and reduce unemployment and poverty among the STs. This is to be implemented in 14 districts where the tribal population exceeds 50 per cent of the population. The poor ST of 164 panchayats and 1330 grams of 30 blocks are to be benefitted from the scheme.
- **Special Central Assistance to Tribal Sub Plan:** The plan aims to increase income and employment of the tribals through special assistance in agricultural and primary activities. It assists in agriculture, horticulture, soil enrichment, water and soil conservation, and forest, management.

(vi) Welfare Schemes for Reduction of Poverty among the Vulnerable Groups

Targeting the Hardcore Poor Scheme (THP)

The scheme aims to reduce extreme poverty among the female-headed households of the STs. For the purpose, various poverty reduction and skill development programs will be initiated with about 2000poor female-headed households of the ST community. It will first be implemented in Dumka and West Singhbhum. About 5 THP will be formed in both districts. Each THP aims to benefit about 200 households.

- **Provision of Subsidized Asset:** Encouraging livelihood is one of the major ways to increase income and reduce poverty. Therefore, the scheme provides asset s at a subsidized rate to the ST, ST, OBC and other minorities for the purpose of starting and enhancing their business.

- **National Family Benefit Scheme:** This scheme aims to reduce poverty among the BPL families whose primary earner has died. It prevents the families from slipping into poverty, by providing a sum of Rs 20,000.

(vii) Welfare Schemes for the Aged Persons/Senior Citizens

- Schools, hostels, old-age homes: The poor, old, weak, disadvantageous, widows, orphans, differently-abled are to be cared for by providing them old-age homes, hospitals, remand homes, children and women homes, and working women hostels.
- **Pension Scheme for the HIV/AIDS persons:** The persons affected with HIV/AIDS are socially dejected which often results in less economic opportunities. Therefore, the scheme provides monthly Rs 600 to the affected persons. 1434 persons have benefitted from the scheme in 2017.
- **State Social Protection Pension Scheme:** The scheme is for the welfare of the disadvantageous groups such as widows, differently-abled, people freed from bonded labour and other weak groups. Persons belonging to such groups who are above the age of 60 can avail the benefits of the scheme. They are provided with financial assistance of Rs 600 per month. In 2015, 1,25,846 persons were benefitted from this scheme. The number of the beneficiaries increased to 2,76,733 in 2017.
- **Indira Gandhi National Old Age Pension Scheme:** A monthly pension of Rs 600 is given to the persons who are 60 years or above with a maximum income of Rs 7995 in rural areas and Rs 9974 in urban areas. In 2015,7,22,053 persons benefitted from the scheme. The number of the beneficiaries has increased to 9,04,270 in 2017. Also, new old age homes have been established in Deoghar, Pakur and Godda. A proposal of 100-beds old age homes has been made in Ranchi, Saraikela and Jamtara. The first part of the construction of 50-beds old age home has been initiated. An "After Care Home" has been inaugurated in Dumka.
- **Indira Gandhi National Widow Pension Scheme:** The scheme was implemented on the recommendations of the Tendulkar Committee. A monthly pension of Rs 600 can be availed by the widows between the age 40-79. The BPL widows are covered under the scheme.

- **State Widow's Honour Pension Scheme:** It is a state-initiated scheme which provides a pension of Rs 600 per month to the widows above the 18 years. The total number of beneficiaries in 2017 was 1,06,828 persons.
- **Workers State Insurance Scheme:** The beneficiaries are the workers of the organised sector which employs a minimum of 10 workers. The workers whose monthly income is or less than Rs 15,000 can avail the benefits of the scheme. It provides health insurance.

(viii) Welfare Schemes for the Differently-abled Persons

- **Differently-abled Welfare Scheme:** The differently abledintellectually/visually/physically challenged can avail the benefits of the scheme by providing them appropriate technological assistance, organizing special workshops and implementing measures for their social and economic inclusion.
- **Education** is encouraged among the differently-abled by providing themscholarships. The **Scholarship for the Differently-abled** provides scholarships to children in schools and colleges. Further, the scheme aims to promote education by providing **hostels for the differently abled**. The hostels will be provided to the school and college going students, who are affected by different disabilities.
- **Indira Gandhi National Differently-abled Pension Scheme:** The poor differentlyabled persons whose income in rural areas is less than Rs7996 or Rs 9975 in urban areas per year, and is affected by 80 per cent disability is awarded a monthly pension of Rs 600. In 2015, the number of persons who benefitted from the scheme was 17,147. The number of the beneficiaries increased to 19,953 in 2017.
- **District Disability Rehabilitation Centre:** A centre is to be established in each state to provide assistance and advice to the differently-abled persons. The centre has been established in 6 districts of Jharkhand, namely, Ranchi, Dumka, Palamu, Hazaribagh, Jamshedpur and Dhanbad. The centre especially assists in rehabilitation, awareness programs and informing about the various welfare schemes.

A **Composite Rehabilitation Centre** will be launched in Ranchi for the education of the differently abled children. **UDID program** has been launched to provide them with disability recognition identity cards. These cards facilitate the procurement of benefits of welfare schemes.

- **Swami Vivekanand Differently-able Self-Reliant Encouragement Scheme:** This is a state-initiated scheme which provides monthly Rs 600 to the differently abled persons. The scheme covers persons from different categories to make most differently abled selfreliant. In total, 1,67,241 persons have benefitted from the scheme in 2017.

Table 15.11: Progress in the Social Welfare Schemes, 2015 and 2017

Social Welfare Schemes	*Number of Beneficiaries*	
	2015	*2017*
State Social Security Pension	125846	276733
Swami Vivekananda Differently-able Self-Reliant Encouragement Scheme	-	167241
Indira Gandhi National Differently-abled Pension Scheme	17147	19953
Indira Gandhi National Old Age Pension Scheme	722053	904270
State Widow's Honour Pension Scheme	-	106828
Pension Scheme for the HIV/AIDS persons	-	1434

Source: Department of Social Welfare, Government of Jharkhand.

Conclusion

Some of the issues that invite attention of the government and development agencies are :

1. Ocial-demographic composition: Jharkhand occupies the 14th position by population among all states and UT's of the country witha population of 32.96 million (census 2011), and a decadal growth of population at 22.34 percent. Out of total population, around 76 per cent is rural and 24 per cent is urban.

Jharkhand is a predominantly tribal state and Scheduled Tribes constitute 26.20 per cent of total statepopulation, which is much higher than the average of 8.3 per cent for all -India. The State has around 32 Tribal Groups andaround one-thirdof the tribal population live in rural areas. Eight out of the 32 tribes of Jharkhand fallunder Primitive Tribal Group (PTG), which are considered to be most vulnerable among the tribal community. Malnutrition is rampant in PTG villages and the access of these communities to the social welfare programmes remains limited.

Child (0-6 years) sex ratio has decreased in the state from 965 to 948 during 2001-11. In ruralregions of Jharkhand state, female sex ratio was 961 while same for the child (0-6 age) was 957girls in 2011. But in urban regions of Jharkhand, both overall sex ratio and child sex ratio aremuch lower at 910 and 908 respectively.

The dynamics of the developmental process on Jharkhand needs to be examined in the context of its predominantly rural population, layered with socio-ethnic multiplicity and increasing need for gender sensitive development in order to foster an inclusive and sustainable policy for its future growth.

2. Poverty and Malnutrition: Despite surging growth, poverty has been a persistent feature of the Jharkhand economy. Povertyin the state is among the highest in the country today, and food security has been a seriousconcern. The 2011-12 poverty estimates by the Planning Commission shows that populationbelow the poverty line in Jharkhand (37 per cent) was second highest in the country and significantly higher than the national average (21.9 per cent).The poverty and deprivation are particularly acute in the interior of thestate with the rural poverty ratio being as high as 40.8 percent.

About 77 per cent of its population are multi-dimensionally poorwith deprivation not only interms of income or consumption expenditure, but the poor also lack access to health, education,housing, good drinking water and sanitation, etc. It continues to suffer from high incidences of malnutrition amongst childrenand anaemia in adults. Stunting and wasting, indicators for malnutrition show high share ofunder-5 children.

The focus of the developmental processin Jharkhand needs to be oriented towards the rampant multidimensional poverty and cases of acute starvation and malnutrition to make significant progress in human development aspects. These issues require in-depth research and analysis.

3. Health and Education and Human development: The human development aspects of health and educational outcomes are essentially the focus areas where development needs to be concentrated. Strengthening rural health infrastructure in the state is essential while addressing the access tohealth facility in rural areas given that most maternal deaths experienced in the state were among poor and non-literatewomen from the rural areas. While infant mortality has declined considerably in the last decade, noticeable gap between urban and rural and across the districts continues to be amajor public health challenge for the state.

The education landscape in the state is characterized by disparity in many areas, including access to quality education, which hinders the overall progress in the state. It faces the disadvantage that out of a total number of 259 blocks in the state, 203 are Educationally Backward Blocks. The disparity in educational attainment in rural vs urban areas are reflected across districts as well as across social groups. Wide disparity in female literacy across districts is also observed

Such issues need to be explored in details in order to attain equitable and sustainable human development worthy of its kind. Identification and reporting the bottlenecks in programme implementation, evaluating and analysing the impact of various government programmes and initiatives targeted towards human development and providing recommendations to the government machinery for inclusive policy formulation will be the fundamental scope of the proposed Centre.

In this effort the Institute would strive to serve as a focal point for tapping the best possible experts through networking arrangements with individuals and institutions.The Institute would have active collaboration with the Government of Jharkhand and other relevant organisations concerned with the development of the state in formulating its research agenda and its implementation. The Centre will be led by a functionary of the Institute andwill beefficiently managed by a Steering Committee with a distinguished academic as its Chairmanalong with nominees of the Jharkhand Government in it. This would ensure that the research concerns of the Government of Jharkhand are fully reflected in the work of the Centre. It is hoped that this effort of the IHD will be useful in providing required input in policy formulation to support the Government of Jharkhand in attaining the Sustainable Development Goals.

Undoubtedly, the State Government has made sincere efforts to ensure the overall development of the tribal and other vulnerable community; albeit it has little achievement to its claim .The status of underprivileged in Jharkhand has shown little improvement since its inception. They continue to lead a deplorable life, with subsistence economy and lack of basic amenities such as drinking water and improved sanitation. Owing to their condition, the human development indicators in the State has showed marginal improvements. Among the underprivileged groups, the tribal community face more problems, given their inability to access resources. Therefore, for an inclusive development, the State requires to focus in specific areas of women development which require attention. The low socio-economic development and their habitation in various ecological and geo-climatic conditions ranging from plains to forest to hills and inaccessible areas are the main reasons for low literacy among the Scheduled Tribe. States has to address the development need of its vulnerable communities.

However, the Ministry is implementing the education-oriented schemes which include PostMatric Scholarship for ST students, Hostels for ST girls and boys, Establishment of Ashram School in Tribal Sub-Plan Areas, Up gradation of Merit through coaching and remedial classes, Rajiv Gandhi National Fellowship for ST students, Top Class Education for ST students and National Overseas Scholarship for ST students to improve the literacy level belonging to the Scheduled Tribe communities, besides usual reservation for ST students. These are supplementary to the efforts made by other Ministries.

Concerns

The status of Tribal in Jharkhand has shown little improvement since its inception. They continue to lead a deplorable life, with subsistence economy and lack of basic amenities such as drinking water and improved sanitation. Owing to their condition, the human development indicators in the State has showed marginal improvements. Among the underprivileged groups, the tribal community face more problems, given their inability to access resources.

Therefore, for an inclusive development, the State requires to focus in specific areas of women development which require attention. The low socio-economic development and their habitation in various ecological and geo-climatic conditions ranging from plains to forest to hills and inaccessible areas are the main reasons for low literacy among the Scheduled Tribe. States has to address the development need of its vulnerable communities.

In this situation we have to find out methods for Financial Inclusion and Digital Payment System for Tribal in Jharkhand

References

Socio-Economic Caste Census, 2011, Census of India, Govermnet of India, Delhi.

Jharkhand Economic Survey 2017-18, Department of planning and Finance, Government of Jharkhand.

Chapter - 9

World of Tribal Women, Work and Leisure with Special Reference to Jharkhand

— Vijay Prakash Sharma, Ivshita Dutta

Tribal women are the prime movers of earning livelihood for their family. They are always on move from here to their performing the household and field services usually with very little leisure time at their disposal.

The rights available to woman) in India can be classified into two categories, namely as constitutional rights and legal rights. The constitutional rights are those which are provided in the various provisions of the constitution. The legal rights, on the other hand, are those which are provided in the various laws (acts) of the Parliament and the State Legislatures. In spite of this, Women in Jharkhand continue to live in extreme deprivation and discrimination. Evident from the recent estimates reported by the NFHS 4, a significant proportion of women continue to suffer from anaemia compared to men.

Moreover, the nutritional status indicated by Body Mass Index, reveals a similar plight of women, i.e., more women are undernourished compared to men in Jharkhand.

Many of those women who could grab the opportunities extended to them have proved that they are capable of discharging the responsibilities assigned to them on par with men.

The nation which neglected almost 50% of its population for several centuries has now understood the necessity of giving equal rights and opportunities to its womenfolk.

The Constitution of India provides equal rights and opportunities to women. It does not make any discrimination on the grounds of sex. Indian women are also responding positively to this changed socio-political situation. This does not mean that our women are completely free from problems. On the contrary, the changing situation is causing them new problems. They are now beset with new stresses and strains. Some of the major problems haunting the modern women may briefly be analyzed here.

Therefore, efforts made by the Central and State Governments in ensuring quality life are indispensable. Despite the diversity of schemes operating in the State for the welfare and protection of women and children, the human development indicators show a dismal picture. High under nutrition rates, drop-out rates, crime rates, human trafficking, etc. is observed among women and children in Jharkhand.

Branding women as witches or 'DAYAN,' they are lynched, raped, tortured, burned or murdered with the intention to ensure the safety of the people in the society. Jharkhand is among one of the 11 tribal major states (Bihar, Haryana, West Bengal, Madhya Pradesh, Maharashtra, Gujarat, Orissa, Chhattisgarh, Assam, Rajasthan and Uttar Pradesh,) mainly where witch-hunting crimes are rampant. The tribal women continue to live in appalling conditions with poor amenities and opportunities. Unfortunately, the women from these communities face a greater disadvantage compared to men. Due to their vulnerability and inadequate access to resources, women require particular attention. The government undertakes the responsibility of providing special care to women and children by implementing various schemes in various areas but is not adequate.

This paper is based on empirical field data and content analysis from secondary sources data from government records.

The rights available to woman in India can be classified into two categories, namely as constitutional rights and legal rights. The constitutional rights are those which are provided in the various provisions of the constitution. The legal rights, on the other hand, are those which are provided in the various laws (acts) of the Parliament and the State Legislatures. In spite of this, Women in Jharkhand continue to live in extreme deprivation and discrimination. Evident from the recent estimates reported by the NFHS 4, a significant proportion of women continue to suffer from anaemia compared to men. Moreover, the nutritional status indicated by Body Mass Index, reveals a similar plight of women, i.e., more women are undernourished compared to men in Jharkhand.

The Constitution of India provides equal rights and opportunities to women. It does not make any discrimination on the grounds of sex. Indian women are also responding positively to this changed socio-political situation. This does not mean that our women are completely free from problems. On the contrary, the changing situation is causing them new problems. They are now beset with new stresses and strains. Some of the major problems haunting the modern women may briefly be analyzed here.

Therefore, efforts made by the Central and State Governments in ensuring quality life are indispensable. Despite the diversity of schemes operating in the State for the welfare and protection of women and children, the human development indicators show a dismal picture. High under nutrition rates, drop-out rates, crime rates, human trafficking, etc. is observed among women and children in Jharkhand.

In 2011, the child sex ratio of Jharkhand (948)was more than some of the Empowered Action Group (EAG) states, that is, Bihar (935), Madhya Pradesh (918), Odisha (941) and Uttar Pradesh (902) but has shown a decline from 2001 to 2011. It was 965 females per 1000 males (between 0-6 years) in 2001 which has declined to 948 (between 0-6 years) in 2011, as per Census 2001 and Census 2011respectively. The childsex ratio has declined in Jharkhand,butthe gender gap in schooling over years has narrowed among the younger groups. According to World Bank Document (2016) the enrolment in education institutions has increased from 62 per cent in 2005 to 82 per cent in 2012 for girls between 6-8 years of age group and for 15-17 years of age group the girls' enrolment has increased from 47 per cent to 74 per cent for the same time period.

As per Jharkhand Economic Survey, 2017-18, the GDP figuresindicate a remarkable growth of 12.1 per cent (at 2011-12 base year prices) for the period between 2011 to 2015-16.Despite increase in household income and improved job opportunities over the years in Jharkhandthe female labour force participation rate (LFPR) tend to remain low for the state.According to NSSO (2011-12), the female LFPR of Jharkhand is among the lowest in the country. Also, the female LFPR of the state has declined from 49 per cent in 2004-05 (as per NSSO, 2004-05) to 30 per cent in 2011-12.

This chapter focuses upon women and their work among the sampled districts of the study. This chapter has two major sections. In the first section we have tried to capture and analyse the women participation in workforce and theircontributionin different sectors of rural Jharkhand. In the second section we have also tried to present the reasons for the women not being in the workforce who belong to the working age group.Within this section, we have also discussed about the practise of dowry system and awareness about the various girl child and women specific schemes.

1. Women Occupational Status

In this study, a total of 3147 female have been surveyed from seven districts (Gumla, Jamtara, Latehar, Dumka, West Singhbhum, Palamu and Simdega) of rural Jharkhand.Among them 17 per cent belong to the age group between 20-30 years, followed 121 by 14 per cent women between the age group of 30-40 years. A major population of them are between the age group of 10-20 years.

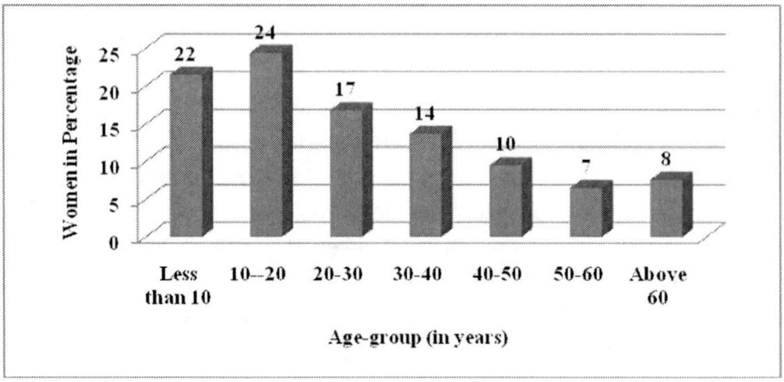

Source: IHD Primary Survey.

Figure 1: Age Structure of the Women.

The following figuredepicts the major occupation status of women. As mentioned in the previous chapters, that livelihood is tough in rural areas; there is a practise of being engaged in more than one occupation, that is, primary occupation and secondary occupation. Figure 2 depicts the primary occupation of the women, that is, the occupation in which they are majorly

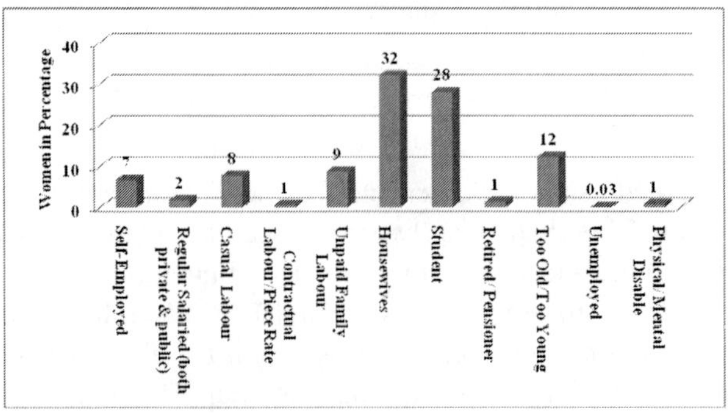

Source: IHD Primary Survey.

Figure 2: Percentage of Women by Usual Status.

engaged. Of the 3147 women, 13 per cent females are either too young/too old, unemployed or physically and mentally disable, while, 28 per cent of them are majorly engaged in education and32 per cent women are housewives/homemakers.

About 27 per cent of the women are engaged in workforce, of which 9 per cent of them are unpaid family labour, that is, those workers who contribute in the productivity of the output at zero wage rates.

The participation of women in the workforce across education groups shows that 61 per cent of the women who work as casual labour are illiterate, while 55 per cent of illiterate women are self-employed. Additionally, 54 per cent of illiterate women are unpaid family labour. Women who are within the salaried job have completed their education upto senior secondary level (30 per cent), while, 26 per cent have completed secondary level. A substantial proportion of women i.e. 17 per cent of them are graduate or hold a degree equivalent to it, 6per cent of them are post graduate and2 per cent of them hold professional degree. Among casual working group 16 per cent of them have completed their education upto primary level, 13 per cent upto middle level while 8 per cent of have completed secondary education. Among the women who are self-employed, 12 per cent have completed their education upto secondary level and 8 per cent are educated upto senior secondary level. Surprisingly, women in the unpaid family labours category, 7 per cent of them are senior secondary pass and 12 per cent of them have completed their education upto secondary level.

Apart from the women in workforce, it was reported that 16 per cent of the housewives/homemakers are secondary pass and 15 per cent of them each have completed their education upto both middle and primary level. Moreover, the proportion of women who have completed their education upto senior secondary level and graduation and above were 6 per cent and 3 per cent respectively.

Based on the discussions with the women, it was observed that restrictions towards women education persists, almost acrossall the districts. When enquired in Andradih village of Gumla district the women stated that they feel the requirement of doing work, to financially supportthe family, but due to lack of education and skills they are unemployed. Further women stated that mostly girls drop out after standard VIII or X. Very few among them have completed Matriculation or Intermediate, and the ones who wereenrolled for Bachelors, could not complete it. In Ghutua village of Latehar district and in Gujharia village of Simdega district it was informed that because of the distance and unsafe conditions, few of the girl students dropped out after Middle School. It was informed that most of the guardians could teach their children especially girls only uptomatric level. In Kharu Kadma village of Dumka district a similar condition is said to persist. Girls belonging from Schedule Tribe and few girls from Muslim community went to high school. In Majhigaon village a different problem were reported, it was complained by the respondents that the co-education school within the village does not have a separate toilet for girls and boys. Early marriage of girls (within 12-13 years of age) has also resulted in the decrease of strength of girls in high school. The girls"Gauna" is done after they attain the age of 4-5 years. It was further pointed that despite the regular visits made by the B.D.O and C.O. the school conditions still continue to remain poor.

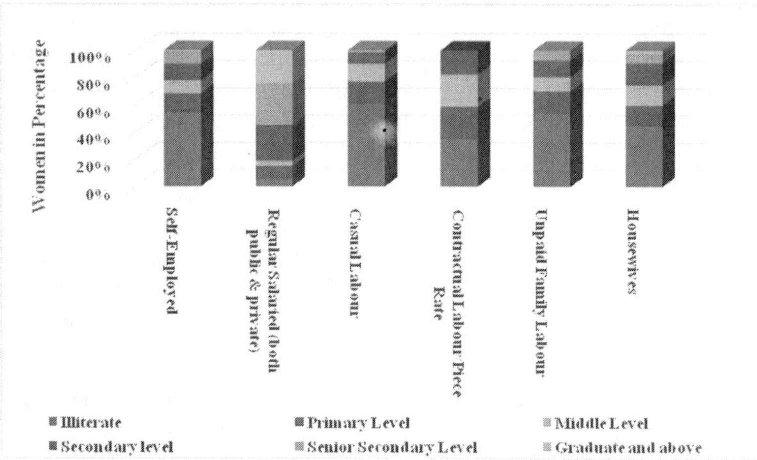

Source: IHD Primary Survey.

Figure 3: Percentage of women by usual status across different level of education.

2. Women Labour Force Participation Rate (LFPR)

The women workforce participation rate varies on the basis of their castes across the districts of Jharkhand. The tribal women are considered to be major contributor in casual labour workforce of Jharkhand.

This has been further explained in the subsequent sections.

3.1 Caste wise occupation

In the following table we have tried to depict the female labour force participation. We have considered the standard working age group, that is, 15-64 years. About 1973 surveyed women come under this age group, of them 773 women are absorbed in different sectors/areas of workforce (casual labours, self-employed, salaried worker, unpaid family labour, contractual/ piece rate earner). A cross district analysis shows that Simdega has the highest female labour force participation rate(0.50) followed by Jamtara (0.45) and then West Singhbhum (0.42) while the lowest women labour force participation rate has been recorded at Latehar (0.27).

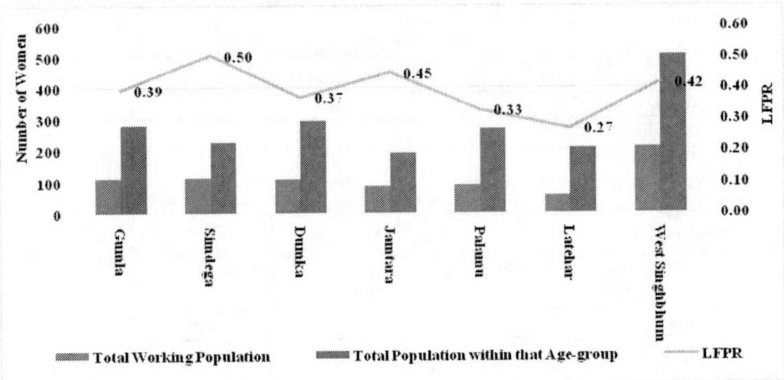

Source: IHD Primary Survey.

Figure 5: Percentage of women in the age group of 15-64 by occupation across districts.

As reported bythe women and others it wasevident that women's role in decision making has increased. They can take astand to call for decision within household and also in other matters. Despite the advancement in the community, in Baradih village of Gumla district women's role in decision making has witnessed no improvement. However, now the women are able to socialize outside their household, which was not allowed earlier though, they are still restricted to attend the village meetings. The meetings with government official held in the villages are attended by men alone and women from the Rajput community are not allowed to attend these village meetings specifically.

3. Women in Workforce

3.1 Women Engaged as Daily/ Casual Earner

In this section we will cover those women who are daily wage/casual labours. Among these 244 women whose primary occupation is working as casual labour, 36 women are either short-term or long-term migrant. Thus, in the following tables those women have been covered who are residents and commuters. A total of 208 women come under this category.Also, along with them, the table includes the contractual labour/piece rate women worker in daily earner/casual labour category.

Thus, a total of 214women who are engaged as casual labour in the labour forcewhich includes contractual or piece rate women workers also (5). It was recorded that of these 214 women, 68 per cent of them are working as casual labour in agriculture sector and 30 per cent of them are working as casual labour in non-agriculture sector.

Table 1: Type of work engagement of women between 15-64 years under casual labour category

Type of Work	*Number of Women*	*Women in Percentage*
Casual Labour in Agricultural Sector	145	68
Contractual labour in Agricultural Sector	1	0.5
Casual Labour in Non Agricultural Sector	64	30
Contractual Labour in Non Agricultural Sector	4	2
Total	214	100

Source: IHD Primary Survey.

Among these 214 women, 211 women lie within the age-group of 15-64 years, that is, the standard working age-group, who have been discussed below. About 96 per cent of 211 women received payment in the form of cash and 4 per cent of them received payment both in form of cash and kind. While 35 per cent of them the received payment within the range of Rs. 100-150,14 per cent of them received the payment between Rs. 200-250.

MGNREGA has played a vital role in bringing changes towards the mode of payment. Earlier, that is before the implementation of MGNREGA most of the payments were made in kind, which was below the marginal labour cost. This was because earlier the main concern was to be able to meet the basic consumption requirements. Now people prefer cash, although in few areas payment in both cash and kind is still practised, for example, along with an amount of Rs.220, 2 kg rice is also provided to them. It was also noted that in some places, along with wages breakfast or lunch is given.

In Andardih village of Gumla district women within the workforce get paid within the range of Rs.100-150 per day, and in some places, they receive both wage and meal. For example, in Jarpi they get meal "haadi" alongwith the wage of Rs. 50 when they work as casual labour in agriculture while in Kochra village, West Singhbhum district they get Rs. 70 and meal while women in Rampur village, Jamtara district receive Rs. 120 and one-

Table 2: Mode of receiving payment by women within the age-group of 15-64 years as casual labour

Mode of Payment	*Number of Women*	*Women in Percentage*
Cash	203	96
Both cash and kind	8	4
Total	211	100

Source: IHD Primary Survey.

time snacks for agricultural work. In Kharu Kadma village in Dumka, the wage for agricultural work is Rs. 120-130 and one-time meal (for Christian) and Rs. 100 (for Muslim) for female. So here, wage varies with religious category. It was stated that women commute to nearby areas during harvest season for sowing and also commute on daily basis to work in crusher machines or brick klins and in construction sector.

Table 3: Average daily earning of the women within the age-group of 15-64 years as casual labour

Average daily earning (if in kind please transfer in Rs) (Per Day)	*Number of Women*	*Women in Percentage*
Less than 100	61	29
100-150	73	35
150-200	32	15
200-250	29	14
250 and above	16	8
Total	211	100

Source: IHD Primary Survey.

About 51 per cent of the women are engaged as casual labour for more than 4-8 months in a year while 17 per cent of them for 8-12 months in a year.As stated above, a majority of them (68 per cent) are engaged as casual labour in agricultural activities while around 30 per cent of them are engaged as casual labour in non-agricultural activates.

About 31 per cent of these women are working for an average of 15-20 days in a month whileonly 2 per cent of them are working for more than 25 days in a month.Also, around 21 per cent of the women work only for 5-10 days on an average in a month.

Table 4: Months engaged for work last year by the women within the age-group of 15-64 years as casual labour.

Number of months you worked last year	*Number of Women*	*Women in Percentage*
Less than 4 months	67	32
4-8 months	108	51
8-12 months	36	17
Total	211	100

Source: IHD Primary Survey.

Table 5:Average days worked by women in a month within the age-group of 15-64 years as casual labour

Average daily earning day you worked in a month	*Number of Women*	*Women in Percentage*
5-10 days	45	21
10-15 days	84	40
15-20 days	65	31
20-25 days	13	6
25 days and above	4	2
Total	211	100

Source: IHD Primary Survey.

Among these surveyed 211 women, 73 per cent of them are working within the village followed by 13 per cent women are working in rural areas within 1-5 km radius from residence. Around 1 per cent of them travel to urban areas within 5-10km from residence for work.

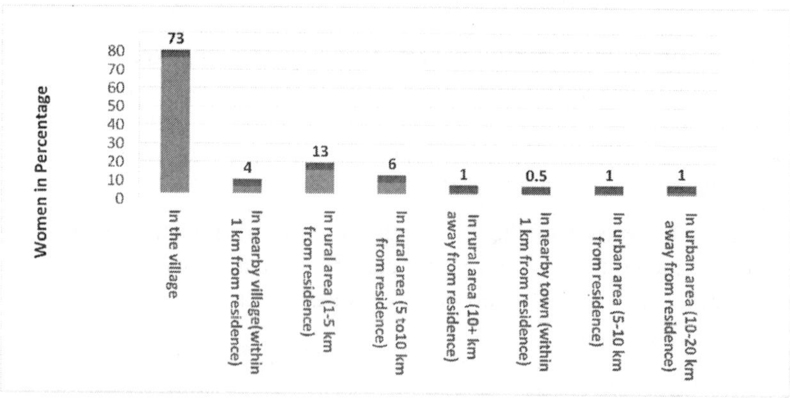

Source: IHD Primary Survey.

Figure 6: Work area of women within the age-group of 15-64 years as casual labour.

3.2 Self Employed

A total of 441 women are engaged as employers or are self-employed in their own activities. Among them, 212 women have self-employment as primary occupation while the rest are unpaid family labour. These women are mostly engaged in their own agricultural land and in other allied activities. Apart from this, they are entrepreneurs too, for example, many of the Santhal women are engaged in making and selling local liquor "hadiya", while Dom women are engaged in basket making and etc. So, on the basis of their religious group their type of work is segregated. Among the 441 women surveyed, about 82 per cent of them are working in their own agricultural land and in other allied activities and 18 per cent of them are self employed, that is, working in their own small or big family business.

Table 6:Type of work engagement of women between 15-64 years under selfemployment category.

Type of Work	*Number of Women*	*Women in Percentage*
Self-Employed in Agriculture and other Allied Activities	362	82
Self-Employed in own Business	79	18
Total	441	100

Source: IHD Primary Survey.

They do not prefer to travel far away for work, a majority of them were found to be working within 1km radius of the village. Very few of them stated that they travel 5-10 km or more away from their residence for work. It was reported that they prefer to work nearby their residence so that they able to manage their household work and very of few of them stated that they are not allowed by theirfamiliesto travel far away for work.

Table 7: Months engaged for work last year by women between 15-64 years under selfemployment category

Number of months you worked last year	*Number of Women*	*Women in Percentage*
Less than 4 months	61	14
4-8 months	270	64
9-12 months	92	22
Total	423	100

Source: IHD Primary Survey.

Among these 441 women, 423 women come under the age-group of 15-64 years, which is the standard working age. When enquired about their engagement for past one year, 64 per cent of them stated that they are engaged for about 4-8 months in this work, followed by 22 per cent of women who stated that they were engaged for 9-12 months in this work, that is, working in full-fledged manner in this area only.

Around 33 per cent of the women stated that they work for an average of 15-20 days in a month, 10 per cent of them stated that they work for 20-25 days in a month while 42 per cent of them stated that they work for an average of 10-15 days in a month. On an average these women are working for 10-20 days in a month.

Table 8: Average number of days worked by women between 15-64 years under selfemployment category

Average number of day you worked in a month	*Number of Women*	*Women in Percentage*
Less than 10 days	32	8
10-15 days	177	42
15-20 days	142	33
20-25 days	42	10
Above 25 days	30	7
Total	423	100

Source: IHD Primary Survey.

As it is difficult to calculate the monthly income when self-employed, so information of only 50 women were recorded. Among them, majority of them (84 per cent) stated that their monthly earning is below Rs.4000 and very few of them (around 4 per cent) stated that their monthly earning is between Rs. 8000-12000.

Table 9: Monthly income of the women between 15-64 years under self-employment category

Monthly Income (Rs.) excluding all expenditures)	*Number of Women*	*Women in Percentage*
Less than 4000	42	84
4000-8000	5	10
8000-12000	2	4
12000 and Above	1	2
Total	50	100

Source: IHD Primary Survey.

Women independence to get out of household to work and to form a group for the betterment of the village and for women empowerment has been encouraged in the surveyed districts. Self Help Groups (SHGs) is one way of making them empowered and giving them their voice. The SHGs werefound to be working actively in almost all the villages of the seven districts. It maybe one or two Tola were they have not been formed. SHGs are mostly a common place were women come together, discuss about the problems of their village, save money for themselves and provide loan to eachother at the time of need. In Ghutua village of Latehar district, it was pointed that more than 85 per cent of the households are connected with SHGs. Mostly they form a group of 5-8 women. They use the saved money to provide it as loan to the women at the time of need.They have to return the loan with an interest of minimum 1 per cent and it exceeds upto percentage depending upon the financial ability of the women of that group. Many of the SHGs accounts are linked with the bank.It was found that in many groups training has been provided as to how to manage the account while in many groups it hasnot, and the groups which donot have the training, agreed upon facing problem with respect to account management.

Certain examples of productive utilisation of loans provided by the SHGs are as follows: Loan provided by SHG in Udaipura village ofLatehardistrict was used to buy a poultry farm, brick kiln and sewing machine. Although 16 women took the training of sewing for 3 months, none of them received the certificate. In Gujahria village of Simdega district the SHGs took the initiative on cutting paddy, providing loan and practise savings.While Sarap Munda village of Simdega district, SHGs provide loan and also gets engaged in harvesting, weeding and transplanting. Weekly saving, poultry farming and goat rearing is also practiced.A shed has been built for goats by Jharkhand Tribal Development Society (JTDS). A similar practise was reported inIndrabanivillage of Dumka district. Also,in Kadhu Karma village of Dumka districts the Public Distribution System (PDS) shops were reported to be run by the SHGs and a similar practise wasrecorded in few otherdistricts also.Apart from this, through these SHGs women have also become empowered, that is, they have started small business or ventures,like, the SHGs in Kochra village of West Singhbhum district, main work is to make utensils and to cultivatepotatoes.

3.3 Salaried

A total of 53 women are engaged in regular salaried work which includes both government and private job. Among them, 43 of them are resident or commuters while the rest 10 of them are either short term or long-term migrants. Also, there are 2 contractual workers who are salaried earners. Thus, in the following tables and figures we will discuss about the 45 women who belong to the age-group between 15-64 years, are salaried earners and are residents or commuters. The migrant women have been discussed in a separatechapter on Migration.

Among these 45 women, 73 per cent of them are in government jobs and 27 per cent of them are in private jobs. Thus,it indicates a larger preference and engagement towards government jobs.

Table 10: Type of Salaried job of women between 15-64 years

Type of Job	*Number of Women*	*Women in Percentage*
Government Job	33	73
Private Job	12	27
Total	45	100

Source: IHD Primary Survey.

As these women are salaried employees, more than 60 per cent of them are working for an average of 25-30 days in a month while 40 per cent of them are working for 20-25 days in a month. Among them 69 per cent of them stated their salary to be below Rs. 5000 followed by 18 per cent women who stated their salary to be within Rs. 5000-10000, while about of 4 per cent of them stated their salary to be both between Rs. 1000-15000 and above Rs. 25000. On an average, most of the women earning ranged between Rs. 5000-10000.

Table 11: Average number of days worked by women between 15-64 years

Average number of working days (In a month)	*Number of Women*	*Women in Percentage*
Less than 20 days	0	0
20-25 days	18	40
25-30 days	27	60
Total	45	100

Source: IHD Primary Survey.

Table12: Monthly income of the wo5men between 15-64 years

Monthly salary (in rupees)	*Number of Women*	*Women in Percentage*
Less than 5000	31	69
5000-10000	8	18
10000-15000	2	4
15000-20000	2	4
20000 and Above	2	4
Total	45	100

Source: IHD Primary Survey.

Around 71 per cent of the surveyed women stated that their work place is within the village, 7 per cent of them stated their work place to be in rural areas and within 5-10km from their residence. Again, 7 per cent of them stated that they travel to nearby town which is 1 km from residence and about 4 per cent of them stated that they travel to urban areas which is 10-20km away from their residence.

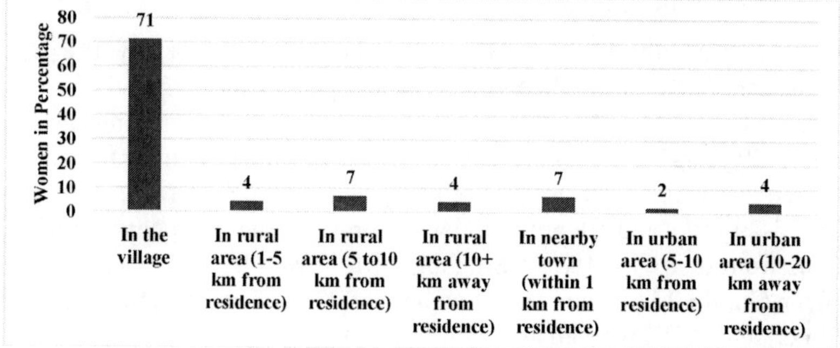

Source: IHD Primary Survey.

Figure 2: Work area of women within the age-group of 15-64 years as salaried worker.

Among these surveyed women, very few of them are recipient of annual gifts/bonus from office. Again, excluding the contractual salaried workers, among 43 women, only 12 per cent of them have Provident Fund (PF) provided by their workplace. Although a good number of womenare in salaried job, very few of them receive the annual gifts/bonus and other facilities from their workplace.

Table 13: Percentage of women within 15-64 years have provident fund (PF)

Whether PF provided	*Number of Women*	*Women in Percentage*
Yes	5	12
No	38	88
Total	43	100

Source: IHD Primary Survey.

4. Women not in Workforce

As per thereport on Women's labour force participation in India by ILO although the women's labour force participation and access to decent work are vital elements for an inclusive and sustainable development process.But still women continue to face the barriers to enter the labour market and to access a decent work. There are multiple ranges of challenges related to access to employment, choice of work, working conditions, employment security, wage parity, discrimination, and balancing the competing burdens of work and family responsibilities. In addition to this, women representation in informal economy is huge where their exposure to risk of exploitation and harassment is high and chances of formal protection is low. These are some of the problems or challenges which are common for all irrespective of rural or urban areas.

In this context, the following section will portray the major reasonspointed out by the women respondents of the sampled districts of the study. In this section the women who are within the working age group of 15-29 years but are not workinghave been discussed. Among the surveyed seven districts, 342 women were the ones who are between the age group of 15-29 years and are not in the workforce. Of these, 20 per cent of them hail from districts of West Singhbhum followed by 17 per cent of them from Gumla, 15 per cent from Latehar and 11 per cent from Simdega. Only 4 per cent of the women are from Jamtara district.

Table 14: Percentage of women (15-29 years) not in workforce across districts

Districts	*Number of Women*	*Percentage of Women*
Gumla	57	17
Simdega	38	11
Dumka	48	14
Jamtara	15	4
Palamu	65	19
Latehar	51	15
West Singhbhum	68	20
Total	342	100

Source: IHD Primary Survey.

A major population of women/girls within this age group are students and few among them are physically/mentally disable. Apart from them, women came up with some of the major reasons for not working. It was reported that social obligation is the first and foremost reason for not joining the workforce (72 per cent). It was followed by an important reason of taking of children/ household chores and lack of opportunity nearby residence (61 per cent and 25 per cent respectively). This clearly shows that women prefer to work in the area near to their residence so that they are able to manage both their household chores and outside work. About 5 per cent of women were the mothers with small children who pointed that due to lack of crèche/ or childcare home at the workplace they are not working and only 1 per cent of them said that lack of transportation facility as the reason for joining the workforce. While discussing with the women in Andradih village of Gumla district. It was recorded that they don't face much transportation problems because buses run to and from Gumla. Thus, it can be said that transportation or communication is not a major reason but its other social and personal problems because of which besides willingness they are not able to participate in the workforce.

Besides the above stated reasonsthere are a certain percentage of women (16 per cent) who stated that since their family is financially stable, or the earning by other household members is sufficient for their household to run properly. Thus, they do not feel the need and the requirement of working.

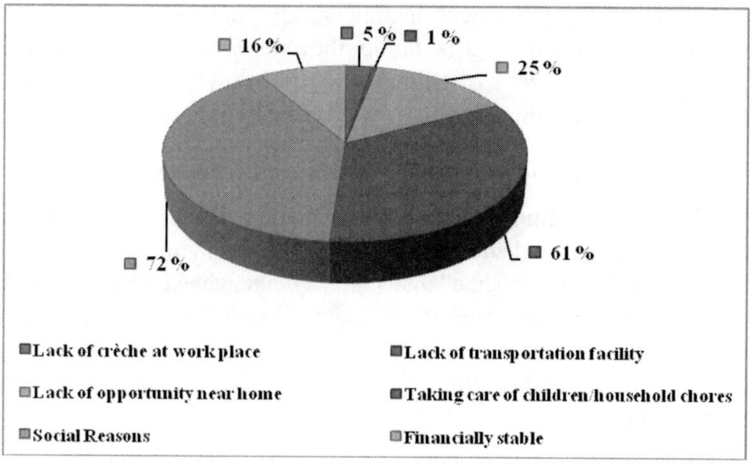

Source: IHD Primary Survey.

Figure 8:Reasons for not being in workforce by women (15-29 years)

4.1 Practise/persistence of Dowry System and superstitious beliefs

While discussing with the women about their condition in the village it was opined that practices such as sacrifice and offerings are still prevalent across all communities. The practice of dowry was also seen across communities in Andradih village of Gumla district. Dowry although considered as a wrong practise by almost all respondents agreed that the system is still prevalent in some areas. In Baradih village of Gumla district, the dowry amount is decided upon the education qualifications of the groom. They pointed that the practise and acceptance of dowry has increased, mostly among Yadav and Rajput communities. In Indrabani village of Dumka district, it was stated that dowry system is prevalent but no incidence of dowry harassment has been seen in the village. They further added that there is no dowry system in the Scheduled Tribe (ST) community but it is present in the Scheduled Caste (SC) community. Also, in Karmatand village of Dumka district, the good economic condition families agreed that dowry system is strongly implemented in theirvillage; marriage does not take place if dowry is not given. While the poor economic condition families of the same village stated that dowry system is not present in their area. Similar conditions were found in Rampur village of Jamtara district, where the dowry system is highly prevalent among the good economic condition families but at the same time 'it is bad for the society'was agreed by the respondents.

In Gujaria village of Simdega district a different system was found to be practised. It was opined by the respondents that from the very beginning girls' family are offered with money, 40 kg grain and 1 kg oil. So rather than taking dowry from girls' family they were rather given. While in the other sampled villages of Simdega district dowry system was neither practised nor were the girls' families given any money and other things.

4.2 Awareness about girl child/womenbenefit schemes

While interacting with the women of some of the villages like Charai of West Singhbhum district and Andradih of Gumla district it was opined by them that "MamtaVahan" visits their village when called and in Murup village of West Singhbhum it was stated that about 12-15 families have received the maternity benefits in last one year. Thus, shows that the people have knowledge and practise of health facilities and schemes forpregnant women in particular.

Also, when enquired about the girl child schemes, it was quite evident that awareness about schemes like Mukhyamantri KanyadaanYojna, Lakshmi Laadli Yojna and Kasturba Gandhi Balika Vidyalaya and Sabla Yojana was present. Apart from knowledge many were beneficiaries of the above stated schemes. It was stated that many girls from different villages were studying in Kasturba Gandhi Balika Vidhyalaya (KGBV). It was also stated that the information about the scheme was provided to them through Sahaiya, Sevikas, from block office and from various panchayat meetings. In Murup village of Latehar district, the Beti Bachao and Beti Padhao scheme was advertised writing it on the walls of buildings. But at the same time, it was also agreed and pointed that although they have heard the name of the schemes but information or knowledge related to them was not present.

5. Conclusion

Women are an important contributor in the workforce. A major group of them are engaged as casual labour and self-employed in both agricultural and non-agricultural sector. But it should be also taken into consideration that still a major proportion woman are housewives/homemakers or are engaged as unpaid family labours. A good proportion of them are engaged into agricultural sector. Apart from this, women who are into salaried job, among them, most prefer and are into government jobs like ANM, cook in primary school, Anganwadi Sevika and etc. Women who are not into workforce are because of social constraints, small children and household workload. Although community specific restrains continue to exists for women, still the women participation in all economic and noneconomic activities has improved. Thus, it can be concluded that women condition is improving in the rural areas of these seven districts. But at the same time, there is a need to provide decent job opportunities to the women so that they can contribute in the economic empowerment of the economy. Further, policies encouraging women empowerment needs to be constructed so as to overcome the gender-specific constraints faced by the women.

References

1. Socio-Economic Caste Census, 2011, Census of India, Govermnet of India, Delhi.
2. Jharkhand Economic Survey 2017-18, Department of planning and Finance, Government of Jharkhand.
3. Rath. Bikash, 2012 The Regional Consultation On Particularly Vulnerable Tribal Groups Of Odisha And The National Rural Livelihood Mission, RCDC, Bhubaneswar.
4. 2. NAC draft recommendations on Development Challenges Specific to Particularly Vulnerable Tribal Groups (PVTGs), 2013, Jun 19,
5. Sharma. V.P 2012 Participatory Development, Ramesh Chandra edited book Tribal Development Administration and Management, DEC, National Institute of Rural Development, Ministry of Rural Development, Government of India, Hyderabad (AP).

Chapter - 10

Economically Challenged People of Palamu, Jharkhand

— *Vijay Prakash Sharma*

Introduction

Through several decades, National programme on rural development has targeted a wide range of issues and challenge faced by over 75% of the countries population living in rural areas. With all the efforts, the physical quality of Life Index (PQLI) of rural community continues to remain far below the levels of expectations envisaged through the National planning process.Grass root reality call for a radical change in developmental approach with focus on public - Private- partnership to pursue the concept of Total Village Management (TVM).This report deals with facts from two field surveys conducted by the author through a scientific study in the year 2004. The result of these studies reported in two parts of the book will help the government to plan a Total Village Development Strategy to develop Socio-economic condition of people in the rural areas of Jharkhand. Jharkhand is rich in mineral and natural resources that have been vastly exploited by the state. The people have very little access to these resources and live in utter poverty. They depend mostly on agriculture for their livelihood. They are not poor but economically challenged people.

The main crop that is sown is paddy, which is heavily dependent on rainfall. Once paddy is harvested few other crops are grown because of lack of irrigational facilities. Only a few cash crops are produced if water is available for irrigation. Thus management of water and land resources for cultivation is essential for water based livelihood development.

Study Area: Palamau District

The District of Palamau lies between 23 degree 50'and 24 degree 8' north latitude and between 83 degree 55' and 84 degree 30' east longitude. It contains an area of 5043.8 square Kms. The administrative head quarter is Daltonganj, situated on koel river in 24 degree 3' north, and 84 degree 4' east. This has takn its name after colonel Dalton, commissioner of Chhotanagpur in 1861.

The distance between Daltonganj and Ranchi is 165 Kms. Now, the old Palamau district is divided into three districts viz. Palamau, Garhwa and Latehar. Dlatonganj renamed as Medininagar after creation of Jharkhand. Among the kings who ruled Palamau Medini Rai was the most famous one.

Table 1: Administrative Unit – Palamau

Sl. No	*Subdivision*	*Block*	*Sl. No*	*Circle*	*Sl. No*	*Educational Block*
1.	Daltonganj	Daltonganj	1	Daltonganj	1.	Daltonganj
					2.	Munispal
		Chainpur	2	Chainpur	3.	Chainpur – 1
					4.	Chainpur – 2
		Patan	3	Patan	5.	Patan – 1
					6.	Patan – 2
		Bishrampur	4	Bishrampur	7.	Bishrampur North
					8.	Bishrampur South
		Panki	5	Panki	9.	Panki East
					10.	Panki West
		Lesliganj	6	Lesliganj	11.	Lesliganj
		Manatu	7	Manatu	12.	Manatu
		Satbarwa	8	Satbarwa		
		Pandu				
2.	Hussainabad	Hussainabad	1	Hussainabad	13.	Hussainabad North
					14.	Hussainabad South
		Hussainabad	2	Hariharganj	15.	Hariharganj
3.	Chhatarpur	Chhatarpur	1	Chhatarpur	16.	Chhatarpur East
					17.	Chhatarpur West

Table 2 : List of villages covered under this study.

Sl. No.	*Name of Village*	*Thana No.*	*No. of House Holds*	*Thana*	*District*
1.	SAKHUI	192	63	PATAN	PALAMAU
2.	PALHE KHURD	193	177	PATAN	PALAMAU

(Contd...)

3.	SIKA	194	164	PATAN	PALAMAU
4.	GARI KHAS	200	176	PATAN	PALAMAU
5.	KATHAUTIA	201	160	PATAN	PALAMAU
6.	KAJRI	202	267	PATAN	PALAMAU
7.	BATSARA	203	201	PATAN	PALAMAU
Total House Holds :-			**1208**		

Study Objectives

- To understand the present Socio- economic situation of the people and the area.
- To identify development needs of the people.
- To identify potential persons with leadership quality.
- To identify available resources in and around the villages for proper channelisation.
- To design sustainable development strategy for the region.
- To understand existing government schemes.

Study Methodology

A full household census was undertaken by the author in the seven villages (table-2 of Patan administrative block in Palamau district of Jharkhand to understand Socio – Economic condition of the people. This includes assessment of the needs & resources of different villages to develop intervention plan.

The study was conducted using PLA (Participatory Learning and Action) techniques like focus group discussions, Key informant interview for qualitative data collection.

Base line household survey of eleven villages was conducted using quantitative techniques of data collection i.e. Pre-coded structured questionnaire cum schedule duly Pilot tested in the field. Tabulation and analysis of quantitative data conducted through computer programming especially developed for the purpose. Qualitative data were analysed using content analysis tables.

Socio-economic Profile of Villages in Palamau

Kajri

This village lies in the west of River Amanat and in the east of River Koyal. NH – 75 is in the south of the village. State Highway is 0.4 Kms east of the village & goes to Patan block. This village is about 10 kms west from Daltongunj and 0.4 km from Patanmor chowk. The Major castes of this village are Rajput, ST and SC. The main occupation of the villagers is agriculture, though some people are involved in transportation business. The total number of households is 267. A primary school exists in the village and for middle school; the students go to Garikhas which is 5 km to the west of the village. A pacca building of Aanganwadi is available in the village. A WLL telephone is also available in the village, but it is dysfunctional presently. Electricity is available in the village. There are about 20 well and 25 tube well available in the village. The depth of water level available in pre monsoon and post monsoon period in the village is 60 ft and 40 ft respectively. The major agriculture crops grown in the village are paddy, maize, wheat, rahar etc. This is the largest village in the project area.

Garikhas

This village is located in the south of River Durgabati. The NH-75 and railway track passes through the village. This village is 15 kms west from Daltongunj and 5 km from patanmor. Major caste of the village is Koeri. The main occupation of the village is agriculture, though some people are involved in business e.g. Shop at the Garikhas chowk. The total number of households in the village is 176. There is a middle school in the village and for secondary school education; students go to Lohara, 3 km from the village. There is an Aanganwadi in the village. This is also used for child education. A government hospital is also available in the village, but due to absence of doctors in the hospital, patients come to Daltongunj for general check up. There is also a facility of a WLL telephone in the village. Electricity is available in the village. There are about 30 well and 6 tube well available in the village. The depth of water level available in pre monsoon and post monsoon period in the village is 25 ft and 15 ft respectively. The major agriculture crops grown in the village are paddy, maize, and Wheat etc. The number of cattle in the village is approximately 800 which mostly survive on stall feeding.

Batsara

This village lies 1 km west to the State Highway running from Daltongunj to Patan block. River Amanat flows in the south-east of this village. That is approximately 10 km to the west of Daltngunj and zero km from Patanmor. The major castes in the village are Rajput, SC, and ST. The villagers are mostly dependent on agriculture. The total number of households in the village is 201. A primary school exists in the village. For middle and secondary school education, students go to Singara and Lohara, 4 km and 10 km respectively from the village. A pacca building of Aanganwadi is available in the village which has been taken on rent. There is also a facility of a WLL telephone in the village which is presently dysfunctional. About 80 wells and 18 tube wells are available in the village. The water level in pre monsoon and post monsoon is about 45 ft and 15 ft respectively. The major agriculture crops grown in the village are paddy, maize, wheat, etc. the number of cattle in the village is 400. 70% of the cattle requirement is met by pasture land that is 2 kms from the village. The rest of the requirement is met by stall feeding.

Sika

This village is located to the west of State Highway going to Patan block, at a distance of 5 km from Meralmor, 7 km from Patanmor and 17 km from Daltongunj. River Durgabati flows in the west of the village. A pacca road is under construction. The major caste in the village is Koeri, SC, ST. The major occupation of the villagers is agriculture. The total number of households in the village is 164. There is a primary school in the village which will soon be promoted to middle school. For secondary school education, students go to Lonhara that is 4 kms from the village. A pacca but damaged building of Aanganbadi exists in the village in which a private school is being run. A WLL telephone is available in the village. About 35 wells and 8 tubewells are available in the village. The water level in pre monsoon and post monsoon is about 45 ft and 10 ft respectively. The major agriculture crops grown in the village are paddy, maize, wheat, chana, masuri etc. The number of cattle in the village is 600 and is entirely dependent on stall feeding.

Kathautia

This village lies to the west of SH going to Patan block, at a distance of 5 km from Meralmor, 7 km from Patanmor and 17 km from Daltongung. River Durgabati flows in the west of the village. The major castes in the village are Teli, SC. The maj or occupation of the villagers is agriculture. The total number of households in the village is 160. There is a primary school exists in the village. For middle school and secondary school education, students go to Lonhara that is 5 kms from the village. There is a provision of WLL telephone in the village. About 44 wells and 30 tube wells are available in the village. The water level in pre monsoon and post monsoon is about 42 ft and 20 ft respectively. The major crops grown in the village are paddy, maize, wheat, chana, matar etc. The number of cattle in the village is approximately 500, totally dependent on stall feeding.

Palhekhurd

This village lies in the west of State Highway going to Patan block, at a distance of 3 km from Meralmor, 5 km from Patanmor and 15 km from

Daltongunj. River Durgabati flows in the north of the village. The major castes in the village are Brahmin and SC. Agriculture is the main occupation of the villagers. Electricity is available in the village. The total number of households in the village is 177. The village has a facility of a primary school. For middle school and secondary school education, students go to Naudiha, 1.5 kms and Lonhara at 6 kms respectively from the village. There is a facility of WLL telephone service in the village. About 25 wells and 20 tubewells are available in the village. The water level in pre monsoon and post monsoon is about 25 ft and 5 ft respectively. The major agriculture crops grown in the village are paddy, maize, wheat, chana, masuri etc. The number of cattle in the village is 100 which are dependent totally on stall feeding.

Sakhui

This village lies in the west of SH going to Patan block, at a distance of 4 kms from Meralmor, 6 kms from Patanmor and 16 km from Daltongunj. River Durgawati flows in the west of the village and in the north flows River Koyal. The major castes in the village are Teli & SC. The major occupation of the villagers is agriculture. The total number of households is 63. For primary school education, students go to Palhekhurd village and for middle school & secondary school education; students go to Lonhara, 7 kms from the village. There are approximately 9 wells and 13 tube wells in the village. The water level in pre monsoon and post monsoon is about 30 ft and 15 ft respectively. The major agriculture crops grown in the village are paddy, maize, wheat, rahar etc. There are approximately 100 cattle in the village which depend totally on stall feeding.

Demographic profile

This survey covered 1208 households with approximately 4832 People residing in the seven villages of coal mine project area at Patan block of Palamau district.

Out of the total population in seven villages in the project area, 54.91% of the people are males and 44.85% females.

Out of the total population in seven villages in the project area 59.12% are married and 38.97% are unmarried. 1% are widow.

Average household size is 4.

There are 30 unsupported widows and 28 unsupported children. Only three beggars could be identified during the survey.

Illages	*Number of HH*	*% Population*			*Average HH Size*	*Sex Ratio (Females/Males x 1000)*
		Total	*Male*	*Female*		
Sakhui	63	96.99	50.47	46.52	4	
Palhe Khurd	177	99.99	55. 72	44.27	4	
Sikka	164	99.75	54.75	45.00	4	
Gari Khas	176	99.43	55.07	44.36	4	
Kathautia	160	99.75	56.77	42.98	4	
Kajri	267	99.59	53.77	45.82	4	
Batsara	201	99.99	54.36	45.63	4	

Cultural Profile

The majority of the inhabitants i.e. 99.66% are Hindus and the rest are Muslims.

Hindus celebrate their numerous festivals at household level. They organise **Akhand- Path** in Palhe Khurd and celebrate **Chatta** as community festival. Muslims commemorate Muharram on community level. ID-UL-FITRE and ID-UL-ZOHA are celebrated at household level. Hindi is the mother tongue of most of the people in the project area. 99.33% of the people speak Hindi and the rest of them speak Bhojpuri and Magdhi.

Housing Characteristics

House Types

There are 93.87 per cent **kacha** houses and 5.13 per cent **pacca** houses in the study area.

Bathroom Type

97.68% of the inhabitants in the project area have no access to bathroom facilities. Only 1.24% of the inhabitants have pucca bathrooms and 0.08% have katcha bathroom facilities. Most of the villagers prefer using open area for nature's call therefore, only upper caste affluent people has adopted urban concept of separate latrine & bathroom.

Kitchen Type

This study reveals the rural house setup having no concept of separate kitchen. 97.43% of the inhabitants in the project area have no kitchen. Only 1.73% of the inhabitants have pucca kitchens, 0.24% have katcha kitchens and 1.24% of the population have pucca kitchens in their homes.

Villages	*% Pucca*	*% Semi Pucca*	*% Kutcha*	*% with Toilet Facility*	*% with Separate Kitchen*
Sakhui	06.34	-	93.65	-	-
Palhe Khurd	04.52	-	94.91	03.95	03.95
Sikka	06.69	-	92.68	01.22	01.22
Gari Khas	07.38	-	89.77	01.13	01.13
Kathautia	05.00	-	94.37	-	01.25
Kajri	05.99	-	92.50	01.87	02.24
Batsara	02.48	-	96.51	0.49	0.99

Infrastructure Access

The access to government infrastructure is difficult as most of the facilities are out side the village area i.e. in Daltonganj, which is situated at a distance of 25 Kms from the villages.

Drinking Water Source

Villages	*Number of Wells*		*Number of Tube Wells*		*River*
	Government	*Private*	*Government*	*Private*	*(Yes / No)*
Sakhui	3	6	5	8	Yes
Palhe Khurd	5	20	5	15	Yes
Sikka	15	20	4	4	Yes
Gari Khas	5	25	6	-	Yes
Kathautia	18	28	18	12	Yes
Kajri	5	15	5	20	Yes
Batsara	40	40	8	10	Yes

Transport and Communication

Road

All the Seven villages are connected with (mettaled as well as non – metalled roads.

Telephone

All the Seven villages have telephone connections or WLL service operating within 2 Kms.

Electricity

Villages	*% Households with Connection*
Sakhui	100.00
Palhe Khurd	99.00
Sikka	04.87
Gari Khas	99.43
Kathautia	56.25
Kajri	98.50
Batsara	100.00

Community Facilities

Table: Number of Community Facilities

Villages	*Anganwadi Centres*	*Community Hall*	*Temple*	*Mosque*	*Cremation Ground*	*School*	*Health Centres*
Sakhui	-	1	2	-	-	-	-
Palhe Khurd	-	-	3	-	-	1	-
Sikka	1	-	3	-	-	2	-
Gari Khas	1	-	-	-	-	2	1
Kathautia	-	-	1	-	-	1	-
Kajri	1	-	4	-	-	1	-
Batsara	1	-	3	-	-	1	-

Community buildings

There are Four Anganwadi centers and one community hall. There are seventeen temples

Drinking Water Facility

The villagers use drinking water from 94 Govt. and 154 private wells, 51 tube wells provided by Govt. and 69 tube wells under private ownership. In addition, except people of Bijra village they also fetch water from River Amanat which flows at a distance of 4 Kms from these villages.

Cremation:

Hindus use riverbank as cremation ground,

Electricity status

In 18.70% of the households in seven villages, there is no facility of electricity whereas the rest of the 81.20% population avail the facility of electricity.

Social Institutions

Banking services are available Self Help Groups are also operative in the area. Some NGO's are also operative from Daltonganj.

Economic Profile

Occupational Profile

Village	*% Main Workers*	*% Marginal Workers*	*Occupational Structure*			
			Cultivators	*Agri. Labourers*	*HH ind.*	*Others*
Sakhui	NA	NA	49.30	20.83	NA	NA
Palhe Khurd	NA	NA	55.57	14.39	NA	NA
Sikka	NA	NA	65.48	07.79	NA	NA
Gari Khas	NA	NA	57.58	14.32	NA	NA
Kathautia	NA	NA	55.78	19.44	NA	NA
Sakhui	NA	NA	49.30	20.83	NA	NA
Palhe Khurd	NA	NA	55.57	14.39	NA	NA

Income and Expenditure

Table % Households in Each Category

Village	*Income*			*Expenditure*		
	Below 5000	*5000 – 10000*	*Above 10000*	*Below 5000*	*5000 – 10000*	*Above 10000*
Sakhui	01.58	63.49	34.92	01.58	39.68	42.85
Palhe Khurd	07.34	53.01	34.46	05.08	54.00	32.20
Sikka	04.87	21.92	62.19	03.65	31.70	36.09
Gari Khas	00.56	62.50	13.06	01.13	62.50	10.79
Kathautia	09.37	32.50	58.12	08.75	25.75	53.75
Kajri	00.74	42.32	27.34	01.12	41.94	24.71
Batsara	00.49	43.24	54.72	01.49	44.27	51.24

Table on Average Expenditure by Items :-Items

Items	*Average Annual Expenditure (Rs.)*
Food	6146
Festivals	2291
Health	2097
Clothing	2015
Education	1164
Transport	1128
Drinks	315
Smoking	145
Electricity	134
Others	450

Average household Income Per Annum

40.06% of the respondents earn an average income of Rs. 10,000 and above per annum. The person earning an income between Rs 5,000 to Rs 10,000 is 45.52%. Only 3.39% of the inhabitants fall under category of income below Rs 5,000 per annum.

Source of Income

The majority of the people earn their income by practicing Agriculture. 45.77% of the respondents are earning their living through agriculture. 18.70% of the people work as labour. 10.14% of them work as daily labourer for their living and 11.25% of the people in the project area are engaged in service.

Average Expenditure per Annum

The expenditure of 37.25% of the people in the project area is Rs 10,000 and above. 43.95% of the people spend between Rs 5000 and Rs 10,000 whereas 3.14% of the people spend less than Rs. 5,000 per year.

Item Wise Expenditure per Annum

In the project area, on an average, the inhabitants spend Rs 6146 on food, Rs 2291 on festivals, Rs 2097 on health, Rs 2015 on clothing, Rs 1164 on education, Rs 1128 on transport, Rs 315 on drinks, Rs 145 on smoking, Rs 134 on electricity, and 450 on other items.

Land Holding Pattern

Village		*Land Holders*		
	% House-holds Landless	*% Owning Below 5 Acres*	*% Owning 5 – 10 Acres*	*% Owning Above 10 Acres*
Sakhui	22.22	60.31	-	-
Palhe Khurd	15.25	72.88	06.78	-
Sikka	01.82	90.24	02.43	04.26
Gari Khas	12.50	77.27	00.56	-
Kathautia	06.87	91.87	04.37	-
Kajri	12.36	74.75	00.74	01.12
Batsara	10.94	76.11	00.49	00.49

Land Holding

78.72% of respondents are marginal farmers having below 5 acres land. Only 0.91% of the population in the project area has land holdings above 10 acres and 2.23% own land between 5 to 10 acres.

Water and Irrigation facilities

There are 835 irrigation wells, 13 irrigation tanks, 7 Lift irrigation facility, 156 pumpset facility and 55 systems for river irrigation are operative in the area.

Household Items

Out of 1208 households, the total number of almiras in the project area is 197 out of which the people use 191. 760 bicycle is used out of 765. Aluminum cooking utensils are 3778 out of which 3768 are used. Steel cooking utensils are 7094 out of which the people use 7058. Earthen utensils in the households' number 3889 and 3865 of them are used. 159 fans are being used out of 160 fans. Hurricane lamps (Lantern) in the households are 1344 in number and 1337 are used. Out of 144 petromax owned by the people181 are used. The number of motorcycles is 88 but the people use only 85. The total number of radio in the villages is 464 out of which 459 are used. 1180 steel boxes are used out of a total of 1183. There are 131 television sets in the project area out of which 129 are used.

All 8 V.D.O / V.C.D are used by the people in the project area. There are a total of 702 wall clocks out of which 696 are in working condition. The number of chairs and tables in the villages are 886 and 357 respectively.

Agricultural Implements

There are 10 tractors in the villages and 642 ploughs in the project area. The number of other agricultural implements in these eleven villages is 1210 that includes KUDALI, HANSUA, GAINTY, HENGA etc.

Occupation

58.99% inhabitants practice agriculture. 2.94% are engaged in service and 0.11% of the population has their own business. The people working as doctors and engineers are 0.01% each. 1.11% of the people in these villages are students. The percentage of population working as labour is 13.88%. The rest of the population works as drivers, home guards and workers. Out of the total female population in the project area 22.54% are housewives.

Employment

Out of the total respondents in the project area only 2.39% is employed and 1.4% is unemployed. 96.20% did not responded.

Agricultural Practices

Cultivation Practices: The major crop in the villages is paddy, wheat and maize followed by pulse crop like rahar khesari. In the Kharif season the crops orown are paddy, maize, rahar, til and nargo. Paddy is grown 12 to 25 mun per bigha and is sold at the rate of Rs. 2 to 5 per kg. In the rabi season the crops grown are wheat, grams, jau, khesari, masuri, tisi and matar. Wheat is the favoured crop during the rabi season. The rate at which it is sold is Rs. 6 to 7 per kg.

Roots Available

Onion is the other major cash crop that is grown by the villagers in the project area. Nearly 16% of the people grow onion. It is followed by garlic, potato and radish (MULEE).

Wood available

The most favored wood is Shisam followed by Gamhar, Mahua and Sagwan. The least favoured wood is Eucalyptus.

Fruits Grown

Mango and Guava are the most preferred fruits that are grown by the villagers in the project area. 8.92% people in the village grow mango and 9.28% Guava. The least preferred fruit is pomegranate. Other popular fruits are Banana, *Bair*, Papaya and *Bel*.

Health and Sanitation

Common Diseases in the Locality

52.15% respondents said that malaria is the common disease in the area. 22.76% said that cough & cold is the common disease, 13.90% said fever is the common disease. 13.90% respondents identified diarrhea as the common disease in the area and 0.57% said T.B is the common disease.

Villages	*Malaria*	*Cough & Cold*	*Fever*	*Diarrhea*	*T.B.*
Sakhui	87.30	03.17	01.58	-	-
Palhe Khurd	67.23	19.20	05.08	01.13	-
Sikka	53.04	29.87	04.87	02.43	00.61
Gari Khas	55.68	25.56	07.95	01.13	00.56
Kathautia	53.75	11.25	20.00	00.62	01.25
Kajri	32.21	37.07	17.97	-	00.74
Batsara	04.75	11.94	27.86	-	00.49

Health Facilities in Government Hospitals

7.94% of the villagers in the project area avail Sub Health Center facilities. Only 2.48% of the villagers avail Primary Health Center facilities and 0.33% have Health Center facilities. 86.83% respondents pleaded ignorance about availability of Govt. health facility in the area.

Health Facilities in Private Clinics

Allopath facilities: 45.19% respondents prefer to visit project area. Ayurvedic and Homeopathic facilities are preferred by in 4.71% and 1.40% respondents respectively in the project area. 46% did not responded.

Knowledge of Family Planning

83.52% respondents in the project area knows about family planning methods whereas 7.27% of the people did not know about these methods.

Family Planning Practices

Out of the total population in the project area 56.37% of the respondents said that tubectomy is preferred device. 0.33% preferred vasectomy. 0.66% of the respondents use condoms as family planning methods.

There is a need for family planning counseling and service to all eligible couples for promotion of condom use as a device against prevention from HIV / AIDS. The health services in the area are very poor. It is suggested that health service activities should be taken up in the project area as entry point activity. Malaria being the major problem, control measures should be initiated on priority basis.

Education & Educational Institutions:

The educated population in the village is 48.8%. At present 2347 children are studying in educational institutions. Out of this 1410 are boys and 937 are girls.

There are eight primary and three middle schools within the villages and three primary, eight middle and one high school outside the villages where children go for education. One private primary school is also operating in the area. Children go to school on foot or on bicycle. Three villages are covered under Surva Siksha Abhiyan of the Govt. This reflects good academic facility in and around villages.

Gender Issues:

Status of Women

84.10% of the population in the project area felt that the status of women in the villages is lower than male whereas only 10.09% felt that their status is high.

Decision Making

In decision-making 92% of the respondents in the project area said that women played a supportive role and only 1.24% of them said that women had authoritative role.

Work Sharing by Women

60.43% of the population in the project area felt that women did not share work with male counterpart and only 3.47% of the population said that they did share workload.

Work and Leisure in productive work

In leisure period, 45% of the women population collects cow dung. 4.38% of the women are involved in firewood cutting and 3.06% in cloth stitching.35.76% did not responded.

Problem of Women

75.91% of the respondent said that women do not face much social problems but 30.71% said that they have to face social problems.71.93% face high economic problems.33.69% said that they face less economic problems.

Government Programmes

Govt. programmes like PMRY, SGRY, PMGVY, IAY, and SGGSY have not reached the people in the area but ICDS & Sarva Siksha Abhiyan are running. It is suggested that :

Programmes	*Number of Beneficiaries*		
	Male	*Female*	*Total*
ICDS	NA	NA	NA
Sarva Siksha Abhiyan	NA	NA	NA

5.7. Alternative village income sources such as following should be promoted.

(a) Bidi making as Kendu leaves is locally available.

(b) Mushroom cultivation.

(c) Leaf plate making.

(d) Cow dung cake making be shifted to coal cake making as source of fuel.

(e) Tailoring.

(i) Animal husbandry – Goat rearing, Piggery & Poultry.

(j) Horticulture etc.
(f) Motor cycle / Bicycle repairing.
(g) TV / Radio repairing.
(h) Carpentry.

Recommendations for Socio-Economic Development of Economically Challenged Areas In Jharkhand

- The Kharif crop is the most important crop for tribal communities in the area and measures need to be put in place to ensure the security of this crop. This leads to both improved agronomic and technical support measures that rest on conserving as much water as possible during the monsoon season. Run off management is thus the key to improve rain fed farming. Therefore, the development strategy should focus at maximizing rainwater conservation through modern technique and water harvesting structures, the use of protective irrigation using traditional irrigation from ponds, streams and wells and agronomic improvements for conserving moisture for longer periods.
- The primary objective should be to promote in predominantly poor and tribal areas a replicable model of self reliant development based on management of water resources for household food security and improve livelihood opportunities and well being.
- Take measures for stablisation of kharif paddy crop by developing irrigational facilities through identification and tapping water resources, efficient management of water resources, and proper channelisation of water resource for equitable distribution of the water to beneficiaries.
- Create an enabling environment for the empowerment of a range of grassroot associations like SHG, Water User Groups (WUG) and Village Development Committee (VDC).
- Promote activities that generate sustainable increases in production and productivity of land and water resources for paddy cultivation. This will include construction and renovation of water harvesting structures for irrigation to improve agriculture practices.
- Help villagers to generate alternate sources of income outside of agriculture, particularly for the landless and marginal farmers e.g. horticulture, goat rearing, pig rearing, Vermi compost and handi-craft items.
- The capacity building exercises should be promoted for a range of interrelated community based institution as including SHG, VDC,

WUG for management of after resources in a way that is compatible with the spirit of extension of Jharkhand Panchayati Raj Act.

Community Development Strategy

- The mobilization of small groups around simple collective action, which are known as SHGs. These SHGs will undertake self defined / need based activities that enhance the sustainability of the project. At least two SHGs per village should be formed.
- Each village will form VDCs comprising 15 – 25 members through Gram Sabha as per Panchayati Raj Act. These VDCs will form Village Developmental Plan and ensure its implementation under various schemes that are availableThe VDC members will meet atleast once in a month.

Health intervention

Special control programme on communicable disease like Malaria & Diarrhea should be taken up.

- Regular health checkup camps can be organized.
- Awareness programme on family planning is needed.
- Medical mobile van service for better coverage may be introduced.
- Possibilities for Promotion of indigenous (herbal) medicine should be explored.

Agriculture

Improved practice of agriculture may be introduced in phased wise manner.

Participatory planning process for land and water management activities, the basic guideline to start with identifying the existing users and the users of both private and common land resources (private land in the area function as common property grazing land after crop harvesting) and evolve alternative development options involving not only the land owners but other existing users called BATAIDARS be initiated.

Water resource management should be taken up by

1. Catchments treatment: Contour / Farm bunding, contour trenching, gully plugs, small earthen check dam, Renovation of existing check dams and other sources of irrigations.
2. Water conservation and optimum use in planned manner.
3. Horticulture, Fishery, Poultry should be promoted through SHG.

4. Cultivation of medicinal and aromatic plants be introduced and promoted.
5. Commercial Promotion of tribal art & craft-through handicraft promotion.
6. Education -Sarva Shiksha Abhiyan to be popularized for involving school drop out children.
7. Some innovative programmes on the lines of EKLAVYA and PRATHAM be introduced.Close coordination with district Education department be maintained for getting support in school education programme.
8. Ensure that every child attends school.

Chapter - 11

The Level of Population Growth of Pahari Korwa of Chhattisgarh

— *Mithilesh Kumar Mishra*

Introduction

The tribal of India constitute 8.6 per cent i.e. 104.28 million (census 2011). Among all states of India, Chhattisgarh has the highest concentration of tribal population. According to census 2011 there are 17, 43,277 tribal household in the state. Total tribal population in the state is 78, 22,902 which includes 38, 73,191 males and 39, 49,711 females. The decadal growth rate of the tribal population during 2001-2011 is 18.2 per cent which is lower than the state decadal growth rate 22.65 per cent. The tribal population of Chhattisgarh forms 30.6 per cent of state total population and 7.5 per cent total tribal population of India.

There are as many as 40 different tribal groups in the state. These groups' shows considerable variation and assimilation of their social and cultural traits, religious beliefs and norms as well as traditional economic pursuits vary from tribe to tribe and region to region. Out of these 40 tribal groups 5 tribal groups have been identified as primitive tribes based on the criteria of low literacy level, pre-agricultural level of technology, stagnant or diminishing nature of their population and subsistence level of economy. PAHARI KORWA, ABUJHAMARIAS, BIRHORS, BAIGAS and KAMARS have been designated as Primitive Vulnerable Tribal Groups (PVTGs) in Chhattisgarh. Out of these five PVTGs, Pahari Korwa and Birhor inhabits Jashpur District. These communities face high level of poverty, malnutrition and limited access to health and nutrition services, manifested in high mortality rates. As a strategy for curtailing the once decreasing population of PVTGs after 1979, Government of India and state government restricted sterilization among these groups, attempting an increase in birth rate rather than a decrease in the mortality rate.

In 1973, Dhebar commission created primitive tribal group as a separate category who are less developed among the tribal groups .In 2006, the government of India renamed the PTGS as Particularly Vulnerable Tribal Groups (PVTGS). PVTGS have some basic characteristics they are mostly homogenous with a small population relatively physically isolated, social institutes cast in a simple mould absence of written language relatively simple technology and a slower rate of change. Particularly vulnerable Tribal Groups 75 such groups in 17 states and one Union Territory have been categorized as PVTGs.

Key Issues

Very few demographic studies have been carried out among the Pahari Korwa tribes of Jashpur district of Chhattisgarh. Till date there is no study available which describe the level of population of Pahari Korwa tribe, based on which one can quantify their population growth? .An attempt has been made in this research to study the population level of pahari korwa tribes.

Objective of the Study

1 To study the level of population growth of Pahari Korwa tribe.

2 To study the ethnographic profile and life cycle of Pahari Korwa tribal community.

3 To examine factors responsible for the slow population growth of Pahari Korwa.

4. To suggest programme for arresting slow population growth of Pahari Korwa.

Research Methodology

The study is based on both primary and secondary sources data. The primary data was collected through structured questionnaire and schedule. Study has been carried out among Pahari Korwa tribes of Jashpur District. A total 100 families were randomly selected from two villages of Manora Block and eight villages of Bagicha block as sample and head of the households were interviewed. Data pertaining to population characteristics viz. population composition and their size, age, sex, education, occupation, marital status, socio-economic status, income expenditure etc. were collected. Focus group discussion has been conducted among elder members for verification of data.

Population growth has four components viz demographic characteristics, birth, death and net migration. Since the primitive tribes are circumscribed tribes they seldom move from one territory to another and hence, their net migration assumed to be zero. Thus, for these populations the balance of birth rates and death rates will determine the level of population growth. The information on births and deaths, thus collected was used to compute the population growth of the Pahari Korwa tribes. Since no separate census data were available on this tribe .An attempt has also been made in this paper to study the level of population growth.

Physiography of the Pahari Korwa Habitation Area Jashpur

Jashpur district is divided into upper and lower Ghats. The upper ghat was previously under Khudia Zamindari comprised of Bagicha and Manora Tribal Development Blocks. It lies in the eastern corner of Chhattisgarh adjoining the border of Jharkhand and Orissa in the eastern side. It is between 22^0 21' 11" and 23^0 15' 21" North latitude and 83^0 24' 15" and 84^0 23' 53" East longitude. The Upper Ghat is an extension plateau covering 1384 sq. Kms which is about 1200 meters above sea level and is covered with the dense forests. This is boundary on north and west by Samri tahsil of Balrampur district. Above it there is another plateau, which is under the Khudia region, and the highest peak in this plateau is 'Pandarapat' which is about 1100 meter high from sea level. The elevated plateau called 'pat' is the main abode of Pahari Korwa. The upper Ghat is drained by the "Lawa and Shank" rivers and their tributaries. The most important river is Ib, which is its source in the Khudia high land and drains the western part of the upper Ghat and leaves Jashpur district boundary at Lawakera. The topographical situation of the khudia plateau, rising as it does to a great elevation above the adjoining area from which the approach lies through perspicuous forests, covered hill passages or Ghats, has however helped in the preservation amongst these people (Pahari Korwa) at the stage of hunting, food gathering and primitive agriculture. Thus, the ecosystem has been inextricably bound with the life of Pahari Korwa.

After the merger of Jashpur state, the whole old Khudia region was divided into two revenue circles i.e. Sanna and Bagicha. Sanna revenue circle comprises 93 villages and Bagicha comprises 103 villages. These are the areas of main concentration of Pahari Korwa on the 'pat' areas and on the slope of the plateau of the Bagicha Block of Jashpur District. Bagicha and Manora Tribal Development Blocks were opened on 2.10.56 and 2.12.63 accordingly. As per the survey conducted by the Pahari Korwa and Birhor Development Agency in the year 2003, Pahari Korwa are found only in 12 villages of Manora and 76 villages of Bagicha Tribal development Blocks.

Settlement Pattern of Pahari Korwa Villages in Jashpur District

The ecological settings of these villages mainly inhabitant by the Pahari Korwa show that their settlement pattern bears definite nomadic character. Another characteristic of the settlement is the detached habitation of the tribe being away from the main villages in the form of hamlets. The origin can be traced to the practice of shifting cultivation resulting in frequent shifting of the settlement. They do not live at a place together to lead a village community life. Each household has its home situated away in some inaccessible spot on the top or on the bottom of hill side of the 'pat' or in the midst of forests at a distance between 1 to 2 kms. When a male member of the family is married, he is separated. He constructs his own house generally near his parent's house. In case of any dispute with the parents, he shifts his house to another suitable place. Their homesteads are thus scattered. A village therefore, obvious has number of hamlets. The number varies from one to even seventeen. The distribution of villages of Manora and Bagicha blocks of Jashpur districts according to the number of hamlet share being displayed in table 1 highlights this characteristic.

Table 1: Percentage distribution of the villages according to number of hamlets

	Manora Block		*Bagicha Block*			
No. of Hamlets	*No. of villages*	*Percentage*	*No. of villages*	*Percentage*	*Total*	*Percentage*
1 to 5	11	90.90 %	48	66.66%	59	69.88
6 to 10	1	9.09%	16	19.44%	17	18.07
11 to 15	-	-	9	9.72%	9	9.84
16 and above	-	-	3	1.17%	3	3.61
Total	**12**	**100**	**76**	**100**	**88**	

Source: Pahari Korwa development Agency, Jashpurnagar (as per special survey 2003).

The above table reveals that in 3 villages, of Bagicha block the number of hamlets is even more than sixteen. These villages of 'pat' region were covered with dense forests in the past which has been destroyed in due course of time.

It has been observed during the study that the settlement pattern is compact mostly in those villages which are forest villages. study has revealed that the in all the villages of 'pat' region of Bagicha and Manora blocks of Jashpur district are generally multi tribe or multi caste village with tribal communities. like Nagesia, Dehari Korwa and Oraon and other castes like Lohara, Ghasia and Ahir.

These Pahari Korwa villages of Jashpur district can be divided into three types of climatic zones viz. hot, cold and moderate. The villages which are on the bottom have hot climate with an average rainfall of about 1250 mm. The villages of pat area which are on higher elevations have cold climate with an average rainfall of about 1550 mm. village which are situated on the slope of elevation have a moderate climate.

Pahari Korwa Villages and Size of Population

The difficult terrain, hard life and almost insufficient development have given rise to the smaller sizes of the villages. The above table reveals that out of 12 villages of Manora block 9 villages have population less than 50 persons. The smallest being Kardana village with population of 03 persons and the largest being Gidha with population of 94 persons. There are 3 villages which have population less than 100 persons. In Bagicha block out of 76 villages, 26 villages have population of less than 50 persons. The smallest being chirodih and Bagdoll with a population of 01 and 05 respectively. The larger village is kamarima with the population of 893 persons Due to undulating terrain and physical barriers like streams and subsequent inadequate availability of agriculture land at one place, larger villages have been divided into hamlets, 5 villages which have population above 400 persons. The details of villages according to size of population is given below in table 7.

Table 2: Villages according to size of population

Block	*Total no. of Villages*	*Less than 50*	***Population***					
			50 to 100	**100 to 150**	**150 to 200**	**200 to 250**	**250 to 300**	**300 and above**
Manora	12	9	2	1	-	-	-	-
Bagicha	80	30	15	4	10	5	2	10
Kunkuri	1	1						
Total	**93**	**40**	**17**	**5**	**10**	**5**	**2**	**10**

Demographic Characteristics

In Jashpur district Pahari Korwa tribal communities are found in Marnora,Bagicha and Kunkuri block . According to a special survey 2015-2016, Conducted by Tribal Reseach and Training Institute Raipur (C.G), The total population of this tribe in Jashpur district is 15012. Block-wise break-up of the families of Pahari Korwa in habiting in three blocks of this district is shown in table 3.

Table 3: Demographic Characteristics

S.No.	*District*	*Integrated tribal dev. Project*	*Block*	*No. of village*	*No. of families*	*Total population*
1.	Jashpur	Jashpu	Manora	12	238	1019
2.		Jashpur	Bagicha	80	3808	13961
3.		Jashpur	Kunkuri	1	9	32
Total				**93**	**4055**	**15012**

Source: Pahari Korwa development Agency, Jashpurnagar (as per 2015 Survey).

The total population of Pahari Korwa in Jashpur district is distributed among 12 inhabited villages of Manora Tribal development Block, 80 villages of Bagicha Tribal development block and 1 village in Kunkuri block . This area comes under Jashpur integrated Tribal development project. As per 2015-2016 survey the total population of Pahari Korwa tribes in Jashpur district is 15012 and the total number of Pahari Korwa families in 4055 i.e. 238 families in 12 villages of Manora block, 3808 families in 80 villages of Bagicha block and 1 village of Kunkuri Block. Among the Pahari Korwa population, 7452 are females and 7528 are males i.e. against every 1000 men there are 990 women. The average size of their family is 3.70. Total 15012 persons (Pahari Korwa) are the member of 4055 families.

Table 4: Demographic details of Pahari Korwa tribes of Jashpur district (Survey 2002-2003)

S.No.	*District*	*Integrated tribal dev. Project*	*Block*	*No. of village*	*No. of families*	*Total population*
1.	Jashpur	Jashpur	Manora	12	143	566
2.		Bagicha	Bagicha	76	2307	10159
Total			**2**	**88**	**2450**	**10725**

Source: Pahari Korwa Development Agency, Jashpur

The total population of Pahari Korwa in Jashpur district is distributed among 12 inhabited villages of Manora Tribal development Block and 76 villages of Bagicha Tribal development block. This area comes under Jashpur integrated Tribal development project. As per 2003 survey the total population of Pahari Korwa tribes in Jashpur district is 10725 and the total number of Pahari Korwa families in 2450 i.e. 142 families in 12 villages of Manora block and 2307 families in 76 villages of Bagicha block. Among the Pahari Korwa population, 5353 are males and 5372 are females i.e. against every 1000 men there are 1003 women.

The average size of their family is 4.37 Total 10725 persons (Pahari Korwa) are the member of 2450 families. Out of 12 villages of Manora Block and 76 villages of Bagicha Block the Pahari Korwa population is 1.42 per cent and 10.78 per cent respectively of the total scheduled tribe population. The block-wise classification of village according to their size of population is given below in table 3 A & B.

Comparative statement regarding number of villages families and population of PahariKorwa in different surveys(1980, 1993, 2003 & 2015). The Pahari Korwa have been original tribe inhabiting the old kudia region of Jashpur district.

But since beginning they have been not numerous as large number of them has migrated in the past to the adjoining forest of Surguja states and onwards. The separate population figures of the Pahari Korwa is not available, According to the census of 1901 (Chhattisgarh Feudatory State), the population of the Korwa Pahari and dehari, was10, 000 in Jashpur state and 16,000 Surguja state. the census handbook of 1941 reveals the population of both the Korwa as 8217 i.e. 24.5% of the total tribal population in Jashpur state(Jashpur Settlement Report 1942).According to the census book of 1961,the total population of both the Korwa19,000 in Raigarh Distinct and out of it Pahari Korwa were 4998.Further the census reflects that the population of both the Korwa have increased by 50.3% during the 1951-1961.the population of the Pahari Korwa according to the census done at the time of the present survey is t the population of both the Korwa have increased by 50.3% during the 1951-1961.the population of the Pahari Korwa according to the census done at the time of the present survey is 5263 in Jashpur tahsil of Raigard district, thus the population of the Pahari Korwa has increased by 15.31% from 1961-1965.

From the point of view of census if the figures in relation to the population of Pahari Korwa obtained in the year 1975 are compared with these obtained in the year 1993, a clear increase of 60 per cent in their population will be noticed. It means that their population is increasing at the annual rate of 3.33 percent. Keeping this in mind that the most of th e primitive tribes are almost on the verge of extinction, the rate of growth is really encouraging. Because during this period itself the national population growth rate is registered to far more below than the above growth rate. Even though among factors might have contributed to the increase in the population of Pahari Korwa at the rate mentioned above, this must also be borne in mind that in the 1975 survey, it is quite possible that many of the Pahari Korwa families and villages might not have been touched by the survey.

The comparative figures from 1975 and 1993 survey regarding number of families and population of Pahari Korwa of Jashpur district is given in table 5

Table 5: Comparative figures of number of villages' families and population of Pahari Korwa (Survey 1975 & 1993).

Name of Districts	*No. of Villages*		*Growth Percentage*	*No. of families*		*Growth Percentage*	*Population*		*Growth Percentage*
	1975	*1993*		*1975*	*1993*		*1975*	*1993*	
Jashpur	68	83	22.00	1259	2195	74.3	5894	9494	61.0

Source : Pahari Korwa development agency Jashpur.

Table 6: Comparative figures of number of village's families and population of Pahari korwa (Survey 1993 &2003)

Name of Districts	*No. of Villages*		*Growth Percentage*	*No. of families*		*Growth Percentage*	*Population*		*Growth Percentage*
	1993	*2003*		*1993*	*2003*		*1993*	*2003*	
Jashpur	83	88	6.02	2195	2450	11.61	9494	10725	12.00%

Source: Pahari Korwa development Agency, Jashpurnagar Distt.-Jashpur (2003)

The table 6 depicts the comparative statements of the number of villages, number of families and population of Pahari Korwa in 1975 and 1993 survey. The above table reveals 22.00 per cent increase in the number of villages, 74.03 per cent increase in the number of Pahari Korwa families and 60.00 per cent increase in the their population. The above table also reveals that, 35.02 per cent of their total populations live in Jashpur district. The total population of 83 Pahari Korwa villages in Jashpur district is reported to be 9494.

The table 6 depicts the comparative statements of the number of village's number of families and total population of Jashpur district. The above table reveals 6.02 per cent increase in the number of villages, 11.61 per cent increase in the number of Pahari Korwa families and 12.00 per cent increase in their population.

The table 7 depicts the comparative statements of the number of village's number of families and total population of Jashpur district. The above table reveals 12.68 per cent increase in the number of villages, 18.60 per cent increase in the number of Pahari Korwa families and 16.77 per cent increase in their population.

Table 7: Comparative figures of number of village's families and population of Pahari Korwa (Survey 2003-2015)

Name of Districts	*No. of Villages*		*Growth Percentage*	*No. of families*		*Growth Percentage*	*Population*		*Growth Percentage*
	2003	*2015*		*2003*	*2015*		*2003*	*2015*	
Jashpur	88	93	12.68	2450	4055		10725	15012	

The illustrated population statistics shows that decadal growth rate of Pahari Korwa is lower than the general population and state average decadal population growth rate 22.6 per cent and also the decadal growth rate of India tribal population 23.7 per cent. (Census-2011).

SELECTED STATISTICS (Fertility &Mortality Indicator)

Table-8

Statistics	*Survey HH*	*Jashpur Distinct*	*Chhattisgarh*	*India*
Crude birth Rate	25.04	22.9	24.4	21.4
Crude death Rate	12.5	9.4	7.9	7.0
Infant mortality Rate	71	62	46	40
Sex Ratio	990	1004	990	940
Total Fertility Rate	3.1	2.6 (estimated)	2.6 (estimated)	2.3 (estimated)

It is notable from the above table that the crude death rate has been estimated to be7.0 for national population, 7.9 for C.G.state and crud death rate of Pahari Korwa has been estimated to12.5 which is higher than the National State and District figure (9. 4 percent).Crude Birth rate has been estimated to be 25.04 Pahari Korwa. The CBR is higher than the CBR of district, state and national population.IMR is very sensitive indicator of mortality indicating pre-natal, natal and post natal care of mother and infants.IMR has been estimated to be 40/1000 India,46/1000 Chhattisgarh state,62/1000 live birth for Jashpur district. IMR for Pahari Korwa is estimated to be 71/1000 live birth which is very high as compared to National State and District figure.

Thus, the higher mortality observed among these tribes is mainly contributed by their higher infant mortality rate. Therefore, the root cause of lower growth rate observed among Pahari Korwa population is their high infant mortality. The fertility records of Pahari Korwa women of various child bearing age groups indicate a total fertility of 3.1 from average parity. Low fertility is another factor for their lower population growth. The causative factors may be many like female illiteracy, early marriages, low birth weight, malnutrition, dysentery, diarrhea etc. Early marriage and repeated pregnancy aggravated the risk of miscarriage, foetal deformities, low birth weight etc. Maximum foetal loss occurred during 0 to 8 days and 10 to 30 days. Among the demographic factors, only age of the mothers had profound effects in foetal and infant deaths. During post natal period, the infant deaths may be due to various problems including weaning of the body with inadequate and improper supplementation of food.

A study of economic factors in context of health care of the Pahari Korwa of undivided Raigarh district conducted by ICMR (Regional Centre Jabalpur, 1991) pin pointed the following salient features ;-(a) Annual average house hold income of Pahari Korwa is Rs.3, 744/ and income per person per month is Rs.69.34 (b) Annual house hold expenditure is Rs.3799.55 and expenditure per person per month is 70.36. It reveals that their economic condition is extremely poor and comes under subsistence economy .The average household expenditure on treatment is Rs 15/ per month.

Socio-Economic Profile of the Surveyed Pahari Korwa Households

In the background of the above mentioned broad picture of the demographic ethnographic profile of Pahari Korwa tribal community which is based on secondary sources are now turn to see and compare the situation at village level. For this purpose we will use the data collected from the primary sources. The data related to household demography and social characteristic has been collected during the survey in 100 households. The same are furnished below:

(a) household population and family size: The Pahari Korwa population covered in the survey was 534 in number. The total population constitutes 284 females and 250 males. Female's population outnumbered the males. The block wise analysis of distribution of household shows 59 males and 64 females in Manora block and 191 males and 220 females in Bagicha block respectively. The average size of the family varies from region to region. The average size of th e family varies in Bagicha block is highest i.e. 4.1 where in Manora block it is the lowest i.e. 3.9 It is peculiar to note that the total average including both the two blocks which is more or less lower than the national average family size i.e. 4.5.

(b) Age wise distribution of the family members: Table 10 depicts the age wise distribution of family members belonging to 100 households. The table shows that the total population of surveyed families is 534(5.34 persons per households), in comprising 250 males and 284 females. 41.01 per cent of the total population is in the age group of 15-45 years, followed by 15.73 per cent in the age group of above 45 years. These two groups together represent 56.73 per cent of the total population. Out of the total population 43.26 per cent fall in the age group. i.e. below 14 years. About

24.34 per cent members of this age group help their families in the fields or cattle rearing, collection of minor forest product (MFP) and domestic activities by taking care of infants in their families etc. 12.23 per cent and 7.11 per cent of the total population fall under the age group up to 46-55 and above 55 years respectively, and most of the old members do not contribute anything to the earnings of their families. Either directly or indirectly these two age groups (below 14 and above 55 years) completely depend on other members of their family. Hence, it can be inferred that the population falling in 15-45 years of age groups accounts for 41.01 per cent of the total population. and this population may be considered as an ideal and effective work force.

(C) Literacy status among family members: Table 11 gives details of literacy among family members. This table clearly shows that total population of surveyed Pahari Korwa households is 534, comprising 284 females and 250 males. 24.34 per cent of the total population is in the age group of 1 to 6 years. Among the children in the age group of 6-14 years, only 97 (18.16 percent) attend schools, and 23.08 per cent children of this age group are non attending and poor participation in educational institution. Lack of awareness of the values of education in the society, lack of parent interest, negligence and inefficiency of teacher are the main reason.

This accounts for 60 per cent cases and in another 30 per cent cases, the children supplement family income, work with parents in the field and forest. In 5 per cent of the cases parents do not visualize the utility of sending their children.

In order to have greater enrolment in schools and ensure larger retention, two measures are required to be taken. First, efforts should be made to bring about change in the attitude of the people towards education. The door to door campaign and involvement of Pahari Korwa tribes in school and Anganwari centre management will be an effective step in this direction; secondly, infrastructural deficiencies should be removed.

This table also clearly shows that in the total population of surveyed Pahari Korwa 56.74 per cent are adult members (303). Out of 303 adult members, only 49.83 per cent are literates and the total literacy rate including school going or enrolled is 50.18 percent. Among the literates 32.0 per cent have received education up to primary level and 5.0 per cent have received education up to middle level. Thus, it can be concluded that economic condition as well as mental outlook of the households are responsible for this sort of situation. It can be said that the Pahari Korwa tribes with relatively better economic back ground believe that the education is at all level useful and they wish to send their children to school and ashram.

(D) Household by occupation: In India, settled agriculture is the predominant source of livelihood among the over whelming majority of the tribal. There are few tribal communities in our country even today who depend entirely on forestry and food gathering. Regarding occupational pattern of the tribal, Roy Burman (1974) has classified tribal communities as (i) Forestry and food gathering (ii) Shifting cultivation (iii) Settled agriculture (iv) Agricultural labour (v) Animal husbandry (vi) House hold industry and (viii) miscellaneous occupation. The occupational pattern of the Pahari Korwa tribal communities in the study area is discussed in Table 6.5.

One of the important indicators of economic development of any region is the occupational pattern of the population. Due to smaller land holding, infertile land and inability to find agricultural inputs, cultivation is not the main occupation of Pahari Korwa. The subsidiary occupation of Pahari Korwa is Agricultural labour and collection of minor forest produce or collection of fuel wood to supplement the food. The analysis shows that the contribution of agriculture to the income of the sample households vary from household to household and only few of them depend on agriculture while others subsists on agricultural labour and collection of minor forest produce.

Table 12 shows that there were wide variations regarding main and subsidiary occupations between Pahari Korwa tribal communities in the study area. The overall picture indicates that agriculture was the main occupation of 65 per cent of sample Pahari Korwa tribal in the survey area. In case of subsidiary occupation, about 23 per cent of Pahari Korwa beneficiaries took various allied activities as their subsidiary occupation to augment their income with the help of government assistance in contrary to this, about 75 per cent of Pahari Korwa beneficiaries reported that the collection of minor forest produce and agricultural labour as their subsidiary occupation.

(E) Land Ownership Status: Land is supposed to be the main assets and agriculture followed by agricultural labour and collection of Minor Forest produce the main source of livelihood of the Pahari Korwa tribal community. The percentage distribution of Pahari Korwa households in the survey area according to size of land holding is presented in table 13. The operational land holding size of the households reveals that 28 per cent of the Pahari Korwa households on the whole hold 2.5 acres of land, 55 per cent possessed up to 5 acres of land and rest 12 per cent semi medium farmers and 5 per cent medium farmers possessed the land up to 10 acres and 25 acres respectively.

Since Pahari Korwa tribes are not much involved in non agricultural activities they are available for service in the fields of other's also. The land ownership status of the beneficiary's households is more or less same in both the blocks but even them we can see that the percentage of households highest in the category of up to 5 acres is in Manora block (66.66 percent). Almost all Pahari Korwa beneficiary households were cultivating on land which belonged to the forest department. As stated by them when their fore–father's settled in these villages, they cleaned the forest land and their family members are still cultivating such land but they are not owners of the land the respondent who had more than 2 acres of land also belong to this category.

(F) Household Annual Income: For the purpose of the present study the sources of gross annual income of the sample Pahari Korwa households are classified under the following main heads: (a) Agriculture and allied activities (b) collection of minor forest produce (c) agricultural wages (d) petty business and service etc. In the present study gross annual income includes both case and kind income earned by the Pahari Korwa. And also, income of these households was computed as the sum of earnings of all the members of a household, derived from all the above sources in a year, on an average during the reference period.

From the table 14 it is observed that the major source of income of the Pahari Korwa household in the study area was agriculture and its allied sectors like poultry, goat rearing etc. (27 per cent of their gross income). It is also evident from the table that majority of the beneficiaries, viz. 46 per cent and 17 per cent earned semi medium as well as low and high level (11 percent) annual income respectively. 35 per cent and 31 per cent sample beneficiaries derived income from agriculture, allied activities and collection of minor forests produce and wages respectively. Only 7 per cent beneficiaries derived income from service employment and petty business. Some people are employed in government department. On the whole the medium and high level of gross income of sample beneficiaries households were increase due to their income from lands and taking various allied activities by utilizing a package of services rendered by government under economic development programme. The average total income of the sample Pahari Korwa households was rupees 15000 per annum.

(G) Annual Expenditure Pattern: In the earlier part of this study a detailed analysis of the Pahari Korwa tribal society their culture, socio-economic pattern, agriculture and living style has been attempted which is adequate to illustrate that these communities not only deferent in social customs habits, religio-cultural beliefs but are also economically poor. Their employment and income levels are low and knowledge of sanitary and health essentials are meager. The standards of consumptions of the Pahari Korwa tribal communities are poor. The Pahari Korwa in general lives a very simple life in the hill areas (Pahari or upland). It is clear from the study that all items of their annual expenditure are expenditure on household consumer items, agricultural operations, live stock, poultry, festival, marriages, medical treatment educational, petty business and intoxicant etc. The favorite's household items that are purchased by the Pahari Korwa normally from the local weekly market are oil, salt, rice, matches, and cloths.

For the study of consumption pattern of the Pahari Korwa households we ask the respondents to give the information about total expenditure during the year under reference 2017-18. The expenditure items have been divided into groups like (a) cereals, including paddy, maize, marua, gondali, kodo, kutaki etc. (b) Pulses (c) vegetables, including meat, egg etc. (d) Miscellaneous, which includes spices, pickle, salt, edible oil, jaggery and all those item which could not be included in above mentioned food items. (e) Clothing includes chadars, blankets, wearing cloths etc. (f) fuel includes expenses on kerosene (g) marriage and ceremony include all the expenses incurred in various ceremonies like birth death, marriages etc. This item also includes expenses on festivals and worship of god etc. (h) educational expenditure (I) health expenses includes all expenses for medical purposes (j) drinks, smoke and tobacco (k) other expenses including expenses on payment like land tax old dues, housing expenditure etc.

House hold expenditure on consumable is so varied and fragmented that in practical very difficult to record it at few sittings with sample households. Therefore we have formed seven broad categories to cover all items as far as possible. These were food items, intoxicants, drinks and entertainments, hospitality etc., social function and worship, health medicine and treatment, education and miscellaneous. Then, we merge the various individual items in this category. It is clear from the study that there is a high positive correlation between annual income and expenditure of the sample households. The average annual household's expenditure is Rs.12825. Food is the most important items of household expenditure which has lion's share in the household income. As many as almost all households claim to have spent larger part of their income on food items. Other important items of expenditure are on social function like birth, death, marriage, religious ceremonies and intoxicant etc. The details of the consumption expenditure pattern of Pahari Korwa household are given in table 14. It is notable from the table- 14 that the percentage share of the total consumption expenditure actually spent on food or related items is as high as 55 percent. Social function like birth, death, marriage consumes another 14.17 per cent of resources spent on consumptions. Pahari Korwa are addict of alcohol or handia, tobacco and other intoxicant and spent a lot of money (10.03 percent) on such things as part of their entertainment, expenses on guests, relatives and friends. A matching percentage share is also spent on religious functions (8.23 percent). On all occasions Pahari Korwa drinks lavishly but most of the drinks are country liquor prepared from mahua and rice bear (handia). If we merge the item 3,4 and 5 indicated in the table we find that around 24.41 per cent of the expenditure is done for unproductive items particularly in economic sense. In the sample household 88 per cent households reported spending on the alcoholic drinks. There is a general tendency of hiding such information among Pahari Korwa respondents unless detailed cross questioning is done at the time of field enquiry. Their consumptions pattern figures indicate that they spent only 2.01 per cent of total consumptions expenditure on the health items. A similar proportion of expenditure consumptions is devoted towards educations (1.36 percent). Though the Pahari Korwa tribes have only little to spend if they decide to educate their children as such facilities are provided free of charge, yet the extent of school going children and total literacy is not satisfactory. The analysis of intergeneration education differential found that literacy is found only with recent origin among them, before this generation the literacy was practically unknown among Pahari Korwa.

The total expenditure of the households was Rs. 7,85,650 which means Rs. 7856 per year Per household expenditure on household consumption. It reveals that their economic condition is extremely poor and still comes under subsistence economy.

(H) Food Consumption Pattern: The staple diet of the Pahari Korwa is coarse, Maize, Maura, Kodo, and rice they supplement their diet with fruits and various kinds of fruits, tubers leaves etc. The root leaves fruits and flowers are collected from the forests. Besides these, various kinds of kanda and fruits are also consumed as well as preserved for further use. The oil is extracted from mahua seed called dorri or bahera are consumed. Food habits and diets of sample Pahari Korwa households were also studied. Table -15 indicating number of diets and item of food taken by surveyed households during the previous year..

The table -16 revealed that during the period of October to December, 80 per cent households get two times meals a day and items of food were mainly crops harvested during the season and few kandas vegetables and fish occasionally. This was the season of goda paddy when they staple rice at least one time a day. Maize was consumed in good quantity, in the form of Chapati (bread) and ghatta (Boiled Bhat). 20 per cent household reported that they had one and half (1/2) meal a day and the other meal used to is not satisfactory and insufficient in quantity. They ate boiled makai (maize) mainly and fish occasionally. They used to eat Gondali, Kutaki, Maize, Pithora Kanda etc. But the second meal what they used to find in the forest i.e. leaf vegetables, fruits, fish and birds were caught and trapped to eat January to March were second better season for the Pahari Korwa. But the start of the season mostly they consumed their harvested crops and vegetables grown in the Bariland (kitchen garden). But maize, maruya, sutru and rahar pulses are available to consume but depend upon the yield of the crops. In case, the yield of these crops is sufficient, it is still for consumption during this season.

The above table also indicate that 80per cent house hold reported that during January to march they had 2 or3 times meal at their disposal and mainly they consumed rice, bread prepared from maruya, boiled maize, rahar and sutru pulses occasionally and Bhat of makai (maize) and fowls decorated their dishes some times. 20 per cent house hold told that they consumed two diet per day and items of food were rice, maruya maize pulses kutaki and kanda etc. some of them reported that they were unable to manage even a full meal for a day in sufficient quantity to fill up the empty stomach. They never draw satisfaction and lived in hunger.

It is found that in the month of April-May and June they entirely depend upon different kinds of fruits and roots. This is the season when fruits are found is abundance. That the most difficult periods is between April & and June where Pahari Korwa get only roots, fruits and leaves. 60 per cent and 40 per cent Pahari Korwa household consumed one or two diets respectively per day and the items of food included rice, kutaki,, Mahua flower, Gate kanda, occasionally fish and hunted animals and birds were also consumed in day meals.. 60 per cent Pahari Korwa households reported that during the month of July to September they consumed two full diet per day and 40 per cent household reported that they consumed one and half diet per day. They did not derive satisfaction from food. Therefore, they called their diet one.

(I) Preparation of Food: Alll types of roots are first boiled and cleaned and then consumed. Flowers and leaves are first boiled and then eaten with salt and chilly. Crops like Gondali, Kutki, first roasted in the earthen pots on chulah, then crushed in Dheki and then boiled like rice to eat. Marua is crushed into powder and then bread is made. Sometimes it is boiled and then eaten. Various pulses are boiled with little turmeric and salt, then eaten. Pulses form side dish to a Pahari Korwa. They consume pulses occasionally, because they are luxury to them. They extract oil from Jatangi sarsso, Toria, Ramtilla, . They prepared bread from the flour of Marua, Bazra, Jwar Rice Sutru, wheat and gram. Pahari Korwa are non–

Vegetarian in nature. Samar, Kotara, Barah, hens, peacocks, titer, fish, goat etc, are killed by them to eat their meat. They do afford mix spices with the meat. Meat is prepared by them in a earthen vessel. They prepared eggs in different ways. Some times they take it boiled with salt. They prepared amlets which they call panna. They mix raw eggs with vegetables too. Food prepared only twice a day, once in the morning and then in the evening. The nature of the food consumed by the Korwa depends upon various factors. All of them, with few notable exceptions, are non-vegetarians. There are differences, however between different people regarding the kind of animal food they would take. Food habits are changing fast. In the village people are satisfied with rice or vegetables or pulses or some non-vegetarian food.

Pahari Korwa are extremely fond of 'Handia' (rice bear) Handia is a kind of food as well as an intoxicant. It is prepared from rice, marua, gondali and maize. This is the favorite drink of the tribe, in case, there is nothing else to eat in the house, and they prefer to drink Handia. It is taken throughout the year but its intake increases during the harvesting season. It is also a peculiarity of Pahari Korwa that they drink Handia beer in a group also. This drink has social as well as economic significance of the Pahari Korwa.

In absence of Handia, Liquor is prepared. Liquor is prepared from Mahua flower. This is unique with Pahari Korwa that he does not drink Liquor alone at the Liquor shop. He always visits the Liquor shop with his wife. The purpose of taking wife to the Liquor shop is to escort him home after he is dead drunk and side by side he feels himself more secure, especially when his wife is young. The wife of Pahari Korwa is always conscious while drinking, so that she may bring back her husband home after drink.

Next to drink, tobacco (TAMAKU) is must to a Pahari Korwa. He is in the habit of chewing tobacco through out the day. Men, women and children above tin years, all chew it. Smoking is also common. A small wooden, plastic or metal box is carried and kept ready for use.

(J) Economic Status of the Households: The table 16 presents details with regard to the economic status of the households. It is evident from the figures depicted in the table that out of total population, 69.29 per cent are earning dependents, which mostly comprises children and the aged. In surveyed Pahari Korwa household family members of Manora block earning dependence are more i.e. 73.17 where as in Bagicha block the earning dependence are less 63.49 percent.

Problems of Pahari Korwa Tribes

The historical background of the tribe and earlier studies reveal that the problems of the Pahari Korwas are many. Prior to Independence their problems were more social and criminal in nature. These problems were due to their socio-economic exploitation by dominant neighboring communities with whom they have long socio-economic articulation. These problems were also due to their ecological settings which kept the tribe more isolated in the extensive forests and difficult terrain. Drinking of "Hadia" (rice bear) has been their greatest weakness. Earlier they had been in the habit of committing petty crimes and went into hiding in the forest thereafter. They did not do it in an organized manner, but due to sympathetic positive attempts made by the government and proper care such activities were controlled and a behavioral change among the community could be realized. Thus criminal offences considerably reduce to stealing of crops, and illegal cutting of the forests. But felling of tress was a bare necessity for them out of survival problem which is more of an issue related human rights.

In present situation the problems are more economical and social in nature. The economic problems are mainly confined to getting two square meals a day, problem related to agriculture, soil conservation, need of cultivable land and land reform and development problem related to drinking waters, health and hygiene, housing problem, social problems and educational problems etc.

Reasons For The Slow Population Growth Of Pahari Korwa Tribes

In this study attempt is made to explore the major factors responsible for their present condition of population growth rate along with suggesions to improve the population status.

(a) Health and Hygine: Progress of any area depends primarily on the progress of its people, however, poor, unhealthy, malnutrition, ignorant and illiterate people can hardly be expected to possess any intense desire to or effectively strive for social change and economic betterment. Health of the people, therefore, should form an important component of any integrated development programme of the people, Since condition of mal-nutrition, adverse health and mental state attuned to these situations relate to ordinary men and women who have responsible identities as members of family groups situated in a particular socio-economic and physical environment. The causes whether environmental or social or economic or a combination of all these factors which contribute to produce adverse health need to be identified according to different geographical conditions.

The health of the Pahari Korwa can not be said to be very bad but their conditions often becomes chronic after repeated infections. The whole region is malarias due to heavy rains and humidity. Water borne diseases, various skin diseases, liver and stomach problems are common among Pahari Korwas. Poor sanitation facilities and hygienic practices have resulted in frequent occurrences of illness in pahari korwa village,due to lack of health care services in pahari korwa village the prevalent illness are not cured immediately

Thus, health care is a major problem in far flung isolated pahari korwa habitation areas.Lack of food security,sanitation,safe drinking water,and high poverty levels aggravate their poor health status.The problem of malnutrition is multidimensional. Health institution are few and far between.

Till recently and abundance of fruits,tubers,roots and leaves in forests on the one hand and indigenous health care systems on the others contributed positively to pahari korwa health.Pahari korwa people have over the centuries developed their own medicinal system based on herbs and other items collected from nature and processed locally. They have their own system of diagnosis and cure .But skill and natural resource,eses are fast disappearing.More over the traditional system can not treat or prevent many diseases that modern medicine can.

(b) High level morbidity among Pahari Korwa: We asked the kind of illness that household has been afflicted by in the previous year.

Hundred households surveyed were studies. The findings of the survey revealed that about 40.07 per cent of the Pahari Korwa population in the surveyed areas suffer from illness every year and 20 per cent of them suffer from malaria, 11 per cent suffer from fever, 5 per cent from stomach pain, 10 per cent from diarrhea and dysentery, 2 per cent from measles, 2 per cent from Jaundice and 5 per cent from cough and cold. The cases of malaria, fever, diarrhea, and dysentery and stomach pain at times spread like epidemic, particularly in Bagicha block. It was reported that the primary health centers and sub centers are required to be render services to large hilly areas. The resources available to the centers are inadequate to meet the challenges of general morbidity conditions.

Pahari Korwas are superstitious and very much afraid of hunting of ancestor's souls. They call "Baiga" for "Ojhai" failing this, they call "Devar" for herbal medicine. They primarily depend upon the traditional method of treatment.

C High level morbidity among women: It is observed that women in general are neglected in respect of their nutrition and health care. A few numbers of Pregnant and nursing mothers are given Pre-natal and post natal care. About 25 per cent pregnant women suffer from swelling anemia, fever and pain. About 30 per cent of the mothers suffer from post-natal complications such as fever, weakness, excessive bleeding and anemia.

Pahari Korwa women are aware that pregnant and lactating womens need extra care and better quality of food. But due to lack of resources and acute poverty, this is not generally given. It is painful to note that Pahari Korwa women (about 25 percent) do not get even two square meals a day during pregnancy and lactation period. Proper prenatal care and neglected during delivery is very common the average fertility rate is about 3 to 4 births. The maximum fertility age is 20 to 30 years of age and there after it rapidly decreases.

Starting from gestation to delivery mothers are left to the mercy of God. During gestation, at least one fifth of the mothers suffer from some complications such as fever, bleeding, pain, anemia, swelling of feet etc. Usually these complications are treated indigenously pre-natal checkup is just unknown to the Pahari Korwas. Some awareness, however, is evident in regard to prevention of mother and child from tetanus and also from polio. Out of 15 pregnant women only 1 pregnant woman is found to have tetanus oxide injection prior to delivery. Delivery is mainly a family affair. The respondents were asked "who attended last 2-3 births in their families". It was observed that most of the village old women was the most popular persons to attend the deliveries in the village. Many mothers experience post-natal complications such as fever, weakness excessive bleeding and anemia are common complications.

D. High Level Morbidity among Children: Korwa children in general are neglected as to health care. Out of children population 30.3 per cent suffer from diarrhea and dysentery. 9.5 per cent suffer from respiratory diseases. 5 per cent become victims of whopping cough, 5.4 per cent get worm infection and 10.5 per cent suffer from malnutrition. Most of the Pahari Korwa children have taken polio drops under Polio eradication programmes.

E. Mortality: Mortality rate in the Pahari Korwa tribal community is not available. Children of 100 Pahari Korwa sample house hold of Bagicha and Manora blocks surveyed were studies. In 100 surveyed house holds 20 per cent child mortality occur in the age group of 0-1 year, 11 per cent in the age group of 1-5 year and another 5 per cent in the age group of 5-14 years. The major causes of death are respiratory infection, rickets, tetanus, prolonged labour pain, pneumonia, malaria, fever, diarrhea and dysentery. It is clear from the household survey that the factor contributing to infant mortality are (i) Ignorance regarding child care (ii) Ill health of mothers, (iii) poor hygienic condition (iv) prolonged dependence on breast feeding and traditionally sanctioned restriction in giving supplementary food (v) Malnutrition.

F. Ignorance about Health Care and Child Care: About 60% of the Pahari Korwa children have been immunized or extended prophylactic treatment. Only children have been immunized for polio under polio-eradication programme. Only 5 per cent ailing persons use primary health center or sub-centre. There is a health sub-centre for a population of 1000. The average distance that a person has to travel to get health facility is nearby about 6 to 10 KM. In the health center availability of medicine is inadequate. About c0 per cent of the respondent and community people are dissatisfied with the existing health facilities in the health centers.

About 72.5 per cent of the babies were delivered at home, attended only by family members or untrained birth attendant .Further more a majority of women eat the same food item same or less than usual during pregnancy raising a serious concern about the care that a pregnant women receive in pahari korwa household.

(g) Poverty and Illiteracy: Poverty and ignorance continue to keep them poor and less dignified. Education can Changes and development gradually for the next generation. There are primary schools in each and every pahari korwa settlements. Moreover, quality education which is, available to the majority is not available to them due to their poverty. Most of the pahari korwa people live for a day and do not plan much for future because they do not have sufficient income to plan for their future if there is any unexpected Incident and spread of diseases etc. occurred in their life that may lead to their mortality also.

Babies born to mothers with no education face almost twice the risk of dying during the newborn period as compared to mothers with at least a secondary education and babies born to the poorest families are over 40%more likely to die during the new born period than those born to the least poor(Unicef).

(h) Poor Anganwadi Services: All most all pahari korwa habitation villages had Anganwadi.It is to be noted that Anganwadi provides limited health services.I.C.D.S scheme provides outreach services to poor families in need of immunization,healthy food .and a learning environment for children and expectant/nursing mothers.In our study village,the majority of women(88%)knew about Anganwadi and 80% of women that knew about it reported of Anganwadi workers visiting them frequently.Allmost all women were aware that Anganwadi provides care for new born babies as well as ensures that all children below the age of six are immunized.Women were also aware that Anganwadi services could be useful for pregnant women.Additionally, the Anganwadi workers are also responsible for providing healthcare and nutritional education to mothers.Nearly no women was aware of health and nutrition educational programme through Anganwadi servicesThe majority did not know that Anganwadi provides health check up,child care and pre school education.These findings suggest that women possibly perceive Anganwadi as a source of supplementary nutrition for their children,not as a platform to learn about healthy life style and welfare of their households.

(i) Nutrition Water & Sanitation: The prevalence and spread of communicable diseases affect the poor households more than households that are better off,leading to the loss of workdays and resulting in the depletion of income and livelihoods.Such communicable diseases are mostly water-born and depend on a number of health related factors, such as living condition of a households,hygine and sanitation and access to safe drinking water.The UNDP reports that some 1.5 die each year from diarrhea-related diseases,often connected to poor sanitation.In pahari korwa society, women are traditionally responsible for domestic water supply and sanitation,as well as maintaining a hygienic home environment .Thus,it is even more important for a women to be aware of healthy life style practices to keep herself and her family free of diseases.

(j) Poor Sanitation and Hygien practices: Inhabitants used open air for toilets.Data suggests (90%)women did not practice washing hands with soap after using the toilet and before eating.Moreover,the majority of women did not purify drinking water.This could be the reason that fever, diarrhea, malaria, weaknesses and other ailments such as stomach pain, headach, tuberculosis, and typhoidwere reported to be the top household concerns by respondents.

(k) Lack of Nutritional Food Intake: Many households consumed staple food,not all consumed protein-rich food.A majority women reported that pregnant women should eat the same or less than usual during pregnancy raising a serious concern about the care that a pregnant pahari korwa women receives.

SUGGESTION FOR ARRESTING SLOW POPULATION GROWTH OF PAHARI KORWA PVTGS

It is critical to recognize and take note of the factors that contribute to the slow or decline in population of pahari korwa PVTGs .These include malnutrition, diseases like anemia, malaria, fever, TB, alcoholic addiction, venereal diseases, skin disease, maternal mortality,infant mortality, and loss of reproductive ability/fertility. Effective preventive and curative health systems should be developed.The health facility should be accessible and affordable.Sanitation programme also needs to be strengthened. IEC companigns need to be stepped up to make PVTGs aware about health hygine programmes.Inthis context, the study highlights the following issues and suggessions.

(a) Health Care: The health progamme is proposed for safe deliveries and adequate brought up of the infants, check up of epidemics and prevention and cure from common diseases. The special diseases of this area will be identified through a health survey. Most common diseases usually prevalent among pahari korwas tribal's are malnutrition, Anaemic disease, water borne diseases, skin diseases, diseases related to liver and venereal diseases etc. The living condition of pahari korwas tribe hiqhly unhygienic. They drinks contaminated water of natural streams, and malnutrition is the result of their poverty. They primarily depend on their traditional method of treatment. They call 'Baiga' for 'ojhai' failing this, they call 'Devars' for herbal medicine.

(b) Health check up: Due to impoverished condition of the pahari korwas many of them die at immature age and get no treatment or bad treatment. They are often victims of liver trouble, tuberculosis. Asthama and other chronic diseases. In addition to these many children suffer from amenic diseases and from diarrhea and dysentery, If they can be covered under the net work of health, many valuable life can be saved and child mortality will go down substantially. This scheme is attempted to this end in view. It is also proposed that they should be provided with health cards which will provide information about the health status of the pahari korwas house holds (including the children's and mothers). The responsibility of distribution the health cards among the family may be entrusted to the members of the peoples committees that will be organized in the panchayat level.

(c) Anaemia Control: It is found that the children and expectant and nourishing mothers from the parade korwas families often suffer from anaemia and anemic diseases like night blindness, ricket, atrophy etc.If adequate dose of iron and vitamins are given they can be freed from these diseases.

(d) Immunization and Prophylactic Treatment: The scope of immunization in this region is quite vast,about 65 per cent children have been immunized and in most of these cases necessary case has not been followed.45 per cent pahari korwas expectant mothers have been immunized against tetanus.The task is stupendous. It requires a group of devoted personnel. For the proper implementation of the schemes. Anganwadi workers,A.N.M. Vaccinators and multipurpose workers called health guides will have to be pressed into the service.

(e) Training of Dais: One of the reasons for the maternity death in this regions is non availability of trained dais. Usually untrained elder women of pahari korwa households or relatives or neighbours take the responsibility of child delivery. They act as a mid wife and cuts the umbilical cord with a knife and sprinkles ash on the naval of child to facilitate healing. for the welfare of pahari korwas childrens and mothers it is felt that in every village there should at least two trained dais. There are 93 pahari korwas villages in Jashpur, so the number of trained pahari korwas dais should be 186. A one week training of ‘ such women’ for delivery seems to be sufficient to impart necessary knowledge regarding delivery, child survival and development.

Since the pahari korwa women may not like to come to block headquarters for training, the camp may be organised at the pahari korwa village. They may be given some incentive in the camp. The expense to be incurred for organising the training camps will have to be born by the pahari korwa development agency. The training may be given by the block medical personnel.

(f) Formation of People’s Committee: In the implementation of development programme and health programme, people participation is essential. It is felt that for effective implementation people’s committee may be formed in the panchayat level. while discussing the organizational aspects of the programme implementation that enthusiastic young pahari korwa youths of every villages may be chosen and trained so that they may actively cooperate and co- ordinate. During the training, they should be informed about the available health and medical facilities for children and women, about family beneficiary development programme and about the bad or harmful effect of liquor. The may be educated about sanitation and hygiene. In short, they will not only look after the delivery system of the inputs but also make the people conscious so the inputs but also make the people conscious so that they receive the services without hesitation.

Since the members of the peoples committee will come from the poor section of the society they may be awarded yearly stipend of Rs. 5000/- each. If one person from one village is chosen, the total number of persons in the committee will be.

(g) Training Camp for Women: The schemes aim at enlighting the married women regarding mother care, child survival and development. In the camp they should know about necessary medical and health care that is required to be given to mother and child and also the concept of balanced died. In addition they should also be given demonstration training about preparation of balanced food through locally available materials.

The trainees should be from the pahari korwas tribal community. Since it is not possible to train all the married women. it is proposed that a group of 2 women from each village may be provided training for 7 days. Thus a total about 186 married women in the district will be trained. Training camp will be organized at Panchayat level. The responsibility ma y be given to those centers which in part training to Anganbari workers. The trained members will in turn motivate the pahari korwas to use their knowledge.

(h) Apart from improving access to health care,the district administration must focus on improving the education of pahari korwa girls who are going to be mothers. There is need for more concentration on the primary health.Since most of the health programmes in the district are centrally sponsored programme .Better monitoring and evaluation strategies is needed in order to ensure proper implementation and access to people.Effort should be made to improve the sanitary conditions and personal hygiene of its people . Health education is also an important means to curb fatal diseases.

(i) Formulate area specific strategies to improve access and utilization of health services.

(j) It can also be suggested that the total 93 Pahari Korwa villages can be divided into 11 or 12 clusters having 10 to 12 villages in each cluster depending upon numbers of households and size of population in respective villages. Further the selection of Pahari Korwa village Pradhan in each village can be done for establishment of better co-ordination among Pahari Korwa villages. One cluster Pradhan from each cluster will also be selected by village Pradhan, so that villages in each cluster can be coordinated properly. These cluster would further help in electing of block head representing the entire block. There can also be a Block Pradhan nominated by Collector to help in establishing link between Pahari Korwa representatives and district administration (Pahari Korwa and Birhor Development Agency, Jashpur nagar) this body will in turn work towards the overall development of the Pahari Korwa villages and Pahari Korwa people as well as help in planning for the active participation of Pahari Korwas in various developmental activities.

(k) Pahari Korwa and Birhor Development Agency should appoint Gram Mitra (Village animator) in the 93 Pahari Korwa villages, they will spread awareness towards Government developmental Programmes, education campaign, health and hygiene, cleanness, institution building i.e. formation of youth club, self help group etc. This Gram Mitra will also help in taking

Pahari Korwa children to the primary school Aganwadi and extend their help in other developmental activities.

(l) The modern medical treatment is accepted if it efficacious and is available and accessible to PTGS. Actually their resources do not permit them to avail the expensive treatment at distance places. As such suggests the strengthening of the local sub center and ANM centers to provide for immediate preventive measures at the household level.

(m) Pahari Korwa should be nominated in Panchayati Raj institutions i.e. Gram Panchayat and Zilla Panchayat. It was observed by the research team that the representation of the Pahari Korwa people in Panchayati Raj System at present is negligible; hence, their problems and needs are not highlighted. By their nature Pahari Korwas are of shy nature and they generally keep themselves away from the mainstream, hence, it is the moral duty of the government to give them exposure, so that they can connect themselves with the mainstream. Further this exposure would help in increasing their pace of development.

(n) Complete ban may be imposed on sell of liquor in this region and also on money lending operations of the money lenders in the scheduled areas and the governmental agency should come foreword to provide liberal consumption loan to the Pahari Korwas. It has been brought during the course of the study that a good number of sample Pahari Korwas households required credit not only for agricultural production but also for their consumption and other social activities like birth, marriage, death and other social functions etc. In this respect, the private money lender and their neighboring community (Ahirs) take undue benefits of their compulsion and exploit them by giving small amount as an advance to the Pahari Korwas to bear unusual expenses and also insist for the repayment in the form of agricultural and minor forest produce at the lowest price, hence, it is strongly recommended that all possible efforts should be made to ensure that the Pahari Korwa Development Agency should meet all the above credit needs of Pahari Korwas tribes timely and adequately on the one side and such credit should be properly linked with the marketing of agricultural and minor forest of the Pahari Korwas on the other side. Unless the arrangements are made as policy frame, it will not be possible to wean away the tribal completely from exploitation of the private money lenders and traders in the tribal areas. Besides this Agro-credit and consumption loans should also be provided.

(o) Land is the major physical resource available to PTGs households. Most of the available land is poor in quality and there is not very much of it . Agricultural intervention in the form of promoting locally relevant crops,drought resistant crop mix along with the agroforestry should be encouraged. Similarly, horticulture and small irrigation schemes should be encouraged.Awareness among the PTGs about the various developmental programmes being implemented for them should be encouraged.

(p) Training should be provided to the PTGs in different income generating activities through setting up more training centers at cluster level, keeping in view the availability of local available raw materials as well as the marketability of the expected produce.

(Q) The first and foremost priority should be in the health and nutrition sectors with proper planning: and the planner must have advocate knowledge regarding the community and should have a lot of knowledge of the traditional society.

Conclusion

The population growth rate of pahari korwa PVTGs was studies. It was observed that the decadal population growth rate of pahari korwa was lower than the general and state average population growth rate 22.6 and also the decadal growth rate of India"s Tribal population23.3 percent. It was also observed that the higher death rates observed in the pahari korwa tribal communities were mainly due to higher infant mortality rates .In order to improve the situation, the level of accessibility and acceptability of maternal and child health care services would have to be enhanced.

Many important issues have emerged from the above discussion regarding health status and socio - economic condition of pahari korwa PVTGs:wherein the intervention in terms of their overall development is still needed in accordance with their existing biological and cultural scenario in general. But, specific problem should be taken care for specific strategies of the development programmes.

Chapter 12

Economic Deprivation among the Lodha Tribe of West Bengal

Rilamala Saren and Ishita Mukherjee

Introduction

India is a country with inhabitants of various cultural groups and a noticeable population of it is of the tribal's. India has a large population of tribal's in comparison to that of the world's population of tribal's.

The indigenous people of the Indian subcontinent are mainly termed as Aadivasis means the first inhabitants or the Indigenous people, as recognised by the Supreme Court of India . According to the census of 2011 the total population of Aadivasis consists of 8.6% of India's population or 104 million people. Aadivasi societies are particularly prominent in the states of Andhra Pradesh, Chhattisgarh, Gujarat, Jharkhand, Madhya Pradesh, Maharashtra, Odisha, West Bengal and Northern states on the Andaman and Nicobar Islands.

West Bengal is one of the states of India which has a large population of the tribal's. According to 2001 Census, Scheduled tribes numbered 4,406,794 persons constituting 5.5 % of the total population of the state. As per the Constitution Order, 1950, West Bengal has a list of about 40 tribes. The major ST population of the state is in the districts of Medinipur, Purulia, Jalpaiguri and Bardhaman.

Jhargram district is the newly formed district from Paschim Medinipur and has a large population of tribal's and one of the most named tribal's are the LODHAS,who are the prime focus of this study. According to the 2001

Census, Lodhas numbered 84,966 and formed 1.9 %of the ST population of West Bengal.

Sangram village is one of the villages of Jhargram district which has a dominant population of Lodhas. Approximately there are 114 households among which there are 67 households of Lodhas.

In Anthropological literature the word tribe is used for them which simply refers to that human aggregates which are at the lowest level of social and economic existence, the nearest to the primitive man. Lodhas also used to live in the forest area of Medinipur which is today known as the Jungle Mahal, who traditionally dependent upon the forest for their living. But when British Raj started in India they were oppressed which gave rise to a revolt. Having being deprived from their livelihood and without any alternatives they took to criminal ways of life and are termed as Criminal Tribes. One of the most important researches on the Lodhas was done by Calcutta University faculty Professor Dr. Prabodh Kumar Bhowmick.

Deprivation: When a person is getting deprived of the basic human rights which others are getting in a society, and is needed to lead a healthy life is known as deprivation.

India is a country where technology is constantly upgrading but on the other hand being a home to about over 84 million tribes they are not getting facilities from this technologies which others are getting living in the same country, this is the tribal deprivation in India. The tribal's are unable to fulfil their basic needs such as food, cloth and shelter and are thus unable to receive other facilities which are very important such as health, education, employment, housing, etc.

Economic deprivation: Lack of material benefits considered to be necessities in a society due to lack of money is known as economic deprivation.

Lodhas were termed as the criminal tribes who used to live in the jungle mahal area of Paschim Medinipur as well as in some parts of Orissa and other places. During the British Raj they were suppressed by the Britishers who has taken their forest which used to be their everything, As a result they were forced to starvation and it is the time when they started their long journey of deprivation. The Lodhas's deprivation was started by the past British raj and now it is not ending because they lack any assistance from the present Government.

The reason behind the deprivation of Lodhas is many but every deprivation results as well as form because of their economic deprivation. The Lodhas lacks all the basic amenities which are needed for everybody's life. While all this amenities are received by other communities such as the upper class Bengalis as well as other scheduled castes of that village but they lacks everything. The Lodhas of the village doesn't have housing facilities, neither education nor health facilities. In fact they don't have a better occupation so that they can lead a healthy life. The Lodhas doesn't have a better economy that's why they doesn't get all this facilities and as a consequence since they doesn't get all this facilities they are remaining economically deprived and their situation is not getting better.

OBJECTIVE OF THE STUDY

The main objective of this study was to know the present situation of Lodhas and the reason behind all their problems. For knowing the current situation, a village named Sangram was chosen. This village is situated in Jamboni Tehsil of Paschim Medinipur/Jhargram district and the nearest town is about 10 km from there that is Jhargram. This village was favourable because it has a noticeable population of Lodhas about 67 households as well as people of other communities also.

RESEARCH METHODOLOGY

This field work is done in the Sangram village which is situated in the Jhargram district of West Bengal. This village has a total population of 67 Lodha households. Different methodologies applied during the field study was observation method, collection of the data through schedule, case study method, census taking, technological aids, method of analysis.

DISCUSSION

Sangram village is one of the villages of Jhargram district which has a dominant population of Lodhas. Approximately there are 114 households among which there are 67 households of Lodhas.

Age Sex Composition of the Lodha Population under the Survey

Age group(in years)	*Male*	*Percentage*	*Female*	*Percentage*	*Total*	*Percentage*
0 – 4	12	8.96	13	10.16	25	9.54
5 –9	19	14.18	14	10.94	33	12.60
10 –14	17	12.69	12	9.38	29	11.07
15 –19	10	7.46	07	5.47	17	6.47
20 –24	10	7.46	14	10.94	24	9.16
25 –29	12	8.95	11	8.59	23	8.78
30 –34	11	8.28	13	10.16	24	9.16
35 –39	12	8.96	11	8.59	23	8.78

(Contd...)

40 –44	07	5.22	06	4.69	13	4.96
45 –49	06	4.48	08	6.25	14	5.34
50 –54	03	2.24	05	3.91	08	3.05
55 –59	08	1.49	04	2.34	11	4.20
60 –64	03	0.75	02	1.56	05	1.91
65 –69	02	0.75	04	3.13	06	2.29
70 –74	01	0	01	0.78	02	0.76
75 –79	01	0	02	1.56	03	1.15
80 –84	0	0	0	0	0	0
85 –89	0	0	01	0.78	01	0.38
90 –94	0	0	0	0	0	0
95 –99	0	0	0	0	0	0
100+	0	0	01	0.78	01	0.38
Total	134	51.15	128	48.85	262	100

Source: Field Data.

The age-sex composition of the sample population reveals higher number of younger persons including children belonging to 0-4, 5-9, and 10-14 age groups. Together these three groups constitute 38.14% of the population. The female population in the higher age groups, particularly beyond the reproductive age, i.e. after 49 years, shows greater number than the males in general. We however, we have not found any age group 65-69 but there were 4 males above 69 years in the population . The interesting aspect about the demography of the Lodhas in this sample in the preponderance of females in almost all age groups (the sex ratio being 89.80). This fact is most revealing in all the young age groups from 0-4 up to 25-29.It only in predominance of males over female.

The Sangram village is situated in the lowest footstep slopes of Chhottanagpur plateau which creates an undulating area with infertile late rite rocks and soil and because of that agricultural land is very less there. So as a result people of that village mostly depend upon the forest resources. But due to the British Government and present state of urbanisation forests are diminishing and from here only there deprivation starts. Whatever scarcity they face everything is somehow related to their economic deprivation.

1. Food Gathering from forest

Since the villagers were mainly forest dwellers, so they collect a large amount of commodities of their daily life from the forest only. They used to collect wood, leaf and skin of sal tree which they used as fuel for their cooking and other uses. They also used to collect Neem stems which are used by them as toothbrush and also they collect coconut leaves from which they used to make broom. They collect fruits and leaves which they used to eat. They also used to collect woods which were used to build their houses. The major forest products were collected by females. Around 16.92% females and 4.54% males used to collect forest product. So as a whole the life of the villagers mainly depends upon the forest products but the forests are decreasing day by day. The wave of urbanisation is restricting their forests and also their forest life. Due to the Forest conservation Act in 1980 they don't go for hunting like they do in the previous times. These acts were provided for the conservation of the forest and also restrict them for taking anything from the forest. They can only take fallen down leaves and stems. They could not cut any tree or hunt any animals. After that the Recognition of Forest Rights Act is passed in India on 18 thDecember 2006. It has also called as Tribal Rights Act, Forest Rights Act, The Tribal Bill, and the Tribal Act. In this Act they can collect only minor forest produce including all non -timber forest produce of plant origin including bamboo, brush wood,, stumps, cane, tussar, cocoons, honey, wax, lac, tendu or kendu leaves, medicinal plants and herbs, roots, tubers.

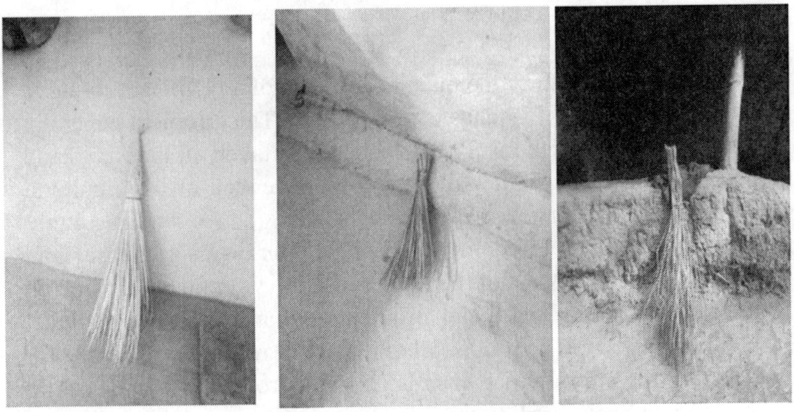

Source: Field.

Different type of Brooms made and used by them.

Hunting

Hunting is not regularly practiced by them neither they used this to earn money. Sometime when got some free time or there is any occasion then only they go for hunting. There they hunt rabbit, some birds and very rarely wild boar. Previously some hunting implements were used by them such as – Bows and Arrows, Net, Hunting trap, Spears etc. But in present they did not practice it regularly because their restricted due to the Forest

Act which prohibited them hunting in the forest. But now a day they only use catapult as a hunting implement. Their traditional occupation was hunting and food gathering and they hunted wild animals but when the Act FRA is passed and implemented the practice of Hunting is stopped and they lose their hunting skill.

2. Fishing

Fishing is the secondary occupation of the Lodhas in this village. So the villagers have various fishing implements in each house. They collect small fishes from the village pond as well as from the agricultural field. Since there is no river present there, so for fishing they totally depend upon these two sources. They collect fish for year round for their own consumption but they don't sell it in the local hats. No fishery cultivation takes place there as the rivers are in very bad condition. Most of the time they remain dry. But now a day's many chemical is used in the 203 agricultural field and water became polluted due to that fishes are lost their life and we cannot found plenty of fish in the agricultural land as well as in the pond also. That's why they could not found fishes for fishing nearby their home.

3. Agriculture

Agriculture is used to be the main occupation of any villager in India. But this is not the case of Lodhas of this village. This problem generally holds its root to the British raj. The Britishers had taken all their land and from that time only most of the villagers don't have their own agricultural land. Only about 15 persons are there who have their own agricultural land. Though the upper class communities bear their own agricultural land but the Lodhas doesn't. Most of the Lodhas used to work in others land on daily basis. Also one of the major problems is that of the geographical condition of that place. The rough soil of that place makes it unsuitable for agriculture as a result only one crop is grown there and it is barley. And also excessive uses of Fertilisers and Insecticides damaged the fertility of the soil and get less products for agriculture produces. So it can be taken that agriculture is not one of the main occupations of the villagers.

4. Daily basis work

The villagers mainly used to work as agricultural labour in others field. Some used to work on daily basis whereas some do on seasonal basis. Around 27.27% male and 38.46% female works as agricultural labour.

People of the village also go to work as daily wage labourer in other places. The percentage of this is higher among the males, that are about

51.14% and about 41.54% females used to work other than agricultural works.

Since the agricultural condition of the village is not so good so people forcibly have to work in other non agricultural sectors, but this doesn't earn them a good earning. They are paid very low which doesn't allow them to lead a good life.

The villagers are also enrolled in the MNREGA works but they haven't work for a single day because no work is actually going there.

5. Business

For the people of the village, business stands for selling simple forest products which they used to collect from the forest and made simple products from them. Such as they used to make broom from the leaves, baskets made from thin stems. They 204 also used to sell woods. But this occupation earns them a very little money, only about 30-70 rupees per day.

Another small business which they used to do is to sell small stone chips which they used to collect from a pond like area in their village. They used to sell this in very low amount about Rs.10 per basket which is used to build houses.

Source: Field.

A Man is collecting stone chips which they use to sell in the market.

Source: Field.

A Girl is collecting the Stone Chips which they use to sell in the market.

6. Domestication of Animal

Domestication of animals is not so common in the village. Some people used to rear goats. The Government has also provided them some animals for domestication but due to lack of knowledge about rearing and interest they have eaten those animals.

7. Skilled Works

The literacy rate of the villagers is very low so skilled work in the perspective of literary works is nil, and skilled works were also not noticeable. But the village children's are very much skilled in their own way. The children used to make beautiful toys made from clay. They usually used to play with this toys but this can also be sold in the market.

Age Group Wise Economic Activities of Female

Age group (in years)	*Owner cultivator*	*Agricultural labourer*	*Non agricultural labourer*	*Forest product collection*
5 - 9	0	0	0	0
10 - 14	0	0	0	01
15 - 19	0	0	01	02

(*Contd*...)

20 - 24	0	05	04	01
25 - 29	0	04	04	02
30 - 34	0	03	05	02
35 - 39	0	05	04	0
40 - 44	0	02	03	03
45 - 49	0	03	01	0
50 - 54	01	01	01	0
55 - 59	0	0	03	0
60 - 64	0	01	0	0
65 - 69	01	01	0	0
100+	0	0	0	0
Grand total	02	25	27	11

Source: field data.

Age Group Wise Economic Activities of Male

Age group (in years)	*Owner cultivator*	*Agricultural labourer*	*Non agricultural labourer*	*Forest product collection*
5 - 9	0	0	0	0
10 - 14	0	02	04	0
15 - 19	0	01	08	01
20 - 24	01	05	04	0
25 - 29	02	04	06	0
30 - 34	01	04	05	0
35 - 39	03	04	04	01
40 - 44	02	01	04	0
45 - 49	0	02	03	01
50 - 54	02	01	0	0
55 - 59	02	0	05	0
60 - 64	0	0	02	01
65 - 69	01	0	0	0
70 - 74	01	0	0	0
100+	0	0	0	0
Grand total	15	24	45	4

Source: field data.

The small household of the population should be viewed in the context of the subsistence pattern of the community. We have not found varied occupational pattern, only four types of occupational scenario, like owner cultivator, agricultural daily labourer and non-agricultural day labourer and forest produce collection. The study revealed that the majority of the male individuals (51.14%) and female individual (41.54%) are engaged in non-agricultural day labourer. We have found agriculture day labourer is more among the male than the female. Few families depend on forest produce collection. According to the villages sometimes they went to migrant labourer and to work as personal house as lease system. Their traditional occupation was hunting and food gathering but because of the FRA they could not do such things for their economy that's why they are now economically deprived.

Conclusion

The Lodhas are the indigenous tribe of India living in some parts of West Bengal and Orissa. In West Bengal they mainly reside in the Paschim Medinipur district. The Sangram village is one of those villages of Medinipur where the Lodhas used to live. This village is situated in the lowest steps of Chotanagpur plateau, so as a result agriculture is not favourable in that harsh land. The people generally depend on the forest products and daily wage basis works. The economy of the village households is generally run by both women and men working in the non agricultural sector and they don't get enough money for that also. So as a result the Lodha peoples are economically deprived and lack every other facility.

The Lodhas of this village usually live in the houses made of wood and mud because they don't have enough money to build houses. The Government has initiated to give them houses under the scheme INDIRA AWAS YOJANA. But this seems like a myth. The amount of puccka houses of the village is very less because the Yojana is not at all working there. Neither the Government nor the workers of the scheme take this seriously and the work is left in the midway. So it cannot be said that the Government has done nothing. Government has proposed this scheme for the welfare of people but there is lack of any scrutiny. So it's necessary that Government should propose any committee that would look after this works and inform the Government administrative.

Since the agriculture is not so favoured by the people because of the poor land and also because majority of the people doesn't bear any land most of the people are engaged in non agriculture work on daily basis. But still they doesn't get enough money to run their family that's why the Government has proposed one scheme which provides them hundred days work during the non agriculture season, named as Mahatma Gandhi National Rural Employment Guarantee Act 2005. Name of many villagers are enrolled in the scheme but in actual they are not working their because no work is going there. So in this case also Government vigilance is lacking.

The village only has one primary school and no secondary school. So children have to leave their study in the mid way. In the data collected it is seen that the literacy rate among the children is very low. But another noticeable thing was that the children were very skilled. They used to play with toys which they used to make from clay. So if they got any training centre where they can learn more about skilled works then they get use it for earning money. The Government can promote these schemes for skill development which have proposed already such as Deen Dayal Upadhyaya Grameen Kaushalya Yojana Etc. The Government can also build secondary school and their skill development classes can be started, with one teacher who will observe every students interest and will appreciate that student to do that particular work. Assistance is needed from the Government in this programme of skill development is that though students will make the clay products but it becomes very difficult for them to sell those products in the city, so the Government also have to help them in this by providing transport facility and a place in the city market.

Source: Field.

Village Children are making toys made out of 'Clay'

Source: Field.

Clay Toy made by the children

Our Prime Minister has promised that every village by 2018 will get electricity and this village has also got that. But if a wire gets detached unfortunately then it takes long months to reconnect it. During the survey only there was no electricity. Electricity is not only needed to lead an easy life but most importantly for the development of the people. Electricity is needed during study and also during any work such as if somebody wants to do stitching during the night time when they get free time. All this are very much needed for their development.

The people of that village also wanted some financial assistance from the government, may be in the form of pension or domestic animals. The government could provide this along with better quality rice, sugar, oil which will help them to run their everyday life with ease. But whatever they would be provided they should be taught about its necessities and how to use it and also how they will avail this.

So it can be noted that for the development of the Lodhas of that village better governing body is needed which will try to understand their problems and will know their scarcities. They will then inform the government about this. Also the governing body will teach them about various schemes offered to them. Time to time survey is also needed. It should be ensured that every person should get at least meal for 2 times a day and every children should get education facility then only their development is possible. Then only the people themselves will understand what is there for them and how would they use that. The NGOs and Self help groups are also needed to be more active.

The Lodhas has saw deprivation for a long time that is from the time of Britishers. So they have come when their deprivation should get ended and they also can lead that life which every other person is leading. For this Government assistance as well as general awareness is needed.

Bibliography

1. Bhowmick, Prabodh Kumar, 1994. The Lodhas of West Bengal. Kolkata: Institute of Social Research and Applied Anthropology.
2. Bhowmick P.K. 1981. Rehabilitation of a 'Denotified Community' The Ex Criminal Lodhas of West Bengal. Royal Anthropological Institute Newsletter. 44:6-8
3. Bhowmick P.K 1966. 'Proceedings of the summer school in Anthropology' Ed. by N.C.Choudhury. Darjeeling: Anthropological Survey of India.
4. Bhowmick P.K 1985. Tribal Situation West Bengal, The Anthropologist, Vol.15, No. 1, pp: 1-19.
5. Chanda, A . 2005. "Tribal Women" in the changing status of Women in West Bengal, 1970-2000 the challenge Ahead. Edited by J.Bagchi, pp. 130-141 Sage Publication: New Delhi.
6. Devi Mahasveta. 1983. Lodhas of West Bengal-1. Economic and Political Weekly, Vol. 18. No.22: 947-949
7. Devi Mahasveta. 1992. "The Story of Chuni Kotal. Economic and Political Weekly, Vol. XVII, No.35,P-1836-1837.
8. Guha, A. 2016. How the Lodhas became criminal or Meeting of the Past and the Present. The Eastern Anthropologist. 69(1): 7188.

9. Mandal, H. et.al. 2002. West Bengal, in India: An Illustrated Atlas of Tribal World. Anthropological Survey of India: Kolkata.

10. Panda, S. and Guha, A. 2013. "Macro-categories of Development and Microlevel Realities: A Case Study of Lodhas in Paschim Medinipur, West Bengal" Journal of Indian Anthropological Society, Vol-48, and pp: 245-255.

11. Panda, S. 2014 " Educational Scenario among the Lodhas of Paschim Medinipur District: A Comparative Account" International Journal of Social Sciences and Humanities Invention Vol.1 No.9 pp-875-890, 2014 [ISSN: 2349-2031]

12. Panda, S. and Guha, A. 2015. " 'Criminal Tribe' to 'Primitive Tribal Group' and role of Welfare State: The Case of Lodhas in West Bengal, India" Nov A Science Publishers Inc. New York, USA.

13. Verma. R.C.1990. Indian Tribes through the ages, Ministry of Information and Broadcasting. Govt. of India.

14. Jha, M. 1994, An Introduction to Social Anthropology, Vikash Publishing House Pvt. Ltd.

Chapter –13

Government Interventions for the Downtrodden in Jharkhand

Vijay Prakash Sharma, Nutan Shasi Tigga

Introduction

India is a welfare State, co©mmitted to the welfare and development of its people in general and of vulnerable sections in particular. The Scheduled Tribes are notified in 30 States/UTs and the number of individual ethnic groups, etc. notified as Scheduled Tribes is 705. the tribal population of the country, as per 2011 census, is 10.43 crore, constituting 8.6 per cent of the total population. 89.97 per cent of them live in rural areas and 10.03 per cent in urban areas. The decadal population growth of the tribal's from Census 2001 to 2011 has been 23.66 per cent against the 17.69 per cent of the entire population. The sex ratio for the overall population is 940 females per 1000 males and that of Scheduled Tribes 990 females per thousand males (Statistical Profile of Scheduled Tribes in India 2013).

According to Article 366 (25) of the Constitution of India, Scheduled Tribes (STs) are referred to as those tribal communities or parts of or groups within such tribes or tribal communities, who are scheduled in accordance with Article 342 of the Constitution. The essential characteristics (first laid down by the Lokur Committee) for a community to be identified as Scheduled Tribes are indications of primitive traits, distinctive culture, shyness of contact with the community at large, geographical isolation, and backwardness. The Constitution further mandates the State to provide for development and welfare of the Scheduled Tribes and development of administration in tribal areas to the level of non-tribal areas and all expenditure incurred are to be taken as "Charged" expenditure in the

Consolidated Funds (Article 275). Special provisions for administration of tribal areas are provided in Schedules V and VI of the Constitution.

Broadly the STs inhabit two distinct geographical areas – Central and the North-Eastern India. Majority of the ST population is concentrated in the eight states of Central India i.e., Madhya Pradesh, Maharashtra, Orissa, Rajasthan, Gujarat, Jharkhand, Chhattisgarh, Andhra Pradesh. The other distinct area is the North-East (Assam, Nagaland, Mizoram, Manipur, Meghalaya, Tripura, Sikkim and Arunachal Pradesh). The share of ST population across the States to the total ST population in India is shown in Figure15.1. The share of tribal population to the total tribal population was highest in Madhya Pradesh followed by Maharashtra.

Figure 15.2 shows the State's share of Scheduled Caste (SC) to total SC population of India. The share of SCs was highest in the State of Uttar Pradesh followed by West Bengal. Four States of India i.e. Uttar Pradesh, West Bengal, Bihar and Tamil Nadu, together account for nearly half of the SC population in India. Under the Constitution, Scheduled Castes (SCs) can only be Hindu, Sikh or Buddhist, while STs can belong to any religion.

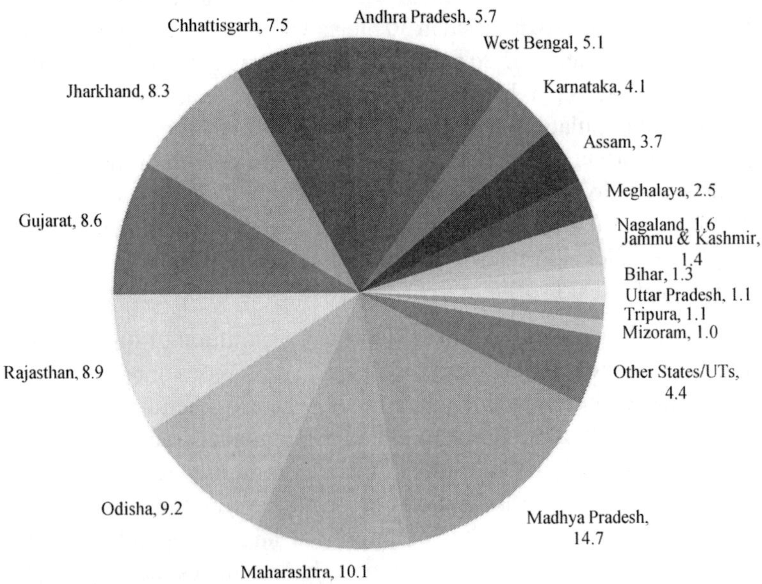

Source: Primary Census Abstract for Total population, Scheduled Castes and Scheduled Tribes, 2011, Office of the Registrar General & Census Commissioner, India[2]

Figure 15.1: State's share of scheduled tribes (ST) to total ST population of India

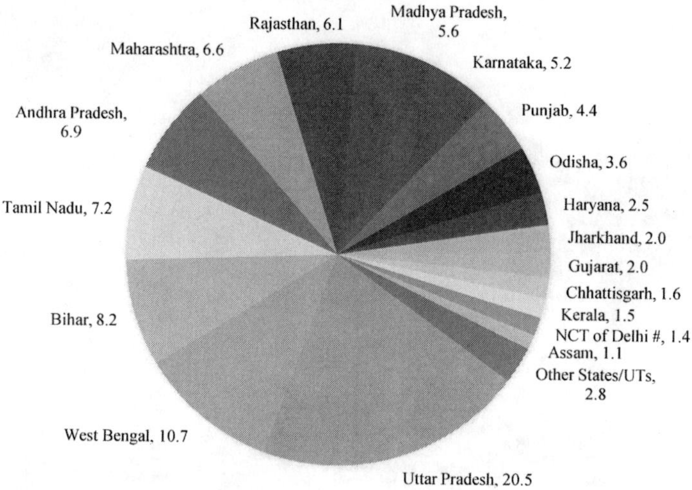

Source: Primary Census Abstract for Total population, Scheduled Castes and Scheduled.

Figure 15.2: State's share of scheduled caste (SC) to total SC population of India.

Tribes, 2011, Office of the Registrar General & Census Commissioner, India[3]

Scenario of Scheduled Castes, Minorities and Disabled Persons

The Scheduled Castes constitutes of 12 per cent of the total population in Jharkhand, comprising of 2 million males and 1.94 million females (Census, 2011). The rural-urban distribution of SC population is Jharkhand was 79 per cent and 21 per cent respectively (Census, 2011).

Table 15.4: Demographic Statistics of SCs in Jharkhand

State	***Year***	***Jharkhand***
Total Population	2001	26,945,829
	2011	32,988,134
Decadal Growth in Percent	2001	22.4
SC Population	2001	3,189,320
	2001	3,985,644
Total Male Population	2001	2,043,458
Total Female Population	2001	1,942,186
Decadal Growth in Percent	2011	25
Percent STs in State to total population of State		12.8
Percent STs in the State to total ST population in India		2

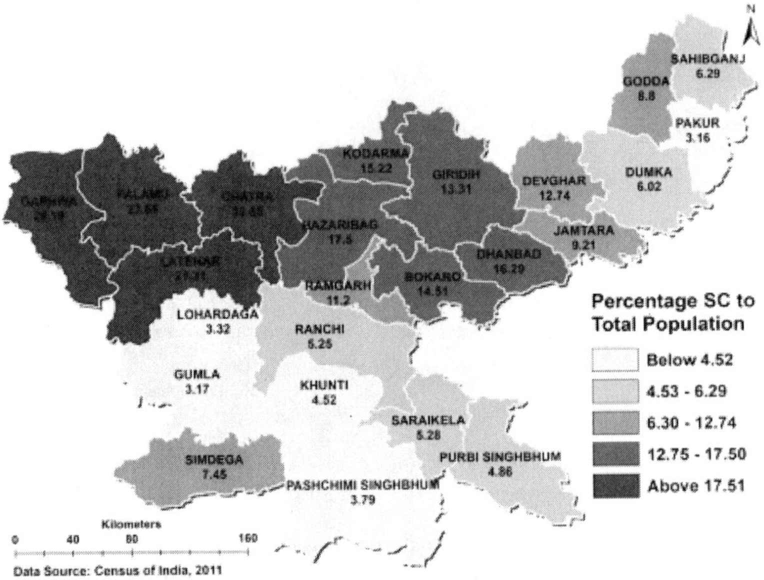

Source: Census of India, 2011.

Map 15.2: Percentage of SC population in Jharkhand.

The minority religious communities in India which comprises of Muslims, Sikhs, Christians, Buddhists, Zoroastrians (Parsis) and Jains are notified as minority communities by Government of India in Gazette under Section 2(c) of the National Commission for Minorities Act, 1992.

Table 15.5: Distribution of Minority population across districts (2011) (%)

Districts	*Muslim*	*Christian*	*Sikh*	*Buddhist*	*Jain*	*Minority Proportion*
Garhwa	14.72	1.30	0.01	0.03	0.00	16.05
Chatra	11.19	0.63	0.09	0.00	0.01	11.92
Koderma	14.94	0.17	0.13	0.00	0.14	15.38
Giridih	20.80	0.60	0.04	0.03	0.06	21.52
Deoghar	20.28	0.40	0.01	0.01	0.02	20.73
Godda	22.02	2.88	0.01	0.01	0.01	24.92
Sahibganj	34.61	7.23	0.02	0.02	0.01	41.89
Pakur	35.87	8.43	0.04	0.03	0.02	44.39
Dhanbad	16.08	0.42	0.36	0.01	0.05	16.92
Bokaro	11.71	0.67	0.20	0.09	0.10	12.77
Lohardaga	20.57	3.63	0.01	0.01	0.00	24.23
Purbi Singhbhum	8.89	1.32	1.68	0.04	0.07	12.00

(Contd...)

Palamu	12.28	0.32	0.04	0.01	0.01	12.66
Latehar	9.60	6.55	0.02	0.02	0.00	16.19
Hazaribagh	16.21	0.99	0.08	0.00	0.10	17.38
Ramgarh	13.59	0.76	0.54	0.01	0.06	14.96
Dumka	8.09	6.54	0.02	0.02	0.01	14.68
Jamtara	20.78	0.56	0.07	0.01	0.10	21.52
Ranchi	14.09	6.66	0.17	0.03	0.09	21.04
Khunti	2.47	25.65	0.01	0.05	0.03	28.21
Gumla	5.02	19.75	0.02	0.05	0.00	24.84
Simdega	2.52	51.14	0.01	0.13	0.02	53.81
Pashchimi Singhbhum	2.54	5.83	0.06	0.03	0.00	8.46
Saraikela-Kharsawan	5.97	0.76	0.10	0.02	0.01	6.86
Jharkhand	14.53	4.30	0.22	0.03	0.05	19.12

Source: Census of India, 2011.

Of the total population in Jharkhand, 19 per cent belong to religious minorities. The proportion of minorities across the districts of Jharkhand is shown in Table 15.5.

Across the minority groups, a large share of Muslim population is found in Jharkhand followed by Christians. The proportion of Muslims was highest in Pakur followed by Sahibganj, while Simdega district had the highest proportion of Christians. The other three minority communities i.e. Sikhs, Buddhist and Jains were meagrely distributed across the districts of Jharkhand. The districts with greater concentration of minority population in Jharkhand were Simdega (53.81 percent), Pakaur (44.39), Sahibganj (41.89) and Khunti (28.21).

The total number of Disabled Persons in India was reported to be 26.81 million, with 7 lakhs disables residing in Jharkhand (Census, 2011). The per cent of disabled person by type of disability is shown in Table 15.6. The proportion of disabled persons who were vision impaired (23.47 percent) was highest in the State followed by those with hearing impairment (21.54 percent).

Table 15.7 details the proportion of disabled persons across the two sectors in India and Jharkhand. The proportion of disabled persons was more or less same across the sectors in India. However, for Jharkhand, the proportion was slightly higher in the rural areas compared to urban areas. In Jharkhand, persons suffering from sight disability were higher in the rural areas, while those suffering from hearing disability were higher in the urban areas. The other forms of disability across the two sectors showed little variation.

Table 15.6: Total number of Disabled Persons with type of Disability

India/ State	*Total number of Disabled Persons*	*Type of Disability*							
		In seeing	*In Hearing*	*In Speech*	*In Movement*	*Mental Retardation*	*Mental Illness*	*Any Other*	*Multiple Disability*
India	2681 4994	5033 431	5072 914	1998 692	5436826	1505964	722880	4927 589	2116698
Jharkhand	7699 80	1807 21	1658 61	4668 4	147892	37458	20157	1123 72	58835
Percent		23.4 7	21.54	6.06	19.21	4.86	2.62	14.59	7.64

Source: Census of India, 2011.

Table 15.7: Total number of Disabled Persons by sector (Rural Urban) with type of Disability.

India/ State	*Sector*	*Type of Disability*							
		In seeing	*In Hearing*	*In Speech*	*In Movement*	*Mental Retardation*	*Mental Illnes*	*Any Other*	*Multiple Disability*
India	Rural	18.80	18.21	7.00	21.66	5.50	2.66	17.67	8.50
	Urban	18.71	20.53	8.49	17.13	5.87	2.78	19.98	6.51
Jharkhand	Rural	23.76	21.21	5.78	19.90	4.80	2.54	14.02	7.98
	Urban	22.45	22.69	7.04	16.80	5.08	2.90	16.58	6.46

Source: Census of India, 2011.

Economic Status of SCs/STs

Map 15.3 shows the SC household in rural Jharkhand which have a monthly income of less than 5000. On an average, 82 per cent rural households in Jharkhand are living with subsistence income. The districts having more than 92 per cent households with a monthly income less than 5000 were Latehar, Khunti, Lohardaga and Pakur.

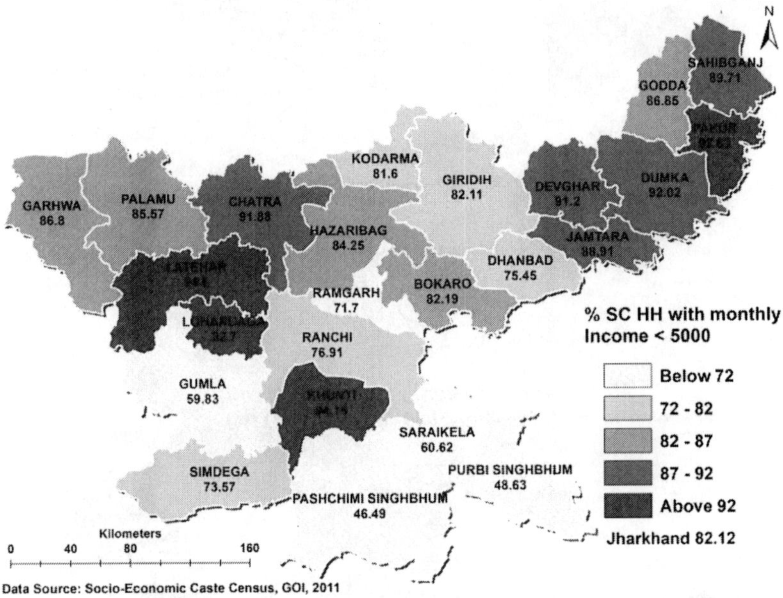

Map 15.3: Percentage of SC households with monthly income <5000 (Rural) (2011) (%)

The rural ST households, compared to the rural SC households in Jharkhand, although reveal a better picture evident from the State average, the disparity across the districts is disheartening. Districts like Pakur, Dumka, Giridih, and Khunti have more than 92 per cent rural ST household with a monthly income below 5000, much higher than the State average (82 percent).

Housing Conditions of SCs/STs

Almost 20 per cent of rural SC households in Jharkhand live-in one room with Kucha walls and Kucha Roof. The proportion of rural SC household living in such conditions was high in the districts of Pakur, Sahibganj, Palamu and Chatra.

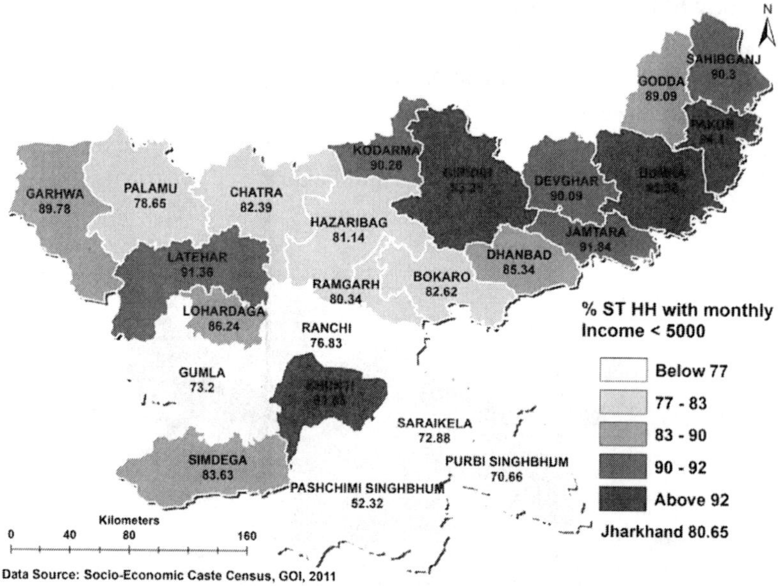

Map 15.4: Percentage of ST households with monthly income <5000 (Rural) (2011) (%)

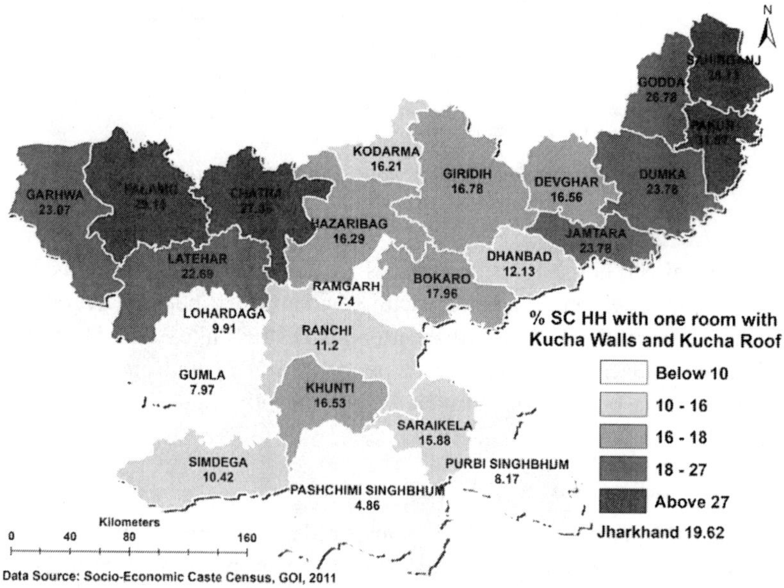

Map 15.5: Percentage of SC households with one room with Kucha walls and Kucha Roof (Rural) (2011) (%)

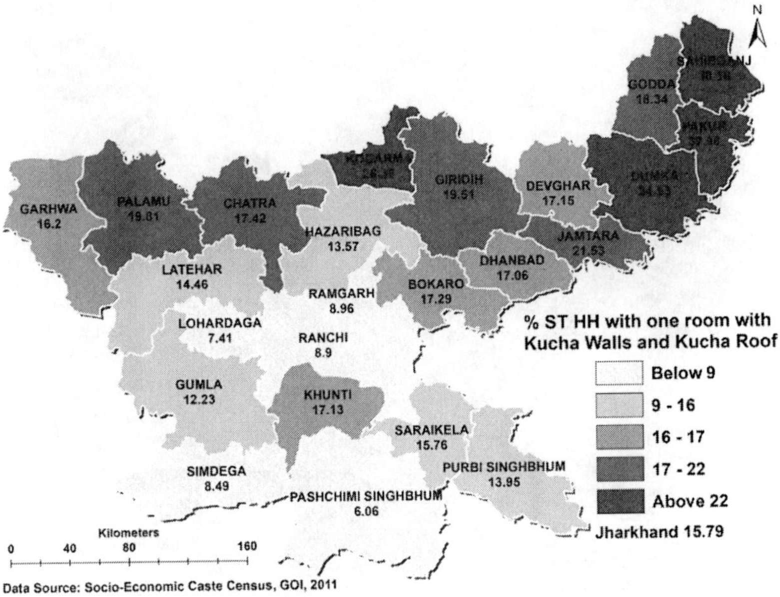

Map 15.6: Percentage of ST households with one room with Kucha walls and Kucha Roof (Rural) (2011) (%)

Even after 17 years of formation of the State, the tribal households in the rural Jharkhand (around 16 percent), are living in one room with Kucha walls and Kucha roof. Across the districts, the proportion is further worse. The district with greater proportion of rural ST households living in one room with Kucha walls and roof is Pakur (32 percent), followed by Sahibganj (30 percent).

Educational status of SCs/STs

In Jharkhand, 41 per cent rural SC households have adults above 25 years with no literacy. Chatra has the highest proportion of SC households with illiterate adults followed by Latehar. On the other hand, Paschimi Singhbhum district had the lowest proportion of SC households with illiterate adults.

The proportion of rural ST households with no literate adults above 25 years was highest in the district of Pakur followed by Sahibganj. The proportion of ST households with no li terate adults in these districts was much higher than the State average of 34 percent.

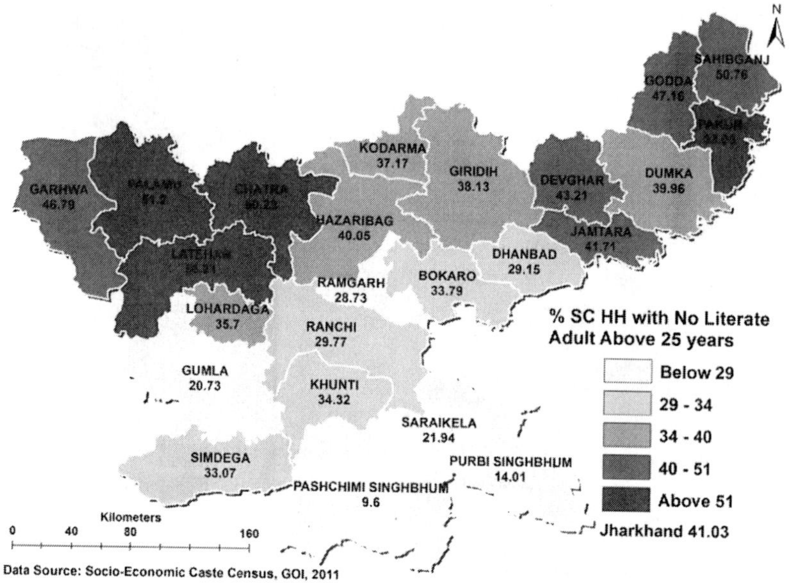

Map 15.7: Percentage of SC households with No literate adults above 25 years (Rural) (2011) (%)

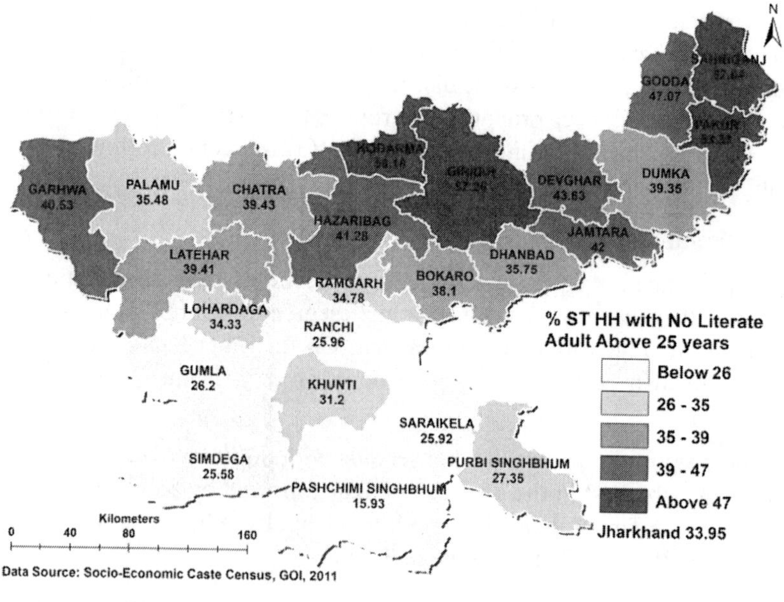

Map 15.8: Percentage of ST households with No literate adults above 25 years (Rural) (2011) (%)

Welfare Department, Government of Jharkhand

The Department of Welfare is mandated to look after the welfare of the most underprivileged sections of the society namely the Scheduled Tribes, Scheduled Castes, Backward Classes and Minorities and the task of bringing all-round development of these sections.

Welfare Schemes for the Tribal and other vulnerable groups in Jharkhand

The Scheduled Tribes (STs), Scheduled Castes (SCs), Other Backward Classes (OBCs), Religious Minorities, Senior citizens or Aged persons, Differently abled are considered as the vulnerable or disadvantaged groups of the society in terms of education, health, social security etc. This section seeks to portray a status report of the various schemes initiated by the Central/State Governments which were operational during the year 2017-18 and review their performance.

Education-related Welfare Schemes for the Vulnerable Groups:

- **Scholarship:** The Scheduled Tribes (STs), Scheduled Castes (SCs) and Other Backward Classes (OBCs) have poor educational attainments as well as poor access to educational infrastructure at all educational levels. To encourage their enrolment, the government provides scholarships at Pre-and Post-Matric levels.
- Pre-Matric Scholarship Scheme provides cash to the poor students belonging to the Scheduled Tribes (STs), Scheduled Castes (SCs) and Other Backward Classes (OBCs) studying at the Primary level i.e. Classes 1-4. The Day-Scholars and Hostellers receive a monthly Scholarship of Rs 50 and Rs 150 respectively for 10 months. In order to promote education at higher levels among these vulnerable groups, students undertaking Middle and High-school education i.e. the students of Class 5-10 are provided with educational incentives in the form of cash through Direct Cash Benefit in their bank accounts. The Day-Scholars and Hostellers among this educational cohort receive a monthly Scholarship of Rs 100 and Rs

  150 respectively for 10 months.

The status of the applications for the Pre-Matric Scholarship targeted for the Minority community during the years 2016-17 and 2017-18 depict that 20625 scholarships were renewed in 2016-17. A total of 15449 scholarships were renewed in 2017-18.In 2016-17, 40411 applied for scholarship, while 68752 applied for the fresh scholarship in 2017-18.

Table 15.8: Pre-Matric Scholarship for the Minorities, 2016-17

District	*Renewed 2017-18*	*Fresh 2017-18*	*Renewed 2016-17*	*Fresh 2016-17*
Bokaro	533	2947	70	1302
Chatra	2970	9979	n/a	6160
Deoghar	80	241	n/a	188
Dhanbad	1247	5209	3329	3272
Dumka	n/a	33	n/a	38
Garhwa	n/a	187	n/a	139
Giridih	n/a	2101	1415	1383
Godda	n/a	89	n/a	67
Gumla	401	1807	n/a	927
Hazaribagh	2412	8685	4584	6208
Jamtara	n/a	567	4	40
Khunti	571	1728	n/a	967
Koderma	34	1988	n/a	148
Latehar	438	4138	243	1040
Lohardaga	324	3855	n/a	1361
Pakur	389	4144	996	3242
Palamu	n/a	290	n/a	95
Pashchimi Singhbhum	148	178	7	256
PurbiSinghbhum	139	977	992	634
Ramgarh	383	1426	439	1259
Ranchi	4632	14970	8162	10089
Sahibganj	12	2059	384	767
Saraikela-Kharsawan	24	131	n/a	112
Simdega	1	663	n/a	717
Total	15449	68752	20625	40411

Source: Department of Social Welfare, Government of Jharkhand.

- **Post-Matric Scholarship Scheme** provides a yearly scholarship upto Rs 50,000 to ST/SC students whose family income is maximum Rs 2.5lakh a year, and OBC students whose family income is maximum Rs 1 lakh a year. Scholarship can be availed by the students enrolled in technical colleges both within and outside the state. Provision of prematric and post matric scholarship in the year 2016-17 amounted to Rs 52839.57 lakh. To provide scholarships in the year 2017-18, Rs 34090 lakh has been estimated for the prematric scholarship and Rs 41389 lakh for post matric scholarship, which has been proposed.

Table 15.9: Post-Matric Scholarship for Minorities, 2016-17and 2017-18

District	Renewed 2017-18	Fresh 2017-18	Renewed 2016-17	Fresh 2016-17
Bokaro	640	1996	678	1885
Chatra	85	360	198	445
Deoghar	20	423	95	698
Dhanbad	789	2996	898	2270
Dumka	364	1079	324	884
Garhwa	23	368	36	82
Giridih	240	810	195	898
Godda	221	1013	364	877
Gumla	70	347	119	193
Hazaribagh	2273	4403	1313	5084
Jamtara	24	216	28	152
Khunti	107	345	128	176
Koderma	22	132	43	218
Latehar	87	180	138	257
Lohardaga	361	530	314	1155
Pakur	454	2336	539	2275
Palamu	145	332	193	590
Pashchimi Singhbhum	59	265	79	214
PurbiSinghbhum	327	1514	346	922
Ramgarh	565	1224	580	1270
Ranchi	79	2172	1094	2331
Sahibganj	334	2198	170	1536
Saraikela-Kharsawan	63	271	54	172
Simdega	20	97	44	252
Total	**8085**	**25677**	**7970**	**24836**

Source: Department of Social Welfare, Government of Jharkhand.

The table 15.9 depicts the application of post matric scholarship for the minority for the years 2016-17 and 2017-18. In total, 7970 scholarships were renewed in 2016-17, while 8085 scholarships were renewed in 2017-18. In the State, 24836 applied for the fresh scholarship in 2016-17, while 25677 applied for the fresh scholarship in 2017-18.

- **Merit cum Means Scholarship:** The scholarship is offered to students from the minority communities in the technical institutions. The students whose family's income is or less than Rs 2.5 lakh per annum is eligible to avail this scholarship.

Table 15.10: Merit cum means (MCM) Scholarship for Minorities, 2016-17 and 2017-18

District	Fresh 2017-18	Renewed 2017-18	Fresh 2016-17	Renewed 2016-17
Bokaro	270	155	398	111
Chatra	66	44	274	54
Deoghar	41	28	93	39
Dhanbad	503	279	542	236
Dumka	66	19	39	9
Garhwa	86	31	112	46
Giridih	169	70	191	70
Godda	104	64	15	52
Gumla	46	14	42	9
Hazaribagh	190	126	305	129
Jamtara	35	7	20	4
Khunti	21	4	12	27
Koderma	43	21	60	n/a
Latehar	33	19	38	8
Lohardaga	32	15	35	11
Pakur	89	21	49	18
Palamu	78	52	132	49
Pashchimi Singhbhum	37	23	58	35
PurbiSinghbhum	272	215	494	260
Ramgarh	71	56	145	79
Ranchi	388	260	530	199
Sahibganj	147	44	123	42
Saraikela-Kharsawan	22	22	33	32
Simdega	8	7	11	55
Total	**2817**	**1596**	**3901**	**1525**

Source: Department of Social Welfare, Government of Jharkhand.

Table 15.10 depicts the application of merit cum means scholarship for the minority in years 2016-17 and 2017-18. The scholarship is provided for education in professional and technical colleges. In total 1525 and 1596 scholarships were renewed in 2016-17 and 2017-18respectively. The total number of fresh scholarship applied in 2016-17 and 2017-18 was 3901 and 2817.

- **Sports Scholarship:** The scholarship aims to encourage the students in sports at District, State and National level. It is awarded to the ST/SC/OBC students for their outstanding sports performance. Other provisions of the scholarship provide assistance in the organization of sports events and provide sports tools and equipments.

- **Exemption from examination fees:** This is state initiated scheme aimed to increase education among the students of the deprived community of ST, SC and OBC. They are exempted from the examination fees in matriculate and Intermediate examinations conducted by the Jharkhand Academic Council. This encourages the students to continue their schooling, which would have otherwise dropped out due to the inability to pay the examination fees. They are exempted from paying Rs 125 in matriculation and Rs 175 in intermediate.
- **Cycle Distribution:** The distance from the school is one of the primary reasons for non-enrolment or low attendance. The problem is more serious among the students of ST/SC/OBC who already have fewer means to send their children to school. The scheme provides Rs 3000 through DTB to the students of ST/SC/OBC and other minority groups enrolled in class 8. About 11.43 lakh students have benefitted through the scheme as on 2016-17.
- **Pahariya Mid-Day Meal Scheme:** The scheme aims to provide the especially backward tribal communities with good education and nutrition. The 32 Pahariya schools in the Santhal Pargana provide books, copies, stationary and other study material. It also provides nutritious mid-day meal to the students. The scheme covers the cost of Rs 10.90 per meal per child. This promotes education and health in the tribal areas of the Santhal Pargana.
- **Guaranteed Education Loan Scheme:** The scheme aims to ensure that the continuation of higher education among the poor students belonging to ST, SC and OBC. The government has launched this new scheme to guarantee the provision of education loan through the banks to such students.

Healthcare related Welfare Schemes for the Vulnerable Groups:

- **Health Assistance:** It provides free medical assistance to the poor families of ST/SC/OBC. The District Welfare Officer provides a maximum of Rs 3000 and District Commissioner provides Rs 10,000 through the district committee.
- **Pahariya Health Scheme:** The health condition among the tribals of Santhal Parganais poor. They often remain excluded and inaccessible to the medical facilities. This scheme makes medical facilities accessible as well as affordable to them. There are

18 Pahariya health-care centers opened in the Pargana area by the Welfare Department. The centers provide facilities of medical checkup, Auxiliary Nurse Midwifery (A.N.M.), Male Health Specialists and medicines. Each centre has received a remuneration of Rs 103596 for A.N.M., Rs 103596 for Male Specialists, Rs 19200 for medical checkups, and Rs 1,40,000 for medicines. Thus, a total of Rs 366392 has been allotted to each medical centre in the Santhal Pargana.

- Rural Hospital: The ST, SC and other minority groups often livein geographically remote areas, making basic facility such as health, mostly inaccessible. Therefore, the scheme aims to provide health facilities in such rural areas by establishing hospitals with both OPD and IPD. Currently, 9 rural hospitals are to be established for the 50 rural identified areas.

Welfare Schemes of Housing for the Vulnerable Groups

- **Birsa Munda Awas Yojna:** The STs have been homeless or live with less stable residence. This makes them more susceptible to health, financial and social exploitation. This State initiated scheme provides ST families with free residence at the rate of Rs 1.35lakh per household.

Welfare Schemes for Social Security and Social Protection of the Vulnerable Groups

The ST and SC are considered minority not just in educational or economic terms, but because they face immense social discrimination and exploitation. The government implements the following Acts to protect them from any acts of atrocity.

- **ST Pension Scheme:** This scheme provides a monthly pension of Rs 600 to the 9 tribes: Asur, Birhiya, Birhor, Birjiya, Korwa, Mal Pahadiya, Sariya Pahariya and Sabar.
- **ST/SC Prevention of Atrocities Act:** This Act protects the members of ST and SC community from atrocities, which can be physical or verbal. The culprit can be charged any amount from Rs 10,000 to Rs 2lakh, depending on the nature and degree of the atrocious act. If such an act leads to the death or inability of the prime earner of the family, then Rs 2lakh is compensated to the family. Further, in case of physical and sexual violation of a female, a compensation of Rs 50,000 is provided.
- **Village Development of the Martyr Scheme:** This new scheme seeks to reward the martyrs of the ST/SC community and promote

rural development. Under the scheme, the villages of such martyrs are developed through road construction, better connectivity, and house construction, provision of drinking water, Anganwadi and health centers. The government provides free residence to the villagers at Rs 2.63lakh per household.

- **Implementation of Forest Rights Act, 2006:** The Act is for the welfare of the STs residing in the forests and other traditional forest-dwellers. Due to the fast rate of industrial development, the tribes who traditionally dwell and depend on the forest, often come in conflict with the outsiders over the use of land and forest. The Act issues legal land rights, patta, to traditional forest dwellers, residing there for more than75 years, and to Scheduled Tribes, who have been residing there for more than 5 years.
- **Citizen Protection Act, 1955:** The Act aims at better governance and prevention of discrimination against the members of ST and SC at public places. It criminalizes discriminatory entry at restaurants, hotels, worship places etc. The District Magistrates are expected to spread awareness through hoardings and street-plays.
- **Article 275(1) of Constitution:** The Act is for the promotion of welfare for the STs of the tribal areas. It provides for the development of Eklavya schools, P.C.C. roads, health centers, rural hospitals, tribal art and culture centers, hostels, solar lights and drinking water. xiii. Welfare Schemes for Livelihood security among the Vulnerable Groups:
- **Grants via Pre-Jha Foundation for Skill Development:** This scheme aims to generate employment among the ST/SC/OBC and other minority groups. Many skill development centers have been opened through the Welfare Department at the district level to provide necessary skills to the unemployed youth. The centers run through the grants provided by the Pre-Jha Foundation. This will increase self-employment and income among such minority groups.
- **Training centre for lac cultivation:** The people from ST still derive their income from the forest resources. To facilitate their livelihood, the government has launched Lac Development Scheme. One of the provisions of the scheme is to provide them with training related to lac cultivation. For the purpose, 98 training centers for lac cultivation have been established.

- Livelihood Training: The scheme aims to encourage self-employment among the ST, SC, OBC and other minority groups. For the purpose, many skill development training centers will be established. These centers will impart skills to the unemployed persons belonging to these disadvantaged groups to be self-employed.
- **Jharkhand Tribal Empowerment and Livelihood Project:** The project aims to increase self-employment, ensure food security and reduce unemployment and poverty among the STs. This is to be implemented in 14 districts where the tribal population exceeds 50 per cent of the population. The poor ST of 164 panchayats and 1330 grams of 30 blocks are to be benefitted from the scheme.
- **Special Central Assistance to Tribal Sub Plan:** The plan aims to increase income and employment of the tribals through special assistance in agricultural and primary activities. It assists in agriculture, horticulture, soil enrichment, water and soil conservation, and forest, management.

Welfare Schemes for Reduction of Poverty among the Vulnerable Groups

- **Targeting the Hardcore Poor Scheme (THP):** The scheme aims to reduce extreme poverty among the female-headed households of the STs. For the purpose, various poverty reduction and skill development programs will be initiated with about 2000poor female-headed households of the ST community. It will first be implemented in Dumka and West Singhbhum. About 5 THP will be formed in both districts. Each THP aims to benefit about 200 households.
- **Provision of Subsidized Asset:** Encouraging livelihood is one of the major ways to increase income and reduce poverty. Therefore, the scheme provides assets at a subsidized rate to the ST, ST, OBC and other minorities for the purpose of starting and enhancin g their business.
- **National Family Benefit Scheme:** This scheme aims to reduce poverty among the BPL families whose primary earner has died. It prevents the families from slipping into poverty, by providing a sum of Rs 20,000.

Welfare Schemes for the Aged Persons/Senior Citizens

- **Schools, hostels, old-age homes:** The poor, old, weak, disadvantageous, widows, orphans, differently-abled are to be cared for by providing them old-age homes, hospitals, remand homes, children and women homes, and working women hostels.

- **Pension Scheme for the HIV/AIDS persons:** The persons affected with HIV/AIDS are socially dejected which often results in less economic opportunities. Therefore, the scheme provides monthly Rs 600 to the affected persons. 1434 persons have benefitted from the scheme in 2017.
- **State Social Protection Pension Scheme:** The scheme is for the welfare of the disadvantageous groups such as widows, differently-abled, people freed from bonded labour and other weak groups. Persons belonging to such groups who are above the age of 60 can avail the benefits of the scheme. They are provided with financial assistance of Rs 600 per month. In 2015, 1,25,846 persons were benefitted from this scheme. The number of the beneficiaries increased to 2, 76,733 in 2017.
- **Indira Gandhi National Old Age Pension Scheme:** A monthly pension of Rs 600 is given to the persons who are 60 years or above with a maximum income of Rs 7995 in rural areas and Rs 9974 in urban areas. In 2015,7,22,053 persons benefitted from the scheme. The number of the beneficiaries has increased to 9, 04,270 in 2017. Also, new old age homes have been established in Deoghar, Pakur and Godda. A proposal of 100-beds old age homes has been made in Ranchi, Saraikela and Jamtara. The first part of the construction of 50-beds old age home has been initiated. An "After Care Home" has been inaugurated in Dumka.
- **Indira Gandhi National Widow Pension Scheme:** The scheme was implemented on the recommendations of the Tendulkar Committee. A monthly pension of Rs 600 can be availed by the widows between the ages 40-79. The BPL widows are covered under the scheme.
- **State Widow's Honour Pension Scheme:** It is a state-initiated scheme which provides a pension of Rs 600 per month to the widows above the 18 years. The total number of beneficiaries in 2017 was 1,06,828 persons.
- **Workers State Insurance Scheme:** The beneficiaries are the workers of the organized sector which employs a minimum of 10 workers. The workers whose monthly income is or less than Rs 15,000 can avail th e benefits of the scheme. It provides health insurance.

Welfare Schemes for the Differently-abled Persons

- **Differently-abled Welfare Scheme:** The differently abledintellectually/visually/physically challenged can avail the benefits of the scheme by pro viding them appropriate technological assistance, organizing special workshops and implementing measures for their social and economic inclusion.
- **Education** is encouraged among the differently-abled by providing themscholarships. The **Scholarship for the Differently-abled** provides scholarships to children in schools and colleges. Further, the scheme aims to promote education by providing **hostels for the differently abled**. The hostels will be provided to the school and college going students, who are affected by different disabilities.
- **Indira Gandhi National Differently-abled Pension Scheme:** The poor differentlyabled persons whose income in rural areas is less than Rs7996 or Rs 9975 in urban areas per year, and is affected by 80 per cent disability is awarded a monthly pension of Rs 600. In 2015, the number of persons who benefitted from the scheme was 17,147. The number of the beneficiaries increased to 19,953 in 2017.
- **District Disability Rehabilitation Centre:** A centre is to be established in each state to provide assistance and advice to the differently-abled persons. The centre has been established in 6 districts of Jharkhand, namely, Ranchi, Dumka, Palamu, Hazaribagh, Jamshedpur and Dhanbad. The centre especially assists in rehabilitation, awareness pro grams and informing about the various welfare schemes.

A Composite Rehabilitation Centre will be launched in Ranchi for the education of the differently abled children. **UDID program** has been launched to provide them with disability recognition identity cards. These cards facilitate the procurement of benefits of welfare schemes.

- **Swami Vivekanand Differently-able Self-Reliant Encouragement Scheme:** This is a state-initiated scheme which provides monthly Rs 600 to the differently abled persons. The scheme covers persons from different categories to make most differently abled self-reliant. In total, 1,67,241 persons have benefitted from the scheme in 2017.

Table 15.11: Progress in the Social Welfare Schemes, 2015 and 2017

Social Welfare Schemes	*Number of Beneficiaries*	
	2015	*2017*
State Social Security Pension	125846	276733
Swami Vivekananda Differently-able Self-Reliant Encouragement Scheme	-	167241
Indira Gandhi National Differently-abled Pension Scheme	17147	19953
Indira Gandhi National Old Age Pension Scheme	722053	904270
State Widow's Honour Pension Scheme	-	106828
Pension Scheme for the HIV/AIDS persons	-	1434

Source: Department of Social Welfare, Government of Jharkhand.

- **Minority Committee:** A Jharkhand Minority Committee has been formed for the welfare of the religious minority community. In 2016, 2854 persons have been sent to the Haz pilgrimage. The number rose to 3133 Haz pilgrims in 2017. Scholarship applications of 44,396 minority students have been sent to the central government in 2016-17. It has been targeted to provide scholarships to 90570 students in 2017-18.

Conclusion

Undoubtedly, the State Government has made sincere efforts to ensure the overall development of the tribal and other vulnerable community; albeit it has little achievement to its claim. The status of underprivileged in Jharkhand has shown little improvement since its inception. They continue to lead a deplorable life, with subsistence economy and lack of basic amenities such as drinking water and improved sanitation. Owing to their condition, the human development indicators in the State has showed marginal improvements. Among the underprivileged groups, the tribal community faces more problems, given their inability to access resources. Therefore, for an inclusive development, the State requires to focus in specific areas of women development which require attention. The low socio-economic development and their habitation in various ecological and geo-climatic conditions ranging from plains to forest to hills and inaccessible areas are the main reasons for low literacy among the Scheduled Tribe. States has to address the development need of its vulnerable communities.

However, the Ministry is implementing the education-oriented schemes which include PostMatric Scholarship for ST students, Hostels for ST girls and boys, Establishment of Ashram School in Tribal Sub-Plan Areas, Up gradation of Merit through coaching and remedial classes, Rajiv Gandhi

National Fellowship for ST students, Top Class Education for ST students and National Overseas Scholarship for ST students to improve the literacy level belonging to the Scheduled Tribe communities, besides usual reservation for ST students. These are supplementary to the efforts made by other Ministries.

References

Census of India 2011 Office of the Registrar General & Census Commissioner, India

Jharkhand Economic Survey 2017-18, Department of Finance, Government of Jharkhand.

Primary Census Abstract for Total population, Scheduled Castes and Scheduled Tribes, 2011,

Office of the Registrar General & Census Commissioner, India. 238.

Chapter - 14

Anthropology and Rural Development

— Vijay Prakash Sharma

Introduction

Honorable Prime Minister of India, Narendra Damodar Das Modi requested the scientists to develop Social Science technique to address the social needs, while addressing the 106th Indian Science Congress on 3rd January 2019. Responding to his call, I would like to present this article depicting the anthropological research technique and its relevance in rural development.

Anthropological studies begin with study of rural (tribal) people round the globe in 18 th century of Christian era. Rural development and social change remained major concern of Anthropologists since the inception of this academic discipline. Anthropologists apply holistic approach in understanding rural problems to suggest the development requirement of a particular community, village or ethnic groups. They assume that there is a connection in social relations, social organizations and development.

Development implies orderly movement of an organism or a social system from a lower level of functioning to a higher level of functioning and integration. Anthropologists generally considered development as a state of society providing for the security and necessities of its members, adopting itself continuously with the changing conception of good life. Development represents an increase in the capacities of the society to organize for its own objectives and to carry out its programmes more effectively.

An examination of development projects indicated that while technical and economic issues are often adequately addressed in the project design, the people related variables frequently get relegated to the background.

Thus, when people do not use irrigation water, which happen quite often, it may not be due to any engineering flows in the construction of channels; the trouble may be due to human factors initially ignored in the project design. Technically and economically sound projects are not necessarily socially sound as well. [Mathura, 1995,]

Environmental issues are two fold in nature- 1) The limit to the natural resources and 2) pollution and stress that result from the exploitation of these resources. Displacement comes under the 2 nd one. Let us examine some cases of displacement in our country and Its Consequences. Ecological control is necessary that deals with both the above mentioned aspects i.e.1) by changing the mix of these resources in favor of renewable resources and 2) by inducing an improvement in resource productivity. For these purposes, it would be necessary to deploy a combination of measures, viz, investment, research for development of environment friendly technologies, economic incentives and disincentives. However, there needs to be a difference in the approach to the problem in the developing countries (including ours) from that in the developed countries. The environmental standards cannot be the same for these two sets of economies. The immediate environmental concerns and issues in developing country like India are- land degradation, soil erosion, disaster management, over chemical treatment of crop production, air and water pollution including ground water pollution, recycling of waste, increasing pressures on life supporting systems, and socioeconomic impact of development projects including human displacement and loss of bio diversity. Since the independence of India, much is being done in the name of Tribal development to bring these millions of people in the mainstream of the advanced and modern cultural groups. Irrigation facilities were created for development of agriculture in 3 rd and 4 th five year plans and also completed by the government.

Poverty focused development strategies can work only if planners try and understand the people for whom they plan development. It is not enough to produce plans, which look excellent on paper. Plans designed to assist development of the poor people must take account of their needs, and their capacity to absorb benefits from the development process.

Most plan failures can be attributed not to technical imperfections in their formulation, but usually to a lack of understanding of socio – cultural realities on the part of both planners and project administrators. [Mathura, 1995]

The development process has failed to end the deprivation faced by the marginalized communities in most of the developing nations. In fact, it has contributed to the social reproduction of marginalization. According to

Human Development Report the marginalized people are emerged as victims of these processes of development. In every society there are some sections of people who are deprived of socio-economic opportunities for their sustenance and are victims of social, cultural and political exclusion. Let us examine some problems of tribal's in Jharkhand and elsewhere.

Importance of anthropology in Development: Global perspective

Anthropologists have long made practical contributions to planned change and policy.

However, many have also studied development as a field of academic enquiry in itself. These studies have challenged the dominant development discourses, its key assumptions, representations, and paved for alternative ways for development. Major issues which call for an anthropology of development include:

- The social and cultural effects of economic change
- The social and cultural effects of development projects

Anthropologists in development

Anthropologists are now employed in growing numbers by development agencies, organisations and private consultancy firms. A discussion of applied anthropology does not therefore simply raise questions of what a professional anthropologist might do. The type of work which professional anthropologists are asked to undertake can vary considerably. They may include applied research to produce supporting data for planned interventions; contributions to the appraisal and evaluation planning of development projects; or attempting to build local participation into the project. Assignments can vary from a short consultancy job lasting a few weeks, to a placement on a project for several years as one of the full-time staff.

Some of the important positions that anthropologists are occupying in development agencies are:

1. Social Development Advisors (SDA).
2. Consultants
3. Research officers
4. Counselors
5. Advocacy role

Apart from the strict routine duties of anthropologists in development agencies, they are increasingly becoming a mediator between the developers and those to be 'developed.' Anthropologists are trained skeptics: they tend to argue that situations and ideas are usually more complicated than is immediately apparent; they believe that no fact or detail is too trivial to be considered; they may prefer quality to quantity; they are rarely ready to offer conclusions or advice in terms of straightforward course of action.

Anthropologists are well equipped to monitor the process of project implementation, which in effect is the task of monitoring social change. To do this, a combination of national and expatriate anthropologists, with both men and women involved, will be able to draw on their different skills and perspectives in order to present different, though mutually reinforcing, and analyses of events.

Anthropologists are involved in project design, appraisal and evaluation by national and international NGOs and aid agencies. Since the Second World War the notion of the project has become central to mainstream development activity, whether centered on large scale infrastructural work such as building of a dam or bridge or softer areas such as health or education provision. Projects tend to pass through a series of staged activities, often known as the project cycle.

By the 1960s and 1970s, the World Bank and United Nations were promoting what they termed "Integrated Rural Development", in which conventional planning methods were cast aside in favor of a measure of community participation in setting needs and a more comprehensive approach to tackling problems on a number of sect oral fronts simultaneously.

In consequence, a number of anthropologists were employed in carrying out impact studies among the local community to whether or not project's objectives have been met.

The appearance of what has been termed 'advocacy anthropology' by its practitioners (Miller 1995) has involved itself with the efforts of indigenous people to gain more control over their lives (Escober 1992).

According to Vidyarthi (1978), "the scope of research in the field of applied research in India is very wide especially when the whole traditional society is in the process of large scale transformation. In proportion to the magnitude of the task, the output to the applied social anthropologists and sociologists has not been adequate. Though, role of the social anthropologists and other behavioral scientists in the various fields of national reconstruction is acknowledged, their impact and contributions have not been as desired. There are many reasons for such a situation of applied social sciences in this country. The role of social anthropologists has not been well defined in the bureaucratic machinery of the State and Central Governments. There is no unanimity even among the anthropologists themselves regarding their roles as analysts, advisers, and co-operators. It seems that the applied social scientists in India should gracefully accept the various roles suggested above if certain conditions are satisfied. Firstly, he should have appropriate status in organizational setup, and secondly, once a subject for investigation is agreed upon through consultation, he must be free to draw up design and the tools of investigations, and thirdly, he must be able to present his findings at the highest policy level."

Writing on categories of applied anthropologists in India Vidyarthi (1978, 176-177) clarify five types such as:

(i) Those who act as consultants on the staff of administration and usually function under the control of the administrators.

(ii) The second types are those who are consultants primarily to the administrators but are outsiders i.e. they are not on the regular pay roll of the organization.

(iii) The researcher and administrator work together as co-administrators.

(iv) A social anthropologist is at least temporarily in actual charge of the development programme of a community which he and his associates are studying.

(v) The fifth category is represented by action anthropology of Sol Tax which can function only in an independent manner and in institutions where an action anthropologist can combine both action and research.

Elucidating the above in Indian context, Vidyarthi mentioned that there are several anthropologists in the first three categories but the fourth is represented only by two cases in India, First, in Tamia Block by B.H.Mehta, who has combined research and development under the auspices of Gondwana Research and Development Centre. The second by P.K. Bhowmik, who successfully combined the two processes of "helping and learning" among an ex-criminal tribe the Lodhas of West Bengal. The fifth category remained unrepresented in India although L.P. Vidyarthi initiated one Action anthropology programme at Neterhat Pat Region of Bihar but remained unfinished.

Applied and Action Anthropological intervention

While metropolitan India is moving along a different tangent, her valleys, ghatis and impenetrable forests provide refuse to cultures which retain elements of great antiquity. These are her advisees- a people with a remote past but no recorded history. If you want to search for the thread of life pattern of another age, take a journey to Jashpur in Chattisgarh, where the hinterland has made pursuit of the wildest tribe- the PAHARI KORWA- impossible.

Scholars like Dalton (1872), Majumdar (1847), and Vidyarthi(1958) have called them 'Primitive'. These tribes are comparatively backward in all spheres of life. Every aspects of their life possess a problem. Illiteracy, Simple economy, lowest standard of production and consumption, Semi nakedness, exploitation are their several complex problems.

Anthropological methodologies in development

The traditional methodology of social anthropology is what is known rather vaguely as 'participant observation': that is, the principle of living within a community for a substantial period of time – 'fieldwork', which might be expected to take one or two years – and immersing oneself in the local culture, work, food and language, while remaining an unobtrusive as possible. Many of the earliest anthropologists recorded their observations in a field diary, taking copious notes on all aspects of life, to be written up later as a monograph or ethnographic text, and without necessarily having a sense of the particular research questions they wished to address until they were well into their period of study or even until after they had returned home.

The blandness of participant observation as a technical methodological term in the 1960s and 1970s was gradually addressed by the growing body of more defined data collection techniques which anthropologists began to use under the general category of participant observation: case study collection, questionnaire surveys, structured and semi-structured interviewing, even computer modeling and the supplementing of qualitative material with quantitative data. Nevertheless, participant observation has retained its centrality to the work of many anthropologists, and anthropologists have in general retained their fondness of qualitative rather than quantitative data.

Applied anthropologists have drawn upon a number of key insights from wider anthropology in order to equip themselves for their work. In terms of research methodologies, the main change is that participant observation my normally now be undertaken within a tightly circumscribed time-frame, with a set of key questions replacing more open-ended blank notebook approach. Furthermore, the applied anthropologists knows that his or her findings will be appreciated far more if they can be presented concisely and made to include at least an element of quantification.

Use of participation

Like many of the currently fashionable development buzz words, the precise meaning of participation is elusive. Adnan et al. (1992) argue that meanings of participation can be broken down into three broad categories:

Participation is simply process in which information about a planned project is made available to the public. This may involve listening to people, more structured survey, or a formal dialogue regarding project options.

Participation may include project-related activities rather than mere information flows. This might involve using labour from the community, or a longer-term commitment by local groups to maintain services or facilities or even to plan for their future use.

There are people's own initiatives. These fall outside the scope of the project agenda. They are therefore, some arguing, the only true form of participation, for they are not imposed from the outside. If mobilization comes from the poorer sections of the community, it also truly empowering.

Participatory Rural Appraisal

The work of Robert Chambers has been extremely influential in this regard, in its attempts to counter excessively formalistic approaches to 'data collection' by development workers and professionals. Participatory Rural Appraisal (PRA) and its variants aim to enable rural people to plan and enact solutions to problems by analyzing their own knowledge of local conditions, facilitated by outsiders.

PRA involves training researchers to go to villages and spend time talking to groups of people 'in situ', encouraging those to express local problems and potential solutions in their own terms. Care is taken to represent as many different sets of interests as possible, and the focus in on mutual learning between researcher and informant.

Participatory research action

It is loose group of methodologies undertaken by agencies – such as NGOs – in areas of Asia and Africa. It assumes that the main objective of development is the fulfillment of the human urge for creative engagement, and does not therefore focus on poverty alleviation, 'basic needs' or structural change as the immediate goals to be tackled.

In practice, typically catalytic initiatives are brought about by educated outsiders, free of party and political allegiances, who encourage groups of people to get together to discuss the reason for their poverty and engage in their own social investigation. Group building follows, combined with discussion of prioritized actions which can be undertaken to address the principal causes of their poverty. External resources can be provided for support, but are not regarded as precondition for problem solving. The aim is to generate a 'progressive actionreflection rhythm' or 'people's praxis'.

Farming systems research

Local knowledge is seen as often situated in practice and in real situations. The emergence of farming systems research in late 1970s reflects many of the concerns that concentrate on local solutions from local knowledge for local problems. FSR focuses on the small farm as a basic system for research and development and attempts to bring about the strong involvement of farmers themselves in every stage of the research and development process (Conway, 1986).

The farmer's decision making is treated as being rational rather than guided, as was often supposed, by ignorance or conservatism. The objective is to improve the relevance and appropriateness of research, and this includes the participation of social scientists alongside biological scientists. FSR is also emphatically holistic, treating decisions and procedures for on crop within the wider farming system and its economic, social and environmental components.

Aid agency/ aid industry/ donors

Development aid or development cooperation (also development assistance, technical assistance, international aid, overseas aid, official development assistance (ODA), or foreign aid) is financial aid given by governments and other agencies to support the economic, environmental, social and political development of developing countries.

Donors today tend to give most aid to countries which they previously colonized: British give most aid to South Asia and Africa. while the Dutch are heavily involved in South East Asia, for example. Despite of several initial beginnings during colonial period, the real start of the administrative processes of aid transfer is usually taken to be the end of the Second World War when major multilateral agencies were established. The IMF and the International Bank for Reconstruction and Development (later to become World Bank) were set up during the Breton Woods Conference in 1944, while the Food and Agricultural Organization (FAO) was created as a branch of United Nations in 1945. In contrast what became known as 'bilateral aid' which was a transfer from one government to another, 'multilateral aid' came to involve a number of different donor acting in combination, none of whom directly controls policy. However, from the outset of donors such as World Bank were heavily influenced by the US and tended to encourage centralized, democratic governments with a strong bias towards the free market (Robertson, 1984). Meanwhile, various bilateral agencies were also established by the wealthier nations. These are the governmental organisations such as the United States Agency for International Development (USAID), or British Overseas Development Administration (ODA), both of which are involved in project and programme aid with partner countries.

Importance of Anthropology and Rural-Tribal Development: Indian perspective

Rural: As per the Webster's dictionary rural means "open land" and according to the United States census rural includes all persons living outside urban area and who live on farm. Agriculture is generally the main occupation in rural areas.

The very concept of rural development requires some elaboration. According to UNESCO, rural development is a process through which a series of quantitative and qualitative changes are brought about in rural areas for improved living conditions.

Rural development can be defined in several ways but for all practical purposes it means helping the poor people living in the villages in their economic development. The major objectives of the rural development programs are:

- To achieve enhanced production and productivity in the rural areas
- To bring about a greater socio-economic equity
- To bring about a spatial balance in social and economic development
- To bring about improvement in the ecological environment so that it may be conducive to growth and happiness, and
- To develop broad based community participation in the process of development

Main Lines of Activity

The activities considered important for rural development can be divided into the Agriculture and related matters, Irrigation, Communications, Education, Health, Supplementary employment, Housing, Training and Social Welfare.

1. Agriculture and related matters: The programme includes reclamation of available virgin and waste land, provision of commercial fertilizers and improved seeds, promotion of fruit and

vegetable cultivation, improved agricultural technique, supply of technical information, improved agricultural implements, improved marketing and credit facilities, provision of soil surveys and prevention of soil erosion, encouragement of the use of natural and compost manures and improvement of livestock.

2. Irrigation: The programme include provision of water for agriculture through minor irrigation works, e.g., tanks, canals, surface wells, tube-wells, etc., the intention being that the agricultural lands be served with irrigation facilities.
3. Communications: The road system on the countryside to be developed to link every village up to a maximum distance of half a mile by feeder roads through voluntary labour of the villagers themselves. Roads to be provided for, and maintained by the State or other public agencies.
4. Education: The community projects to provide for social education, expansion and improvement of primary and secondary education. Vocational and technical training be emphasized in all the stages of the educational programme.
5. Health: The Health Organization to provide primary health in the Development Blocks and a secondary health unit equipped with a hospital and a mobile dispensary at the headquarters of the Project area and serving the area as a whole.
6. Supplementary Employment: The unemployed and the under-employed persons in the village community be provided with gainful employment to such extent as is possible, by the development of cottage and small-scale industries, construction of brick kilns and saw mills and encouragement of employment through participation in the tertiary sector of the economy.
7. Housing: Apart from the provision of housing under various schemes, provide demonstration and training in improved techniques and designs for rural housing.
8. Training: The training of farmers, village level workers, project supervisors and other personnel to be carried out for skill up-gradation and enhanced efficiencies.
9. Social welfare: Make provision for audio-visual aid for instruction and recreation, for organizations of community entertainment, sports activities and fairs.

The rural development in India is expected through the initiative of external change-agents and outside resources, with the mutual involvement of the rural population. The external forces or resources can be useful to the extent of people's participation and, thus, rural development is a people's programme. The external agencies should phase out when villagers are educationally and economically advanced to carry on their own.

In general, it seems that the goal of rural development in India is eradication of poverty and unemployment which are the major twin causes of rural - poverty in India. All most all government programmes, (baring a few), are targeted in this direction but lack of proper implementation poses a big question mark.

Eradication of rural poverty is possible only by generation of income and employment opportunities for the rural poor especially for those who are at the lowest rung of the social order. Somehow, our modern development planners ignored employment and skill development potential inbuilt in our village Jajmani system since time immemorial. It is important to emphasize here that certain amount of diversification in the occupational opportunities available in the rural areas, have to be revived in non-farm sector as it has still many openings for absorbing a large number of rural people by inculcating in them the requisite skills in the context of emerging trades and demands.

Most people in rural and tribal areas are engaged in their traditional occupations which are land and forest based and therefore, had developed an orientation to think of their occupational life in terms of interaction with land and what so ever it can produce. In view of the constraints of providing land to a large number of landless people, certain attempts have to be made to create employment opportunities in non-land based occupations, mostly in small-scale, cottage and household industries. In the new strategies of development, the role of education as instrument of socio-economic-transformation has become more important.

The symbiotic relationship between education and rural economy is now being appreciated by policy makers and planners.

The emerging concept of development lays emphasis on people's participation which is a welcome departure from the yore of imperial rule. The role of education has been reexamined in the process of nation development. Education has been considered important source for developing human potentialities, increasing production and nations overall development. Kothari commission of education (1964-66) has recommended that there should be educational revolution and radical reform through internal transformation of the system of education so as to relate education to life's need and aspiration of the nation, but a lot has to be done in this area. Educational Institutions like universities can contribute a lot for rural development planning and implementation. For any machinery to work effectively, it needs to be placed in well trained hands. This becomes even more crucial in programme implementation initiative. Some of when it is about governance machinery.

The village governance initiative should aim to facilitate smooth functioning of Panchayati Raj Institutions and empowering grass root leadership. This should be done by training various stakeholders of village society through workshops and seminars by anthropologists. The idea is to help stakeholders get a perspective on various issues and help them in getting clarity about their roles and responsibilities. This should be done to build responsible and accountable leadership capacities at the grassroots level. Thousands have been deprived of benefits from NRGEA because of the present haphazard rural development the issues that people should be sensitized as part of this programme about government schemes, participatory planning, empowerment, communication skills, leadership skills, gender issues, stress management, social audit, Right to Information. (Sharma 2018).

Contribution of prof. Prabodh Kumar Bhowmik in applied and action anthropology

Writing about Prof. P.K. Bhowmick, Prof. Parlay Kumar Deb, Dean of Kalyani University, accepts that "indisputably the greatest doyen of Action Anthropology in West Bengal, remarkable for his critical perceptiveness and constructive judgment, Dr. Prabodh Kumar Bhoumick (1926-2003) was at once a fine scholar and an able teacher."——— "Dr. Bhoumick was a prolific writer both in English and Bengali."—— The tradition of anthropological/ sociological studies established by Dr. Bhowmick, still continues and will continue for all the time to come.(Deb 2006)

I would like to share some of my memories with Professor Probodh Kumar Bhowmick. He was an indefatigable scholar and great teacher as well as doyen of Action Anthropology in India. I came in his contact in 1974 at this institute. Since then, I always remained near and dear to him. I remained his associate. Prof. Bhowmick believed that it was possible – indeed necessary-to be interested in many things, a capacity he brought to the generosity and inclusiveness of his teaching and collegiality as well as to his scholarship. The range of his professional involvements was breathtakingly broad. He touched all most all aspects of anthropology, the science of man as well as the man itself (LODHAS).

Following professor P.K.Bhowmick, who successfully combined the two processes of "helping and learning" among an ex-criminal tribe the Lodhas of West Bengal-a model of Applied And Action Anthropology, today,

I have chosen to speak on His contributions in the field applied and action anthropology in India. Following his model the author also attempted a successful project for rehabilitation of PAHARI KORWAS in Chhattisgarh. Following professor P.K.Bhowmick's model of applied and action anthropology this paper presents the case study of a successful effort in the category to bridge the gap between knowledge and practice that is the felt need of the hour to have a clear understanding of contemporary situation of the above mentioned primitive tribal groups in ecological setting of Jashpur District of Chattishgarh for better planning and implementation of need based development programmes by the district authorities.

It was proposed in 1997 that an Applied and Action Anthropology programme be commissioned urgently to study contemporary life and culture of these people with special emphasis on their ecology and problems and to implement some kind of development project to better their lives.

The author started Applied and Action Anthropology intervention programme among PAHARI KORWA of Bagicha and Manora block in 1997 in collaboration with Tribal and Rural Development Institute of Jashpurnagar, Madhya Pradesh now Chhatishgarh.

There has been considerable fund allocation through all the 11 five years' plans of Government of India for development of these groups but the ground reality indicates towards their grim situation.

There are as many as 40 different tribal groups in the state of Chhatishgarh. These groups show considerable variation and assimilation their social and cultural traits, religious beliefs and norms as well as traditional economic pursuits vary from tribe to tribe and region to region. Out of these 40 tribal groups 5 tribal groups have been identified as primitive tribes based on the criteria of low literacy level, pre-agricultural level of technology, stagnant or diminishing nature of their population and subsistence level of economy. Pahadi korwa, Abujhamarias, Birhors, Baigas and Kamars have been designated as Primitive Vulnerable Tribal Groups (PVTGs) in Chhattishgarh. Out of these five PVTGs, Pahari korwa and Birhor are inhabits in Jashpur District. These communities face high level of poverty, malnutrition and limited access to health and nutrition services, manifested in high mortality rates. As a strategy for curtailing the once decreasing population of PTGs after 1979, Government of India and state government restricted sterilization among these PVTGs groups, attempting an increase in birth rate rather than a decrease in the mortality rate.

Though there were many anthropological studies conducted in the past about their life and culture as scholarly exercises but the regional variations in cultural pattern could not attract attention. Thus, the development plans made on the generalized findings were of little help.

The Phari Korwa Habitttion Area Jashpur

Jashpur district is divided into upper and lower Ghats. The upper gnat was previously under Khudia Zamindari comprised of Bagicha and Manora Tribal Development Blocks. It lies in the eastern corner of Chhattisgarh adjoining the border of Jharkhand and Orissa in the eastern side. It is between 22^0 21' 11" and 23^0 15' 21" North latitude and 83^0 24' 15" and 84^0 23' 53" East longitude. The Upper Ghat is an extension plateau covering 1384 sq. Kms which is about 1200 meters above sea level and is covered with the dense forests. This is boundary on north and west by Samri tahsil of Balrampur district. Above it there is another plateau, which is under the Khudia region, and the highest peak in this plateau is 'Pandarapat' which is about 1100 meter high from sea level. The elevated plateau called 'pat' is the main abode of Pahari Korwa. The upper Ghat is drained by the "Lawa and Shank" rivers and their tributaries. The most important river is Ib, which is its source in the Khudia high land and drains the western part of the upper Ghat and leaves Jashpur district boundary at Lawakera. The topographical situation of the khudia plateau, rising as it does to a great elevation above the adjoining area from which the approach lies through perspicuous forests, covered hill passages or Ghats, has however helped in the preservation amongst these people (Pahari Korwa) at the stage of hunting, food gathering and primitive agriculture. Thus, the eco-system has been inextricably bound with the life of Pahari Korwa.

After the merger of Jashpur state, the whole old Khudia region was divided into two revenue circles i.e. Sanna and Bagicha. Sanna revenue circle comprises 93 villages and Bagicha comprises 103 villages. These are the areas of main concentration of Pahari Korwas on the 'pat' areas and on the slope of the plateau of the Bagicha Block of Jashpur District. Bagicha and Manora Tribal Development Blocks were opened on 2.10.56 and 2.12.63 accordingly. As per the survey conducted by the Pahari Korwa and Birhor Development Agency in the year 2003, Pahari Korwa are found only in 12 villages of Manora and 76 villages of Bagicha Tribal development Blocks.

Pahari Korwa Villages and Size of Population

The difficult terrain, hard life and almost insufficient development have given rise to the smaller sizes of the villages. The above table reveals that out of 12 villages of Manora block 9 villages have population less than 50 persons. The smallest being Kardana village with population of 03 persons and the largest being GIDDHA with population of 94 persons. There are 3 villages which have population less than 100 persons. In Bagicha block out of 76 villages, 26 villages have population of less than 50 persons. The smallest being Chirodih and Bagdoll with a population of 01 and 05 respectively. The larger village's kamarima with the population of 893 persons. Due to undulating terrain and physical barriers like streams and subsequent inadequate availability of agriculture land at one place, larger villages have been divided into hamlets, 5 villages which have population above 400 persons. The details of villages according to size of population is given below in table 7

Table – 2 Villages according to size of population

Block	*Total no. of Villages*	*Less than 50*	*Population*					
			50 to 100	*100 to 150*	*150 to 200*	*200 to 250*	*250 to 300*	*300 and above*
Manora	12	9	2	1	-	-	-	-
Bagicha	80	30	15	4	10	5	2	10
Kunkuri	1	1						
Total	93	40	17	5	10	5	2	10

Source: Pahari Korwa development Agency, Jashpurnagar (as per 2015 Survey).

V.P.Sharma Model and Process of Intervention: The AAA Approach:

Another famous anthropologist Dr. Vijay Prakash Sharma's Applied and Action Anthropology approach is worth mentioning here. His associate's regular interaction with Pahadi Korwa of Jashpur resulted into confidence building. A Socio- Economic survey was carried out to know their problems and with the help of local government many developmental programmes were implemented by the Institute.

PRA exercises were conducted; training programmes were organized to bring these hill dwellers in the main stream of national life. A great Tribal congregation of PAHARI KORWA was organized at Hrrapat in 2000 where the institute developed the idea of bringing them on plains as plain settlers.

Regular interaction resulted into confidence building among most primitive tribal group PAHARI KORWA of Chhattisgarh. Counseling exercises were conducted; training programmes were organized to bring these hill dwellers in the main stream of national life by rehabilitating them on plains. A Tribal congregation of PAHARI KORWA was organized at Hrrapat in 2000 where the institute developed the idea of bringing them on plains as plain settlers.

After long persuasion 13 families agreed to settle down on plains. The Institute convinced government to sanction PTG Housing scheme for them. Finally, thirteen families themselves volunteered to construct their own houses. A cherished dream of TRDI, under Applied and Action Anthropology Programme became reality in 2004.

Now, it was important to introduce livelihood development programme for these most primitive tribal group PAHARI KORWA of Chattishgarh. For this, the institute implemented an UNDP supported Technology Management Programme (TMP). Under this programme, the institute has established block level Technology Resource Center (TRC) for Jashpur block in collaboration with Regional Research Laboratory, Bhopal.

Technology, employment and tribal each one of these terms has baffled and divided both the academicians and the practitioners since long, especially during last few decades. (Sharma and Singh, 1988)

Gurnar Myrdal, commenting on employment policy, emphasized in his epic study about Asia that" If by a miracle, the cultivators in South Asia could be induced to work more diligently, Production would rise dramatically".

Technology has been widely acknowledged as a critical parameter in the production system.

Generally speaking in a broader sense of the term, it has been identified practically with each and every aspect involved in the process of development or change, in fact technology represents in a way the unending human struggle for a better existence in his/her environment. "

If employment is to be generated in a tribal region, it should be and can be best done by promoting and strengthening the existing modes of production of the people with the inputs of modern science and technology in a manner that the advantages of the existing system as well as those created by men to exploit the resources are combined." (Quoted in Sharma and Singh, 1988).

The basic idea behind the project was to promote the traditional occupation and to introduce people's friendly new rural technology, upgrading of their skills, provision of raw materials and modern equipments, credit support and marketing facility for the development of livelihood of rural and tribal people.

In specific terms, the project aimed at setting up a Common facility centre for training, demonstration and popularization of small scale industrial packages for identified cluster of 6 villages in Manora block.

To strengthen the existing units under initial stage and to introduce new technologies that is tested in other tribal areas, two institutions UNDP and IFAD were approached through Government of Madya Pradesh and Government of Chhattisgarh, Tribal and Rural Development Institute adopted some villages under UNDP programme and introduced Mushroom production, Beekeeping, Beehive box manufacturing, Production of Herbal pesticides, production of fishing trap, Cultivation and storage of medicinal plants, wooden handicraft, MANDAR(beating drum)production, Bamboo basket production, Broom making and marketing, Leaf mat, leaf bowl and leaf plate production etc. were introduced in the Cluster of 25 tribal dominated villages in Manora block of Jaspur district.

In the second step, International Fund for Agricultural Development (IFAD) sanctioned watershed projects covering 6 villages for three years duration, Micro watershed code 4G2B6G -1. Total geographical area of the Watershed was 1109.214 hectares out of which750.826 hectares were treatable area. There were 299 households inhabited by 1714 people(Male-884,Female-830).

The institute completed three years **Shaila watershed project** (2003 - 6) covering Six villages sanctioned by CGTDP, Government of Chattisgarh, funded by International Fund for Agricultural Development (IFAD) and undertook following important activities:

1. 15 days training to 20 farmers on Fish Farming and Nylon net weaving.
2. Seven days training to 80 farmers on Bee –Keeping.
3. Two months training to two persons on Bee-box making skill.
4. Fifty two farmers were trained on Vermi-compost and construction of permanent pit.
5. Four farmers were trained in PAIRRA Treatment.
6. Three Anganwadi centers, one each in Shaila, Chattauri and Chirotoli village were constructed.
7. One EGS building was constructed at village Kardana.
8. Two water ponds were constructed at village Chattauri and are used for fisheries.
9. Sixteen Indira Awas for Primitive Tribal Group (Pahari Korwa) were constructed in village Chattauri. This is first ever novel attempt to inhabit hill dwellers on plane. The 16 Pahari Korwa families themselves contributed their labour in construction of their own houses. This is one of the most successful programme of the Institute.

10. Construction of 207 meters RRC village approach road at village Shaila using local M L A fund.
11. Under Goat Farming activity 45 goats were distributed to 14 Shelf Help Groups for pursuing sustained livelihood.
12. Construction of 14 Goat sheds in PTG colony of Chattauri village.
13. Building for Vocational Training centre was constructed at Village Chattauri.
14. Construction of one Stop –check- dam with canal at village Shaila.
15. Vegetable mini kits were distributed to 60 farmers.
16. 600 kgs Potato seeds were distributed among 34 members of BPL –SHGs.
17. 25 Women were trained in Bamboo craft through three months training programme.
18. 40 Women were provided training in Tailoring and Knitting works and they are earning livelihood through these skills.

Visible Impact of AAA Programmes

Activities and results under AAA programme enumerated in detail and the visible impacts of Applied and Action Anthropology intervention may be summarized as follows:

Self Help Groups

1. Regular saving habits inculcated among members.
2. Several members increased their income adopting income generating activities promoted by the institute.
3. Easy access to financial services ensured.
4. Collective decision- making promoted by institute now institutionalized.
5. SHG members taking up community development works.
6. Women are running Fare Price Shops successfully in the area.

Land and Water Management Programme

1. Waste- land converted into farm land helped the villagers in increased crop production.
2. In last Monsoon season, earthen and check-dams constructed by the Institute provided protective irrigation in moisture stress.
3. In canal constructed area some farmers took up two crops this year against one earlier. Some farmers extended their area of Kharif Crops.

4. Tanks constructed by institute helped in fish farming and supplementary irrigation.
5. Boulder and earthen checks proved to be of great help in checking soil erosion in the area.
6. Construction of proper approach road in village Chattauri is of great help in transport and communication to villagers.

Awareness campaign

1. The demonstration effect of transparency and timely payment of wages in the programmes run by TRDI generated high faith and enthusiasm among the tribal community.
2. Migration appears to have lowered down in comparison to previous years due to Creation of wage employment.

References

Allan R. Holmberg, 1955 "Participant Intervention in the Field," Human Organization, XIV, 1, 23–26. [Google Scholar]

Anthropology and Rural Economic Development, Nicholas, Pages 168-173 | published online: 10 Mar 2014.

Bhowmik, P.K.(1966) An Integrated Plan for the Development of Lodhas and other Tribal of Midnapur in West Bengal,Vanyajati,Vol. XIV, No-2.

C. C. Wrigley, 1964 "The Changing Economic Structure of Buganda," The King's Men, L. A. Fallers, ed. (London), 16–63. [Google Scholar]

Clifford Geertz, 1963Agricultural Involution (Berkeley). [Google Scholar]

Dalton, E.T. (1872) Descriptive Ethnology of Bengal (Reprint) Superintendent, Govt. Printing,

David Lewis. (2005). Anthropology and development; the uneasy relationship. London: LSE research online. Click here

David W. Brokensha, 1966 Social Change at Larteh, Ghana (Oxford,). [Google Scholar]

Donald N. Levine, 1965 Wax and Gold: Tradition and Innovation in Ethiopian Culture (Chicago). [Google Scholar]

E. E. Evans-Pritchard, 1940 The Nuer (Oxford,). [Google Scholar]

Elliott P. Skinner, 1960 "Labour Migration and its Relationship to Socio-cultural Change in Mossi Society," Africa, XXX, 375–400. [Google Scholar]

Emile Leynaud, 1966 "Fraternités d'âge et sociétés de culture dans la Haute-Vallée du Niger," Cahiers d'Etudes Africaines, VI, 41–68. [Google Scholar]

G. I. Jones, 1961 "Ecology and Social Structure Among the Northeastern Ibo," Africa, XXXI, 117–134;

Gardner, K., and Lewis, D., (1996). Anthropology Development and Post-modern Challenge. London: Pluto Press. Most of this note is taken from Gardner and Lewis's book. This is still the best book on development and anthropology so far I have seen Gilles Sautter, 1966 De l'Atlantique au fleuve Congo, une géographie de sous-peuplement (Paris,). [Google Scholar]

Harold K. Schneider, 1959 "Pakot Resistance to Change," Continuity and Change in African Cultures, W. H. Bascom and M. J. Herskovits, eds. (Chicago), 144–167. [Google Scholar]

Harold K. Schneider, 1966 "Turu Ecology: Habitat, Mode of Production, and Society," Africa, XXXVI, 254–268. [Google Scholar] http://sumananthromaterials.blogspot.com/2012/05/anthropology-and-development.html

J. van Velsen, 1961 "Labour Migration as a Positive Factor in the Continuity of Tonga Tribal Society," Social Change in Modern Africa, Aidan Southall, ed. (London), 230–241. [Google Scholar]

Jacques Daget, 1956 "La pêche à Diafarabé: étude monographique," Bulletin de l'Institut français d'Afrique Noire, ser. B, XVIII, 1–87. [Google Scholar]

Jean Gallais, 1967 Le delta intérieur du Niger: étude de géographie régionale, Mémoires de l'Institut Fondamental d'Afrique Noire, LXXIX (Dakar). [Google Scholar]

John Middleton, 1966 The effects of economic development on traditional political systems in Africa south of the Sahara (Paris), 12. [Google Scholar]

Lloyd A. Fallers, ed. 1964 The King's Men (London,). [Google Scholar]

Lucy Mair, 1957 Studies in Applied Anthropology, London School of Economics

Monographs on Social Anthropology, No. 16 (London,). [Google Scholar]

Majumdar. D.N (1959) Indian Anthropologists in Action, Journal of Social Research,Vol-II,No1-2

Majumdar. D.N (1973) Races and Cultures of India, Asia Publishing House, Bombay, 2nd reprint.

Mathur, Hari Mohan.1995 Anthropology and Development in Traditional societies, Vikas publishing House Pvt. Ltd. New Delhi.

Nicholas S. Hopkins, "Leadership and Consensus in Two Malian Cooperatives," The Anthropology of Development in Africa, David Brokensha, ed. [Google Scholar]

O'Driscoll, E. (2009). Applying the 'uncomfortable science: the role of anthropology in development. Durham Anthropology Journal. click here

Pierre Idiart, 1961 "Métayage et régimes fonciers dans la région du Faguibine (Cercle de Goudam-Soudan)," Etudes Rurales, II, 37–59; III (1961), 21–44. [Google Scholar]

Polly Hill, 1963 Migrant Cocoa Farmers of Southern Ghana (Cambridge,). [Google Scholar]

Polly Hill, 1963Migrant Cocoa Farmers of Southern Ghana (Cambridge,). [Google Scholar]

Raghabendra Chattopadhyay, Bhaskar Chakrabarti and Suman Nath. (2010). Village Forums or Development Councils: People's participation in decision-making in rural West Bengal, India. Commonwealth journal of local governance. click here

Robert Le Vine, 1966 Dreams and Deeds: Achievement Motivation in Nigeria (Chicago,). [Google Scholar]

Robert M. Netting, 1965, "Household Organisation and Intensive Agriculture: The Koyfar Case," Africa, XXXV (422–429;

Robert M. Netting, 1968Hill Farmers of Nigeria: Cultural Ecology of the Kofyar of the los Plateau (Seattle,);

S. F. Nadel, 1942 A Black Byzantium (London,). [Google Scholar]

Sachchidanand (1973) Planning, Development and Applied Anthropology in India, Indian Anthropologist, Vol.3.

See Kathleen Gough, 1968 "Anthropology: Child of Imperialism," Monthly Review, XIX, 11 (), 12–27. [Google Scholar]

See Philip Mayer, 1962 "Migrancy and the Study of Africans in Towns," American Anthropologist, LXIV, 576–592. [Google Scholar]

See Walter Goldschmidt et al., 1965 "Variation and Adaptability of Culture: A Symposium," American Anthropologist, LXV, 400–447;

Sharma, Vijay Prakash. 2014Thinking about Tribal Development through Integrated Village Development Model in Jharkhand, P. Dash Sharma edited book Livelihood and Health, Serial Publication, New Delhi,

Sharma, Vijay Prakash.2018 "Marginalization and Development", V.P.Sharma edited book Dreams and Reality of Rural Development in India, Kalpaz Publications, New Delhi. 2018

Sharma, Vijay Prakash.2018 An Introduction to Rural Development in India. Next Gen Publications, NewDelhi, Simon Ottenberg, 1959 "Iboo Receptivity to Change," Continuity and Change in African Cultures, W. H. Bascom and M. J. Herskovits, eds. (Chicago,), 130–143. [Google Scholar]

Simon Ottenberg, 1968 "The Development of Credit Associations in the Changing Economy of the Afikpo Igbo," Africa, XXXVIII (), 237–252. [Google Scholar]

Sol Tax(1959) Action Anthropology, Journal of Social Research, Vol-II, No. 1-2

Swapan Kumar Parmanik et.al. (2006) Explorations In Anthropology, The Institute of social research and applied anthropology, Bidisa.

Vidyarthi, L.P, (1972) Problems and Prospects of Tribal Development, Indian Anthropologist, Vol.2, N0. 2.

Vidyarthi. L.P, (1968) Applied Anthropology in India, [Ed.] Kitab Mahal, Allahabad.

Vidyarthi. L.P, (1978) Rise of Anthropology in India, Vol. II, Concept Publishing Company, Delhi.

Viviana, Paques. 1953 "Dans un village soudanais, est-il possible, est-il souhaitable, d'améliorer la productivité?" Productivité française, XIX-XX. [Google Scholar]

William J. Barber, 1967 "Urbanisation and Economic Growth: The Cases of Two White Settler Territories," The City in Modem Africa, Horace Milner, ed. (New York), 9–125. [Google Scholar]

Chapter - 15

Tribal Deprivation and Identities in Assam: A Sociological Study based on Deuri Tribe of Lakhimpur District in Assam

— Dilip Kumar Bhuyan, Sri Himeswar Borah

Introduction

People come across a number of crises in their personal, professional, cultural, political, religious and social interaction. Therefore crisis is part of human civilization. Most of the major conflicts occurred in history based on ethnicity. In ethnicity people are united and feel secured. North East India experienced a number of conflicts based on ethnicity. In this connection, it may be stated that people of the North East are not satisfied with the central government and its policies towards the Assam. As a result of there is tension among the tribes as well as non-tribal people of the state of Assam in order to preserve their identity. Most of the North East states do experience ethnic conflicts due to which the region has a bad reputation and this has also adversely affected the developmental activities of the region as well.

The North East India comprised of eight states peopled by tribes and communities majority of which are culturally and ethically different from the rest of India. The North East region is still lagging behind as compared to many states of India. As a matter of fact it can be stated here that people of this region have facing inequalities and deprivation in socioeconomic aspects still now. After India's independence, the Government both of the state and central level has been implementing several development programme for reduce on poverty alleviation, employment, infrastructure, education, agriculture etc apparently to positively 'transform peoples' lives in the region. In spites of these initiatives, several decades of intensive development programmes and strategies has somehow seen more failures than success. While development should have brought a positive change in peoples' lives. But it has become more and more emerging inequalities and deprivation in the field of socioeconomic, socio-political and socio-environmental conditions among the tribes and other communities in Assam. In this regard some quest to be arisen in our mind why is happening, how did it happen and how can this problem be solved are the questions being asked. The quest for identity is a basic sub-concern of globalization process, where the creation of viable identities was a fundamental issue. It is acknowledges to global economy, on the other, it also cautions the increasing levels of inequality, poverty and social conflicts and the threat that globalization puts to local and regional identity as a result of overwhelming processes of globalization.

The concept of identity is closely associated with the idea of culture. Identities can be formed through the cultures and subcultures to which people belong o r in which people participate. Stephen Frosh describes the view that identity draws from culture but is not simply formed by it. Recent sociological and psychological theories have stressed that a person's identity is in fact something multiple and potentiality fluid, constructed through experience and linguistically coded. In developing their identities people draw upon culturally a available resources in their immediate social networks and in society as a whole. The process of identity construction is, therefore, one upon which the contradictions and dispositions of the surrounding socio-cultural environment have a profound impact. The term identity first gained salience through the work of the psychologist Erikson (1968). Erikson uses the term identity crisis to refer to individuals who have lost a sense of sameness or continuity. Although Erikson theorizes on identity from a psycho-analytic point of view, he also emphasizes the role of the environment, and particularly the social environment.

Tribes of North East India is the homeland of a large number of tribal groups and it has own cultures. The Constitutional name for them is Anusuchit Janajati (Scheduled Tribe). The scheduled tribes are indigenous, have their own distinctive culture, are geographically isolated and are generally living in lower socio- economic conditions. After Independence, Government of India scheduled tribal groups in the constitution and provided special provisions for their welfare and development as in the case of SCs. There are about 654 ST communities across the States in India and 75 of the STs are most backward and are termed as the Primitive Tribal Groups. Due to this, infrastructure and development facilities in tribal areas for education, roads, health care, communication, drinking water, sanitation etc. have lagged behind compared to other areas which have resulted in further widening the gaps of development between the tribal people and the general population for a long time.

The most important trend that has emerged in recent years is the assertion of tribal identity. Assertions have been made on the basis of region, ethnicity, language, among other elements. All tribal movements today are an expression of the deeply felt-sense of identity. The socio-economic forces of modernization and development have no doubt brought some benefits to the people of some areas, but the benefits accrued to them have been largely outweighed by the harm. Development induced displacement; involuntary migration and resettlement have caused the marginalization of the tribal people and presented enormous problems to them. The new economic regime has led to the privatetization and marketisation of the economy reveling it to be a powerful threat to the survival of tribal communities.

North East India is a politically vital and strategically vulnerable region. It is virtually a land-locked area since it is connected with the rest of India through a narrow, thirtykilometer corridor of foot hills land in North Bengal. Such unparalleled location of the region has invariably converted the North East India into an isolated pocket, where a feeling of alienation and separation find it easy to get developed. In the state of Assam, the population is so much heterogeneous in nature. It consists of many different caste, classes, race, language, religion etc. In this situation, various ethnic, linguistic and religious groups demand their separate identity and they are opting for identity movements, autonomy movements etc.

Tribes of North East India: India is the homeland of a large number of ethnic groups and cultures. These communities, believed to be the earliest inhabitants of the country, live in the forests, hills, plateaus and naturally isolated region and are differently term as Vanyajati (forest caste), Vanavasi(forestinhabitants),Pahariya(hillmen),Adimjati (Primitivecaste), Adivasi (Original settler), Janajati(folk communities) and several such other names signifying either their ecological or economic or historical and cultural characteristics. Among these nomenclatures the most popular term is "Adivasi" while the constitutional name for them is Anusuchit Janajati (Scheduled Tribe). The scheduled tribes are indigenous, have their own distinctive culture, are geographically isolated and are generally living in lower socio- economic conditions. After Independence, Government of India scheduled tribal groups in the constitution and provided special provisions for their welfare and development as in the case of SCs. There are about 654 ST communities across the States in India and 75 of the STs are most backward and are termed as the Primitive Tribal Groups. Most of the tribal areas of the country resulting in the by passing of general developmental programmes where Deuri peoples lived. Due to this, infrastructure and development facilities in tribal areas for education, roads, health care, communication, drinking water, sanitation etc. have lagged behind compared to other areas which have resulted in further widening the gaps of development between the tribal people and the general population for a long time.

Objectives of the study: The study is planned to examine the socio-economic conditions and their inequalities among the Deuri tribe of Assam. Attempts have been made to analyse inequality in the access to basic amenities. It is tried to quantify the level of facility deprivation and socio-economic deprivation and to make some suggestions to resolve the deprivation and inequalities of the Deuri tribe.

Methodology: In this present paper, descriptive and analytical method has been adopted and required information are collected from secondary sources such as books, journals, newspapers, census report and office record etc. as well as primary data.

North East India is full of diversified ethnic groups living together generation after generation having distinctive historical and structural setting. As a result have been struggling for upliftment on the basis of their ethnic distinctiveness and for this reason they are indulge in identity movement.

In the following the scribe makes an attempt to give a brief idea about the Deuri Community, in which enlisted as scheduled tribe (plain) in Assam.

Deuri Tribe: Among the different tribal communities of Assam the Deuri community is a distinct tribal tribal group who are traditionally engaged in the priestly activities in the Royal Temples of the Chutiyas, and they numerically dominant Mongoloid population of Upper Assam (Gait:1905). According to Kakoty (1967) the word 'Deuri' is originated from Sanskrit word'Deva-Grihika'. That is, the word Deuri means in charge of a Temple or the Priest. The Deuri community comprises of four main sub-sections or khel(territorial group), namely the Dibongiya, the Tengaponiya, the Borgonya and the Patorgonya. They are maintaining their own culture which distinguishes them as a separate ethnic group.

The Deuri tribe is categorized as the Scheduled Tribes by the Constitution. North East India presents a resource abundant economy which continued to remain backward in comparative perspective with other regions. However, the backwardness of the economy could be attributed as much due to geo-political constraints as to retrograde policies pursued by the constituent states, a fact which impeded the process of transformation of traditional economy to having the semblance of a modern one. Tradition and identity issues had lulled the region to a zone of complacency and inaction and the only grace point was the safety net of the region which operated through the community based socio-economic structure prevailing in the tribal areas.

The quest for deprivation as well as identity is a basic sub-concern of globalization process, where the creation of viable identities was a fundamental issue. It is acknowledges to global economy, on the other, it also cautions the increasing levels of inequality, poverty and social conflicts and the threat that globalization puts to local and regional identity as a result of overwhelming processes of globalization.

The most important trend that has emerged in recent years is the assertion of tribal identity. Assertions have been made on the basis of region, ethnicity, language, among other elements. All tribal movements today are an expression of the deeply felt-sense of identity.

The socio-economic forces of modernization and development have no doubt brought some benefits to the people of some areas, but the benefits accrued to them have been largely outweighed by the harm. Development induced displacement; involuntary migration and resettlement have caused the marginalization of the tribal people and presented enormous problems to them. The new economic regime has led to the privatetization and marketisation of the economy reveling it to be a powerful threat to the survival of tribal communities.

Discussion and Result: The study is based on analysis of access to basic amenities, namely drinking water, toilet facility and electricity facility. The study also planned to examine the socio-economic conditions of the Deuri tribe. Socio economic deprivation is constructed and based on selected seven socio economic indicators: per cent of Houseless population, per cent of Housing shortage, per cent of poverty rate, unemployment rate, illiteracy rate, male illiteracy rate, female illiteracy rate.

A majority of India's population does not have access to sanitation facilities in their dwellings and lack of sanitation facilities. Like this scenario was found in the tribal villages. It was observed that majority of Deuri people has access to drinking water from a tap or hand pump/tube well situated within or outside the premises, it is considered as having access to safe drinking water. Access to electricity is a basic amenity and an index of industrialization. The economic backwardness of the Deuri is evident from 0their low income.

Education is considered as means to enhance capability, overcome constraints, enlarge choices, and power to cope with resilience for standard of living. It bridges the gaps in communication and encourages people's participation in social and political life. The educational attainment has its positive impact on the people's wellbeing and changes the perceptions, aims, means and ability of an individual as well as community. It is the determining factor of formation and application of new technologies. In the Deuri's villages it was found that there have not any proper hospitals for health care as well as lack of awareness regards to health.

As a whole initiatives should be taken to expand capabilities (opportunities freedoms) and to support people's agency (process freedom) among the weaker Deuri population of backward villages. Both State and Central Government should focus on economic infrastructure i.e. transport, communication and energy, social infrastructure i.e. education, health, housing, water supply, sanitation in the tribal areas in Assam.

References

1. Kakoty, B.K, 1967: Mother Goddess of Kamakhya, Lawers Book Stall, Guwahati.
2. Gait,Sir Edward, 1905 : A History of Assam, 1905,Surjeet Publication, Delhi.
3. Sonowal,C.J (2010): Quest for Identity, Autonomy and Development: The Contemporary Trends of Ethnic and Tribal Assertion in Assam, vols I, II, Akansha Publications p. 486, vols. 2.
4. Gupta, N (2018): "Ethnicity in north east India: A challenge to identity" International Journal of Advanced Educational Research, ISSN 2455-6157, VOL. 3, ISSUE 2, March 2018.
5. Debasis Neogi (2010): "Disparity in socio-economic Development and its implications on communal conflicts", International Journal of Humanities and Social Sciences, Vol 4, No 2, 2010.

Chapter - 16

The Impact of Economic Deprivation of Santhal Tribe on Ajodhya Hill Area, Purulia

— *Tarak Mohan Hazari*

Introduction

The tribal population is identified as the aboriginal inhabitants of our country. They have been living a simple life based on the natural environment and have developed cultural patterns congenial to their physical and social environment The term 'tribe' have not been defined clearly anywhere in the Indian constitution. Only the term 'Scheduled Tribe' explained as "the tribe or the tribal communities or parts of or group within tribes or tribal communities" (Ministry of Tribal Affairs, Annual report 2010-11).

India is home to more than five hundred tribal groups, whose population is close to ten crores. In other words, the indigenous population is 10 per cent of the total population. About three quarters of them were settled in Madhya Pradesh, Maharashtra, Chhattisgarh, Rajasthan, Jharkhand, West Bengal, Odisha, Gujarat, and Bihar. Of course, in the states like Mizoram in North-East (94%), Nagaland (89%), Meghalaya (86%), and Arunachal Pradesh (64%), the number of indigenous population in the population is not only in the tribal states of India but also in all Adivasis are minorities in the state. Although they are large in number but the total population of these states is much higher, their relative density becomes small.

In the Scheduled Castes and Scheduled Tribes Order (Amendment) Act, 1976 (Number 108 of 1976 dated 18.09.76) as many as 564 groups of tribes besides a number of sub-tribes inhabit different parts of the Indian sub-continent and constitute about 10% of its population. There are 38 groups of tribes are inhabited in West Bengal (Baskey, 1999, p.1 0). The

Santhal are one of the most important and numerically the largest homogenous tribe of India, mainly concentrated in the South-Eastern plateau of Jharkhand (formerly Bihar), especially in its division of Santhal Parganas. They inhabit at in West Bengal, Orissa and Assam also. Moreover, they are also found in neighbouring countries like Nepal and Bangladesh. According to Skrefsrud the word 'Santhal' comes from 'Saontal' and Acharya Suniti Kumar[5]http://www.guruchandali.com/default/2018/05/10/1525914367382.html Chatterji says that 'Santhal' comes from 'Samantapal' (i.e., Samantapal~ Samanta-al ~ Saontal~santal).[6]

What is Deprivation

The deprivation usually refers to not giving his ability to a person or a community. It is a situation in which, people do not have basic thing that they need to live a comfortable life. On the other hand, taking away someone's property or rights is also called deprivation.

Example of Deprivation on Indian Tribes

India is home to more than four hundred tribal groups, whose population is close to ten crores. In other words, the indigenous population is 10 per cent of the total population. About three quarters of them were settled in Madhya Pradesh, Maharashtra, Chhattisgarh, Rajasthan, Jharkhand, West Bengal, Odisha, Gujarat, and Bihar. Of course, in the states like Mizoram in North-East (94%), Nagaland (89%), Meghalaya (86%), and Arunachal Pradesh (64%), the number of indigenous population in the population is not only in the tribal states of India but also in all Adivasis are minorities in the state. Although they are large in number but the total population of these states is much higher, their relative density becomes small.

Studies by many, including Walter Fernandez, have been shown how millions of indigenous people of India have been driven out of their settled lands - somewhere in the dams, somewhere in the mines, somewhere in the name of development through the tourism luxuries, organized a great deal of deprivation. Most of the people who are being affected by this development are Adivasis. As a survey, 40% of the people evicted in the name of development are indigenous - but only 10% of their population.

There are numerous examples of such eviction or deprivation in India. In the year 1956, the dam on the Mayakakshi River was completely submerged in the 144 acres of fertile area of Santhal Parganas. Then the tribal people of that village were forced to sit in the dry land of[6] https://photius.com/religion/india_tribal_religions.html the Birbhum-Dumka border. Those who used to eat rice for their cultivation this time, they became starving overnight, half-hearted day-labourers. And this way the economic life of the indigenous people has been uprooted repeatedly.

The people of the indigenous people have to go away and get to the address. Millions of indigenous people of Santhal Pargana, Chotanagpur have to leave Villa ge-Jangle-Jhorna in Assam, in North Bengal the people of non-indigenous communities started gathering in indigenous areas through changing land ownership. In 1856, the tribal population of Kolhundi was 63 percent; today it has changed to 33. Chhotanagpur-Santal ParganaMidnapur-Purulia-Mayurvjan is an intolerable experience of indigenous border settlement everywhere. It is also an example of deprivation.[7]

Objective of the Study

The present study aims to appraise the effect of economic Deprivation on the social life of Santhal community of Ajodhya hill area with particular focus on their economic life also. With these purposes, the study sets following objectives.

1. To understand the present condition of Santhal people of those area.
2. To understand the Development status in those backward area.
3. To find out their present social, economic and health status.
4. To understand that, how economic deprivation effected their daily life.

Research Questions

1. What are the changes of their daily life for the increase of the price of essential commodities?
2. What are the major impacts of current political economic activities on their life?

Methodology

Sample Size and Data Collection

The total 80 households were covered during this study. The present study is based on primary data, collected from each household, about the effect of deprivation, with a well designed and structured schedule and face-to- face interview and the secondary data are collect from the journal, book and internet. Key Information method and in depth interviews are the chief methods for data collection for the study. Besides, Non participant observation is also an important method used.

Tools and Technique

Mainly qualitative aspects have been taken into consideration for the study. The methodology followed was a schedule-based survey among the tribal of the selected villages. The schedule consisted of 20 items on various aspects. A case study among Santhal tribes of Ajodhya hilltop was initially conducted to test the validity and reliability of the schedule. \Subsequently certain items were dropped and certain others were modified for better elicitation of results.

Table 1: Tools and Technique

Technique	*Tools*
In depth interview	Semi structure schedule
Observation	Observation Notebook
Secondary data	Internet, book and journal

Limitation

In some case, there were many limitations in the study of those areas of the Ajodhya hill

1. Time was a factor in the survey of the region, not all of the family was available anytime. Besides, there was the obligation to finish work before the evening in those village surround by the jungle.
2. There are a lot of problems in conversations with illiterate people in those areas of Santali language.
3. Many women of different houses did not want to answer for many reasons.
4. Surveying in those hilly areas surrounded by jungle was very hard, which caused some obstacles in our surveys.

Study Area

The present study was carried out in 4 villages situated in the Ajodhya hill area of Baghmundi block, the distance is about 40 kilometers far from Purulia town. Name of this 4 villages are Puniashason, Churingsara, Chhatni and Darudi. The study was specifically confined to the Santhal community.

Among the 80 sample collected from those 4 villages, 23 sample were collected from Puniashason, 13 from Churingsara, 39 from Chatni and 5 sample were collected from the village Darudi.

About Purulia District

Purulia district is one of the twenty-three districts of West Bengal state in Eastern India. The city of Purulia is the administrative headquarters of the district. Purulia lies between 22.60 degrees and 23.50 degrees' north latitudes and 85.75 degrees and 86.65 degrees' east longitudes. Compass declination 0º22'W. The geographical area of the district is 6259 km². This district is bordered on the east by Bankura, Paschim Midnapur districts, on the north by Bardhaman District of West Bengal state and Dhanbad District of Jharkhand state, on the west by Bokaro and Ranchi districts of Jharkhand state.

In 2011, Purulia had population of 2,927,965 of which male and female were 1,497,656 and 1,430,309 respectively. There was change of 15.43 % in the population compared to population as per 2001. In the previous census of India 2001, Purulia District recorded increase of 14.02 % to its population compared to 1991. The initial provisional data suggest a density of 468 in 2011 compared to 405 of 2001. Total area under Purulia district is of about 6,259 km2.

Average literacy rate of Purulia in 2011 were 65.38% compared to 55.57% of 2001. If things are looked at gender wise, male and female literacy were 78.85% and 51.29% respectively, compared to 73.72% and 36.50% in 2001. Total literate in Purulia District were

1,656,940 of which male and female were 1,021,455 and 635,485 respectively. In 2001,

Purulia District had 1,182,284 in its total region. With regards to the sex ratio in Purulia, it stood at 955 per 1000 male compared to 2001 census figure of 954. The average national sex ratio in India is 940 as per latest reports of Census 2011 Directorate.8

About the Block

Baghmundi is located at 23°122N 86°032E. Baghmundi CD Block is located in the southern part of the district. The Subarnarekha forms the interstate boundary between West Bengal and Jharkhand in Jhalda I CD Block and a small portion of Bahgmundi CD Block. The Bagmundi-Bandwan uplands is an area that has descended from the Ranchi Plateau. In the Baghmundi and Balarampur areas, the Ajodhya Hills form the main highlands, forming the drainage divide between the basins of the Subrnarekha and the Kangsabati. The elevation ranges from 475 to 700 m. Thousands of tourists come to visit Baghmundi to witness the charm of natural beauty of Ajodhya Hills and Bagmundi dams like Murguma. It is located 41 km from Purulia, the district headquarters.

Baghmundi CD Block has an area of 427.95 km^2. It has 1 panchayat samity, 8 gram panchayats, 92 gram sansads (village councils), 142 mouzas and 138 inhabited villages. Baghmundi police station serves this block.[11] Headquarters of this CD Block is at Patardi. As per the 2011 Census of India Baghmundi CD Block had a total population of 135,579, all of which were rural. There were 69,520 (51%) males and 66,059 (49%) females. Population below 6 years was 21,992. Scheduled Castes numbered 14,042 (10.36%) and Scheduled Tribes numbered 34,038 (25.11%). Baghmundi block had a total population of 112,388, out of which 57,650 were males and 54,738 were females. Baghmundi block registered a population growth of 13.64 per cent during the 1991-2001 decade. Decadal growth for Purulia district was 13.96 per cent.[15]Decadal growth in West Bengal was 17.84 per cent. Other villages in Baghmundi CD Block are (2011 census figures in brackets): Ajodhya (1,468), Patardi (1,609), Birgram (3,722), Kalimati (1,961), Serengdi (305), Tunturi (2,037), Suisa (2,649) and Matha (624).[9]

About Ajodhya Hills

The area of Ajodhya Hills is about 320 Sq Kilometers which covers portions of Jhalda, Baghmundi, Balarampur and Arsha Blocks in Purulia district. The word 'Ayodhya' (locally called'Ajodhya') is derived from a Dravidian word 'Ajhaida' (Ajhai=large, Da=daha)i.e. there was a large abyss (daha). In Ajodhya Hill there are 70 hamlets containing 15-20 thousand inhabitants, two Gram Panchayats, Ranga and Ajodhya, a library, an office of Comprehensive Area Development Corporation, Ajodhya Hill hospital, water project etc. The height of Ajodhya Hill is about 2200 feet. The figure of Ajodhya Hills is somewhat L- shaped covering 32 miles in length and 10 miles in width. It is treated as sacred by the tribal communities of Purulia district. In Santhal language the word 'buru' denotes 'paha'r (Hill) like Gagaburu, Gargaburu, Mathaburu, Chemtuburu etc. The large boulders, rough rocks, gravels, large sand particles are found in profusion on the river beds which are called 'rahr' in local language. It is for this reason that Purulia is also recognized as the 'rahr' district of West Bengal.

Several concealed water sources have emerged from Ajodhya Hill like Kansai, Rupai, Kerensai, Saharjuri, Samarbishi, Bandu, Chatuhasa, Kumari, Kulbera, Shakha, Shova, Bane, Kadrugara, Machkanda, etc. which flow over areas with abundant herb, climber, shrubs and vegetation. The tribal communities settled in Ajodhya Hill belong to Santhal, Birhor, Munda, Bhumij, Ghashi, Paharia, and Kheria tribes whose main source of earning is Agriculture. During Buddha Purnima (the full moon-birth day of Gautam Buddha), the tribal groups used to hunt in Ajodhya Hill by using traditional hunting weapons to kill fox, porcupine, deer, pig, rabbit, snake, dove, parrot, squirrel etc. and gather the bodies as source of food. Community Area

Development Corporation also renders medical collaterally promotes farming, poultry, dairy, nursery, water supply, irrigation, construction and maintenance of roads, literacy, ration shop, tea garden etc. inhabitants of Ajodhya Hill. There are two routes. to reach Ajodhya from Purulia, One may follow the route from Purulia to Ajodhya either via Sirkabad via There are also vehicle facilities for tourism from morning to evening and 'Niharika' and 'Sagarika' housings were constructed accommodating tourists.[10]

Demography of the study area

1. Puniya Shasan is a Santali tribal village in Purulia district of West Bengal. Geographically, this area is bounded on the north by Chhanti village, on east by Simulbera village. Churingsara and Ajodhya village are situated in west direction and Gobariya village in south west. This village is geographically characterized by a very less rainfall, dry climate and sparse vegetation. Punia Shasan is a village which is located in Bagmundi Block of Puruliya district, West Bengal with total 55 families residing. The Punia Shasan village has population of 287 of which 147 are males while 140 are females as per Population Census 2011.

Table 2: Demography of Puniya Shasan Village

Particulars	*Total No. of Houses*	*Populati on*	*Child (0-6)*	*Schedule Caste*	*Schedule Tribe*	*Literacy*	*Total Worker*
Total	55	287	71	0	287	134	183
Male	-	147	39	0	147	79	98
Female	-	140	32	0	140	55	85

Source: Census 2011.

2. Churingsara is a Santali tribal village in Purulia district of West Bengal. Purulia district is placed in the western part of the state of West Bengal. Geographically, this area is bounded on the north by Chhanti village, on east by PuniaShasan village. Churingsara and Ajodhya village are situated in west direction and Gobariya village in south west. This village is geographically characterized by a very less rainfall, dry climate and sparse vegetation. Churingsara is a village which is located in Bagmundi Block of Puruliya district, West Bengal with total 27 families residing. The village has population of 143 of which 77 are males while 66 are females as per Population Census 2011.

Table 3 : Demography of Churingsara village

Particulars	*Total No. of Houses*	*Population*	*Child (0-6)*	*Schedule Caste*	*Schedule Tribe*	*Literacy*	*Total Worker*
Total	27	143	67	0	143	65	62
Male	-	77	38	0	77	39	34
Female	-	66	29	0	66	26	28

Source: Census 2011.

3. Chhanti is a tribal village in Purulia district of West Bengal. Purulia district is placed in the western part of the state of West Bengal. Geographically, this area is bounded on the north by Ajodhya village, on east by Ushuldungri village. Churingsara and Ajodhya village are situated in west direction and Punia Shasan village in south west. This village is geographically characterized by a very less rainfall, dry climate and sparse vegetation. Chhatni is a village which is located in Bagmundi Block of Puruliya district, West Bengal with total 87 families residing. The Chhatni village has population of 423 of which 222 are males while 201 are females as per Population Census 2011.
4. Darudi is a Santali tribal village in Purulia district of West Bengal. Purulia district is placed in the western part of the state of West Bengal. Geographically, this area is bounded on the north by Bhursabera village, on east by Ushuldungri village. Simulbera village are situated in west direction and Kalijharna in south west. This village is geographically characterized by a very less rainfall, dry climate and sparse vegetation. Darudi is a village which is located in Bagmundi Block of Puruliya district, West Bengal with total 29 families residing. The Darudi village has population of 153 of which 82 are males while 71 are females as per Population Census 2011.

Table 4: Demography of Darudi Village

Particulars	*Total No. of Houses*	*Population*	*Child (0-6)*	*Schedule Caste*	*Schedule Tribe*	*Literacy*	*Total Worker*
Total	87	423	67	0	423	177	294
Male	-	222	38	0	222	106	159
Female	-	201	29	0	201	71	135

Source: Census 2011.

Deprivation on Government Schemes for Tribal Development

Looking at the initial aspect, it cannot be said that the tribal community of India is totally deprive. Since the time of independence, the central government and also various state governments have been taking special care for the development of indigenous people. For the development of them, many sections have been added to the Constitution, and have been introduced many different laws for them. There is also a special arrangement for reservation for tribal people in the government sector.

But after all this, looking a little better, it can be seen that many indigenous communities in India have been deprived even today. In spite of having so many official facilities, many tribal people in many places do not get those services properly for a variety of reasons. And so, all those tribal inhabited regions of Ajodhya are still hill area so backward even today. Such as……

1. Various scholarships are offered for indigenous students to improve the quality of study from the primary level. There are also separate hostels in different school colleges and universities for indigenous students. But due to one kind of government's indifference and family poverty, many students were forced to leave their studies. As a result, many tribal students are totally deprived of these facilities.
2. In order to make people self-reliant in the economically backward areas, indigenous people have been provided free loans. And keeping their traditions in mind, different birds and animal husbandry were arranged for the development of the tribal people. Even though such initiatives are taken in some big villages, the general public of most small villages does not know anything about this.
3. There are many pension plans for older indigenous people. However, due to inadequate communication, due to lack of proper application at the right time, many are deprived of this pension.
4. In various tourism areas, the traditional culture of indigenous people has been utilized for the purpose of earning their money. But in this area, there has been no official initiative taken by the government in this purpose.

Others Finding of this Survey

Seeing economically, indigenous people are deprived of all aspects.

1. Once upon a time, hunting was one of the sources of income of tribal community, one of the pillars of living of the indigenous

people. Sometimes they used to sell the meat of their hunting in the market area, and sometimes they would eat to meet their hunger.

But standing in present India, not talking about hunting, little torture on any animal is also a punishable crime. In those circumstances, the oldest process of income and living of the tribal people are now closed. And this is one of the greatest examples of tribal deprivation in the mask of law.

2. At one time, the indigenous people had free access to forest. From every morning to night, they had deep relations with the forest in every step. Plants, fruits, wood, leaves, and everything in the forest are closely related to their daily life. Not only that, the cultural and economic life of indigenous people is totally incomplete without them.

   But now, by the name of law, the rights of indigenous people are being taken away from the forest. Which has become a sign of an inhuman activity towards them? In such a way, the continuous deprivation of them is going on, in addition to that, forests are being destroyed one by one in many areas for the development and modernization. As a result, they are not only deprived of it, but are slowly becoming panic day by day.

3. The same condition is seen in the Ajodhya hill area. As a tourist area, the Ajodhya hill is famous today, all over the India. In the name of development of these tourism infrastructure, many land of the tribal people of the area have been bought at low prices, some have lost their homes also. In addition to that, many trees have been cut for various reasons, which have affected the life of indigenous people in that place. In spite of such a large tourism area, there are no arrangements any employments for tribal people in those areas today. If it were done correctly, the figure of socio-economic life would change of the common people in that area. And this is one of the worst examples of economic deprivation towards indigenous people.

Suggestions

1. For the development of those areas, first of all, there is need to proper implementation of various government projects.
2. It is must necessary to establish a primary and high school in those area to give the best opportunity for the student to continue their study.

3. In Ajodhya hill areas, it is very necessary to establish good road to provide better connectivity, hospitals and ambulance for health services.
4. Keeping their traditions in mind, it is worthwhile to cooperate with them to expand the handicrafts of forest produce.
5. Their cultural heritage can be used for the expansion of tourism, which will lead to economic development. Apart from this, using the solitary of forests, HOME STAY can be arranged through SELF HELP GROUP, obviously with the government help.
6. Different domestic birds and animal can be arranged by making them aware of the negative aspects of hunting.
7. Without hurting their traditions, the primary responsibility of conservation of forests can be given to them by making them aware about the different forests act at the government level.

   Apart from providing housing facilities to homeless people, providing drinking water facilities, improving communication system, providing suitable facilities for different government projects at the right time, it is possible to free a lot of indigenous people from this deprivation.

Bibliography

1. Baskey. D. August 2002. THE TRIBES OF WEST BENGAL, Subarnarekha, MG road, Kolkata, 2002.
2. Sen. S. June 2013. The Sandals of Jungle-Meals, Akashdeep, Kolkata 2013.
3. Pradhan, Niladri. 2014 TRIBAL EDUCATION IN INDIA: CHALLENENGE AND STRATEGIES, Firma KLM private limited, Kolkata.
4. Rao, M V. 2012 PRESISTENCE AND CHANGE IN TRIBAL INDIA, Concept Publishing Company, New Delhi.
5. Mukhyopadhay J. 1992 Gabesonapatra Onusandhan o Rachona, Ananda, Kokata.
6. Bera, G K & Svd K J. Tribal India's Traditional Wisdom And Indigenous Resource Management.
7. Bodding, P.C. 1942 'Traditions and Institutions of the Santals, Oslo: A.W. Broggers Boktrykkeri.
8. Bose, Nirmal Kumar.1971 'Tribal life in India,' National Book Trust, New Delhi.

Websites

http://www.guruchandali.com/default/2018/05/10 1525914367382.

htmlhttps://photius.com/religion/india_tribal_religions.html

http://www.guruchandali.com/default/2018/05/10 1525914367382.html

https://en.wikipedia.org/wiki/Purulia

https://en.wikipedia.org/wiki
Baghmundi_(community_development_block)

https://en.wikipedia.org/wiki/Ajodhya_Hills

Index

A

Aamar Baari Schemes, 62
Agricultural Implements, 146
Agricultural Laborers, 20
Agricultural labour, 164
Agricultural Practices, 146
Agricultural wages, 165
Agriculture and allied activities, 165
Agro-credit and consumption loans, 178
Ahir Sonar, 23
Ajodhya hill area, 247, 254
Ajodhya Hills, 249, 250
Ajodhya hilltop, 248
Alcoholic addiction, 174
Alipurduar, 54
Alipurduar district, 56
All Jharkhand Student Union, 75
Ancient Indian history, 30
Andaman and Nicobar Islands, 182
Andaman Nicobar & Lakshadweep, 30
Andhra Pradesh, 32, 33, 91, 95, 181, 196
Andhra Pradesh, Telengana, 70
Andre Beteille, 39
Anganwadi centers, 233
Anganwadi Sevika, 133
Animal husbandry, 149, 164
Annual average house hold income, 162
Annual Employment, 89
Annual house hold expenditure, 162
Annual Plans, 46
Anthropological literature, 182
Applied And Action Anthropology, 228
Applied and Action Anthropology, 234
Arunachal Pradesh, 32, 33, 47, 196, 245, 246
Aryan Hindus, 29
Asia and Africa, 224
Assam, 32, 33, 47, 56, 66, 116, 196, 239, 246
Auxiliary Nurse Midwifery, 106, 210
Average Expenditure per Annum, 145
Axe, 86
Ayurvedic and Homeopathic facilities, 148

B

Babasaheb Ambedkar, 44
Backward Class, 23
Backward Classes, 103, 205
Badjamda and Kiriburu connects, 80
Baghmundi CD Block, 249
Bagicha block, 154, 158
Bagicha Block of Jashpur District, 155
Bagmundi dams, 249
Bagmundi-Bandwan uplands, 249
Bahgmundi CD Block, 249
Bahujan Samaj Party, 75
Bali and Sugriva, 29
Bamboo basket production, 233

Bamboo craft, 234
Bangladesh, 246
Bankura, 249
Bardhaman District, 249
Barpeta, 54
Bee-box making skill, 233
Beehive box manufacturing, 233
Beekeeping, 233
Below Poverty Line, 89
Bengal, 23
Bhagalpur, 16
Bharat Sevashram Sangh, 86
Bharnobari tea garden, 56
Bhopal, 232
Bhuiya and Dusadh, 20
Bhumij tribe, 45
Bhuria Committee, 70
Bhutan, 53, 56
Bicycle repairing, 150
Bidi making, 149
Bihar, 116, 196, 245, 246
Bihar Peasant Life, 17
Birbhum-Dumka border, 246
Birhor Development Agency, 155, 177, 230
Birhor inhabits, 153
Birsa Munda Awas Yojna, 106, 210
Birsa Munda Revolt, 66
Body Mass Index, 116, 117
Boiled Bhat, 167
Bongaigaon, 54
Bows and Arrows, 185
Breton Woods Conference, 224
British colonial period, 56
British colonization, 42
British crown, 66
British Economist, 53
British Government, 184
British Overseas Development, 225
British Raj, 43, 182
British rule, 43
British rulers, 65
Broom making, 233

C

Calcutta University, 182
Caste Census of India, 92, 93, 95
Caste wise occupation, 120
Census operations of Bihar, 18
Central and North-Eastern region, 91
Central and North-West region, 41
Central India, 33
Central tribal region, 30
Central Vindhya region, 28
Cha Bagan Workers Union, 61
Chamars of Bihar, 17
Chatra, 100
Chatra district, 20
Chhatishgarh, 222, 229
Chhatni, 248
Chhattisgarh, 33, 70, 91, 95, 116, 154, 181, 196, 245, 246
Chhattisgarh Feudatory State, 159
Chhattishgarh, 229
Chhotanagpur, 54, 58, 136, 247
Chhotanagpur origin, 54
Chhottanagpur plateau, 184, 190
Chik Baraik, 54
Children of the tea labourers, 59
Churingsara, 248
Citizen Protection Act, 107, 211
Coal mine project area, 140
Collection of minor forest produce, 165
Colonel Dalton, 136
Common Diseases in the Locality, 147
Communicable disease, 151
Communication between Afghan and Iranian, 42
Communication skills, 228
Community Area Development Corporation, 250

Community buildings, 143
Composite Rehabilitation Centre, 110, 214
Consolidated Funds, 196
Constitution of India, 31, 195
Contaminated water of natural streams, 175
Coochbehar, 54, 56
Cow dung cake making, 149
Creation of wage employment, 235
Cremation ground, 143
Criminal Tribes, 44, 182
Cultivation of medicinal and aromatic plants, 152
Cultivation Practices, 146

D

Daltonganj, 136, 138, 139, 140, 142, 144
Daltongunj to Patan block, 138
Damodar Valley Corporations, 27
Darudi, 248
Death and death rites, 17
Deoghar, 109
Depressed Classes, 15, 65
Deuri peoples, 242
Deuri tribe of Assam, 242
Dhanbad, 66, 110
Dhanbad District, 249
Differently-abled Welfare Scheme, 110, 214
Dipankar Gupta, 48
Direct Cash Benefit, 104, 205
Disabled Persons, 200
District Disability Rehabilitation Centre, 110, 214
District Welfare Officer, 106, 209
Domestic animals, 192
Domestication of animals, 188
Dominant Castes, 24
Dooars region, 54, 55, 59
Dowry system, 132
Dravidian tribe, 30
Dravidians, 28
Drinking Water Facility, 143
Dubari, 54
Dumka, 101, 118, 201
Dumka and West Singhbhum, 212
Dumka district, 120, 127, 132

E

East Dooars, 54
Eastern Blocks of Birbhum, 48
Eastern India, 249
Ecological control, 218
Economic backwardness, 243
Economic deprivation, 182
Economic Problems of Scheduled Caste of Bihar, 18
Economic Status of the Households, 169
Educational Institutions, 148
Educational status, 203
Empowered Action Group, 117
Eradication of rural poverty, 227
Establishment of Ashram School, 215

F

Female illiteracy rate, 243
Fish Farming, 233
Fishing boats, 93
Five Year Plans, 45
Focus on poverty alleviation, 224
Folk communities, 241
Food and Agricultural Organization, 224
Food Consumption Pattern, 167
Food gathering, 164
Food Gathering from forest, 184
Food items, 166
Forest region, 66
Forest-grown food, 39
Forestry and food gathering, 164
Francis Buchanan, 16
Franz Boas, 39
Fruits Grown, 147

G

Gandharvas & Kirata, 30
Gandhian Approach to untouchability, 18
Ganguram Champia, 81
Garhwa, 20, 136
Gauhatu Toli, 81
Geo-climatic conditions, 215
Gerua Hill, 67
Giridih, 101, 201
Goalpara, 54
Goat Farming activity, 234
Goat rearing, 149
Gobindapur under Dhanbad district, 67
Godda, 109
Goldsmith, 23
Gonds, 28
Gondwana Research and Development Centre, 221
Government of India Act, 15
Government of Jharkhand, 16
Gram Mitra, 177
Gram Sabha, 70, 71, 151
Great Kol Revolt, 66
Guaranteed Education Loan Scheme, 105, 209
Gujarat, 23, 32, 33, 70, 91, 95, 116, 181, 196, 245, 246
Gumla, 100, 118, 130
Gumla district, 121, 122, 131, 132
Gurnar Myrdal, 232

H

Harkara Hill, 67
Haryana, 116
Hazaribagh, 110
Health and Hygine, 170
Health care, 175
Health check up, 175
Health Facilities in Government Hospitals, 147
Health Facilities in Private Clinics, 148
Health institution, 171
Health intervention, 151
Health services, 148
Herbert Hope Risley, 39
High economic problems, 149
High incidence of poverty, 16
Himachal Pradesh, 70
Horticulture, 150
Hostels for the differently abled, 214
House hold industry, 20, 164
Household Items, 146
Human Development Report, 219
Hunting trap, 185

I

Ignorance regarding child care, 172
Ill health of mothers, 172
Illiteracy rate, 243
Implementation of Forest Rights Act, 107, 211
Indian Anthropology, 17
Indian nomadic tribes, 29
Indian tribal community, 43
Indian tribal society, 41
Indira Awas Colony, 80
Indira Awas for Primitive Tribal Group, 233
Indira Gandhi National Differently-abled Pension, 214
Indira Gandhi National Old Age Pension Scheme, 109, 213
Indira Gandhi National Widow Pension Scheme, 109, 213
Indo Genetic basin, 30, 42
Infant mortality rate, 89
Integrated Rural Development, 220
Integrated Tribal Development Programme, 46
Integrated Tribal Development Project, 46
International Bank for Reconstruction and Development, 224

International Fund for Agricultural Development, 233
Intoxicants, 166
Island region, 30
Item Wise Expenditure per Annum, 145

J

Jalpaiguri, 56
Jamshedpur, 110
Jamtara, 118
Janani Suraksha Yojana, 36
Jashpur, 222
Jashpur District, 153
Jashpur Settlement Report, 159
Jashpur tahsil of Raigard district, 159
Jhalda I CD Block, 249
Jhargram district, 182, 183
Jharkhand, 19, 33, 65, 66, 69, 70, 91, 92, 95, 99, 100, 101, 116, 136, 181, 196, 201, 203, 219, 230, 245, 246
Jharkhand Academic Council, 105
Jharkhand Economic Survey, 117
Jharkhand Minority Committee, 215
Jharkhand Mukti Morcha, 75
Jharkhand Panchayati Raj Act, 151
Jharkhand Shiksha Pariyojna, 86
Jharkhand state, 249
Jharkhand Tribal Development Society, 127
Jharkhand Tribal Empowerment and Livelihood Projec, 108
Jharkhand Vikash Morcha, 75
Jog-Manjhi, 66
Jog-Paranik, 66
Jungle Mahal, 182

K

Kalchini Block, 56, 57
Kalyani University, 228
KanyadaanYojna, Lakshmi LaadliYojna, 132
Kasturba Gandhi Balika Vidhyalaya, 132
Kendu leaves, 149
Kerala, 90
Kharia, 54
Kharif Crops, 234
Khudia region, 230
Khudia Zamindari, 155, 230
Khunti, 100, 101, 201
Kinship system, 17
Kitchen garden, 168
Knowledge of Family Planning, 148
Koderma, 100
Kokrajhar, 54
Konarko Toli, 81
Kondhs, 28
Kothari commission of education, 227
Kshatriya caste, 45
Kucha Roof, 103, 201
Kucha Roof (Rural), 102
Kucha walls, 103, 201
Kunkuri Block, 158

L

Labour co-operatives in tribal area, 45
labour force participation rate, 117
Lac Development Scheme, 108
Lack of nutritional food intake, 174
Lad Sonar, 23
Large sized Multi-purpose Cooperative Societies, 46
Latehar, 118, 136, 201, 203
Latehar district, 127
Leaf bowl and leaf plate, 233
Leaf mat, 233
Leaf plate making, 149
Limited employment opportunities, 16
Liquor shop, 169
Livelihood Training, 108
Lohardaga, 20, 201
Lohra, 54
Lokur Committee, 31, 195

M

M.K.Gandhi, 18
Madan Mohan Malviya, 65
Madhu tea estate, 57
Madhu Tea Garden, 56, 59
Madhya, 95
Madhya Pradesh, 32, 33, 70, 91, 95, 116, 181, 196, 229, 233, 245, 246
Madya Pradesh, 233
Mahabharata, 29
Maharashtra, 23, 32, 33, 91, 95, 116, 182, 196, 245, 246
Mahatma Gandhi National Rural Employment Guarantee, 49, 190
Mahli, 54
Maithan Dam, 67
Male illiteracy rate, 243
Manipur, 32, 33, 47, 196
Manjhi, 66
Manora block, 154, 165, 230, 233
Manora Tribal development Block, 155, 158, 230
Manual casual labour, 93
Maternal malnutrition, 91
Mayakakshi River, 246
Medical mobile van, 151
Medininagar, 136
Medinipur, 190
Meghalaya, 32, 33, 47, 196, 245, 246
Metropolitan tribe, 46
Micro watershed code, 233
Migrant tea worker, 61
Ministry of Tribal Affairs, 245
Minor Forest produce, 164
Minority Committee, 215
Minority community, 205
Mizoram, 32, 33, 196, 245, 246
Mughal invasion, 42
Mughal Reign, 43
Mughal rulers, 42
Mukhyamantri, 132
Munda, 54
Munda of Bokna village, 81
Munda of Jharkhand, 83
Mushroom cultivation, 149
Mushroom production, 233

N

Nagaland, 32, 33, 47, 196, 245, 246
Narendra Damodar Das Modi, 217
Nathdwara in Rajasthan, 18
National Commission for Minorities Act, 198
National Family Benefit Scheme, 109, 212
National Overseas Scholarship, 216
Nawamundi block, 79
Naxal movement, 32
Nepal, 246
Netarhat firing range, 27
Nilgiri Hills, 42, 43
Non-agriculture sector, 122
Non-vegetarian food, 169
North Bengal, 247
North East, 32, 33, 91
North East India, 239, 240, 241, 242
North East region, 239
North Eastern region, 30
North Indian Gonds, 41
North- Eastern region, 56
North-East, 196, 245, 246
North-East Himalayan areas, 41
North-Eastern India, 196
North-Eastern tribal region, 30
North-Western tribal region, 30
North Eastern Area, 32
Nutrition Water & Sanitation, 174
Nutritional status, 115
Nylon net, 233

O

Odisha, 182, 245, 246
Official development assistance, 224

Old-age homes, 212
Opportunities freedoms, 244
Ore Rich Saranda forest division, 79
Original habitant area, 58
Original settler, 241
Orissa, 32, 33, 66, 91, 95, 116, 190, 196, 230, 246
Orissa Human Development Report, 90
Other Backward Classes, 69, 104, 205

P

Pahadi Korwa of Jashpur, 231
Pahari Korwa, 153, 154, 155, 230
Pahari Korwa Development Agency, 156, 178
Pahari Korwa tribal community, 164, 172
Pahari Korwa women, 161
Pahariya Health Scheme, 106
Pahariya health-care, 106
Pahariya health-care centres, 106
Pakaur, 20
Pakaur and Gumla, 21
Pakota Sahi, 81
Pakur, 109, 199, 201, 203
Palamau district, 137, 140
Palamu, 20, 118, 136
Panch Dravid, 23
Panch Gaud, 23
Panchayati Raj, 228
Panchayati Raj Act, 151
Panchayati Raj Institution, 66, 69
Panchayati Raj institutions, 178
Panchayati Raj System, 178
Paranik, 66
Participatory Rural Appraisal, 224
Particularly Vulnerable Tribal Groups, 91
Paschim Medinipur, 182, 183, 190
Paschim Medinipur district, 190
Paschim Midnapur districts, 190, 249
Paschimi Singhbum, 100
Patan administrative block, 137
Patan block, 137, 139, 140
Patna, 16
Petty business and service, 165
Physical environment, 170
Physical quality of Life Index, 135
Piggery & Poultry, 149
Pithora Kanda, 168
Polio eradication programmes, 172, 173
Poor hygienic condition, 172
Poor sanitation and hygien practices, 174
Post-Matric Scholarship Scheme, 206
Post Matric Scholarship, 207, 215
Poverty and Illiteracy, 173
Pre-British India, 31
Pre-Matric Scholarship Scheme, 205
Pregnant and lactating womens, 172
Pregnant and nursing mothers, 171
Pregnant women, 174
Preparation of food, 168
Primary Health Center, 86, 147
Primitive Tribal Groups, 241
Primitive Vulnerable Tribal Groups, 153, 229
Problems of Pahari Korwa Tribes, 169
Probodh Kumar Bhowmick, 39
Production of fishing trap, 233
Production of Herbal pesticides, 233
Prof. P.K. Bhowmick, 228
Prof. Parlay Kumar Deb, 228
Provident Fund, 129
Provision of Subsidized Asset, 108
Puberty customs, 17
Public Distribution System, 127
Pucca bathrooms, 141
Puniashason, 248
Purnea, 16
Purulia, 249
Purulia district, 251
Purulia town, 248

Q

Qualitative data, 137

R

Radio repairing, 150
Rajasthan, 23, 32, 33, 91, 95, 116, 196, 245, 246
Rajiv Gandhi National Fellowship, 215
Ramayana age, 29
Ranchi, 36, 110, 136
Ranchi districts, 249
Ravana, 30
Ravana battle, 30
Reduction of Poverty, 108
Regional Centre Jabalpur, 162
Regional Research Laboratory, 232
Rehabilitation problem, 58
Religious Minorities, 205
Research officers, 219
Reserve Forest.Agriculture, 81
Revitalizations of caste in India, 23
Right to Information, 228
River Amanat, 137, 138
River Durgabati, 138, 139, 140
River Koyal, 140
Roots Available, 147
Royal Temples of the Chutiyas, 242
Rural Hospital, 210

S

Sahibganj, 199, 203
Samri tahsil of Balrampur district., 155, 250
Sanitation programme, 175
Santhal, 246
Santhal community, 248
Santhal Pargana, 105, 209, 247
Santhal Parganas, 209, 246
Santhal Revolt, 66
Santhal Tribe, 66, 248
Santhal tribesmen, 48
Santhali, 54
Sarva Siksha Abhiyan, 149
Satali tea estate, 57
Satali tea garden, 57
Schedule Tribe, 120
Scheduled and Tribal Areas, 70
Scheduled Area, 70, 72, 74
Scheduled Castes, 19, 21, 22, 69, 103, 196, 197, 205
Scheduled castes of Bihar, 17
Scheduled Tribes, 16, 17, 31, 32, 45, 89, 91, 99, 103, 182, 195, 205, 215, 245
Scholarship for the Differently abled, 214
Senior citizens, 205
Settled agriculture, 164
Sex ratio, 20, 22
Shahabad, 16
Shaila watershed project, 233
Shifting cultivation, 164
Shodhganga, 90
Shubhasini tea garden, 56
Sickle, 86
Sikkim, 32, 196
Simdega, 100, 118, 121, 130
Simdega district, 119, 127
Singara and Lohara, 138
Sixth and Seventh Five Year Plans, 46
Skill development programs, 212
Social and political development, 224
Social Development Advisors, 219
Social problems, 149
Source of Income, 145
South Asia and Africa, 224
South East Asia, 224
South-west region, 90
Southern Tribal region, 30
Spade, 86
Special Central Assistance, 212
Special Central Assistance to Tribal Sub Plan, 108
Sri Lanka, 29
ST Pension Scheme, 210

State Highway, 139
State Social Protection Pension Scheme, 109, 213
State Widow's Honour Pension Scheme, 110, 213
Statistical Account of Bengal, 17
Status of Women, 148
Stephen Frosh, 240
Sub Health Center, 147
Sub-Saharan Africa, 90
Subhasini tea estate, 57
Suniti Kumar Chatterji, 41
Supplementary, 225
Supplementary employment, 225
Supreme Court of India, 181
Surajit Sinha, 39
Surguja state, 159
Surva Siksha Abhiyan, 148
Swami Vivekanand Differently-able Self-Reliant, 214

T

Tailoring and Knitting works, 234
Tamil Nadu, 43, 196
Tana Bhagat movement, 66
Targeting the Hardcore Poor Scheme, 212
Tea migrant labourer, 60
Technocratic approaches, 43
Technology Resource Center, 232
Tendulkar Committee, 89
Territorial group, 242
Tilka Manjhi Revolt, 66
Tirilpi Toli, 81
Tondanghatu Toli, 81
Total Village Development Strategy, 135
Total Village Management, 135
Traditional environment, 48
Traditional political system, 75
Traditional power structure, 44
Training and Social Welfare, 225
Training centre for lac cultivation, 108, 211
Tribal Advisory Council, 32
Tribal and Rural Development Institute, 233
Tribal and Rural Development Institute of Jashpur, 229
Tribal children, 36
Tribal communities, 66, 91, 95, 195
Tribal communities in Mughal period, 42
Tribal development, 43
Tribal Reseach and Training Institute Raipur, 157
Tribal Sub-Plan Areas, 215
Tribes Advisory Council, 73
Tribes and Castes of Bengal, 17
Tripura, 32, 47, 196

U

Unemployment rate, 243
Unemployment Survey, 89
United Nations, 220, 224
United States, 225
United States Agency for International Development, 225
Upadhyaya Grameen Kaushalya Yojana, 191
Upper Ghat, 230
Urban tribe, 44, 46
Uttar Pradesh, 116, 117, 196

V

Vaisnava religion, 42
Vanavasi, 241
Vedic age to pre-Mughal era, 43
Vedic antiquity, 28
Vedic Aryans, 40
Vedic period, 18, 29
Vermi-compost, 233
Village Development Committee, 150
Village Development of the Martyr Scheme, 210

Village Developmental Plan, 151
Village Jajmani system, 227
Vindhya region, 28
Vocational Training centre, 234
Vulnerable Groups, 205, 210
Vulnerable Tribal Groups, 31, 95, 154

W

Walter Fernandez, 246
Water and Irrigation facilities, 146
Water User Groups, 150
Welfare Department, 205, 211
Welfare Schemes for Reduction of Poverty, 212
Welfare Schemes for the Aged, 109
Welfare Schemes for the Tribal, 205
Welfare Schemes of Housing, 210
West Bengal, 44, 54, 56, 58, 66, 116, 182, 183, 190, 196, 228, 245, 246, 249
West Bengal government, 61
West Dooars, 54
West Singhbhum, 118, 121, 130, 132
West Singhbhum district, 122, 127, 132
West Singhbhum district, 79
Western Blocks of Birbhum, 48
Western modernity, 48
Western tribal region, 30
Women in Jharkhand, 116
Women Labour Force Participation Rate, 120
Wood available, 147
Wooden handicraft, 233
Wooden plough, 86
Work and Leisure in productive work, 149
Work of Robert Chambers, 223
Work Participation Rate, 22
Work Sharing by Women, 149
Workers State Insurance Scheme, 110, 213
World Bank, 220, 224
World Bank Document, 117

Y

Yadav and Rajput communities, 131
Yaksa and Rakshas, 30

Z

Zilla Panchayat, 178
Zoroastrians (Parsis) 198